THE
GREAT
TRAINS

THIS BOOK HAS BEEN CREATED AND PRODUCED BY EDITA LAUSANNE

THE GREAT TRAINS

Editor: Bryan Morgan   Assistant Editor: Alan A. Jackson

with contributions by: John Snell • Arthur D. Dubin • Charles Owen •
John Foster White • K. Westcott Jones • Philip Unwin • David Tennant •
David Elliot
Foreword by Sir John Elliot

BONANZA BOOKS New York

Published 1985 by Bonanza-Books,
distributed by Crown Publishers, Inc.

Library of Congress Cataloging in Publication Data
Main entry under title:

The Great trains.

Reprint. Originally published: Cambridge [Cambridgeshire]: Stephens, 1973.
Includes index.
1. Railroads-Express-trains-History. I. Morgan, Bryan, 1923-   .   II. Jackson, Alan Arthur.   III. Snell, J.B.
TF573.G72 1985   385.09   84-28512
ISBN 0-517-52807 X

Printed in Italy and bound in Switzerland

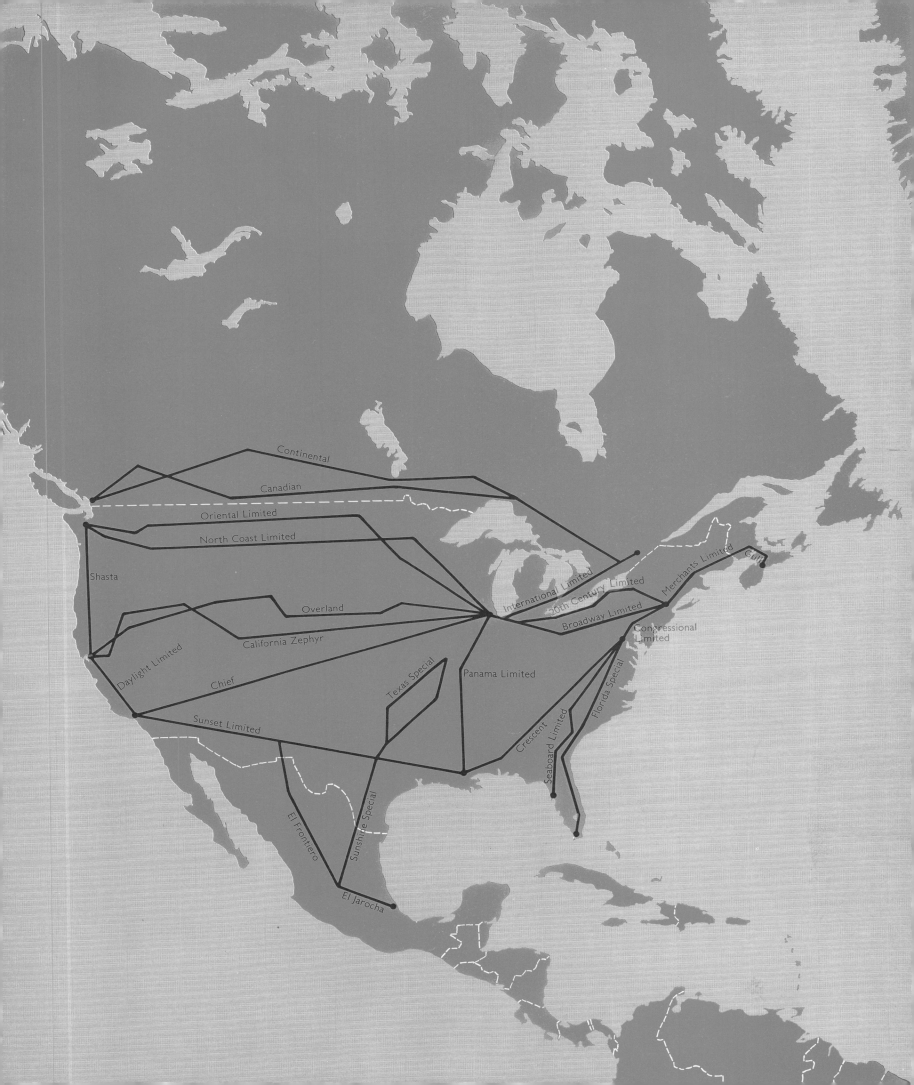

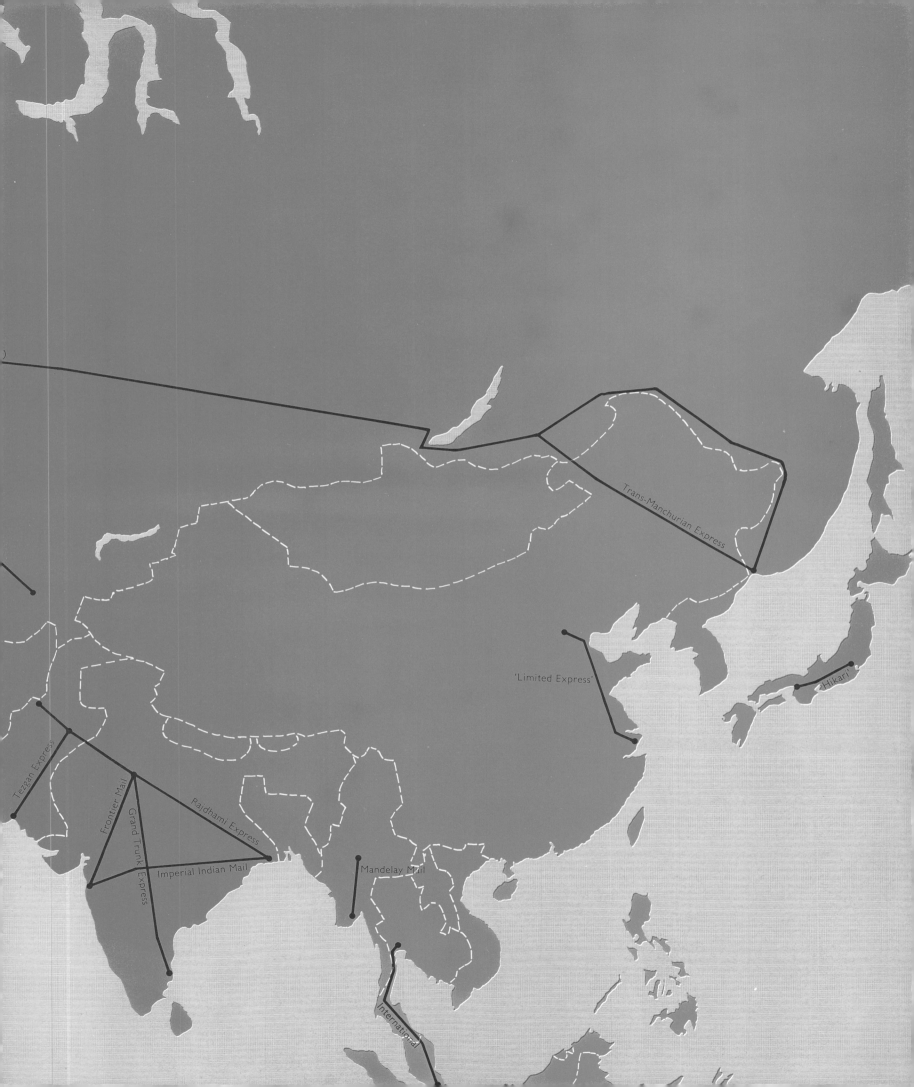

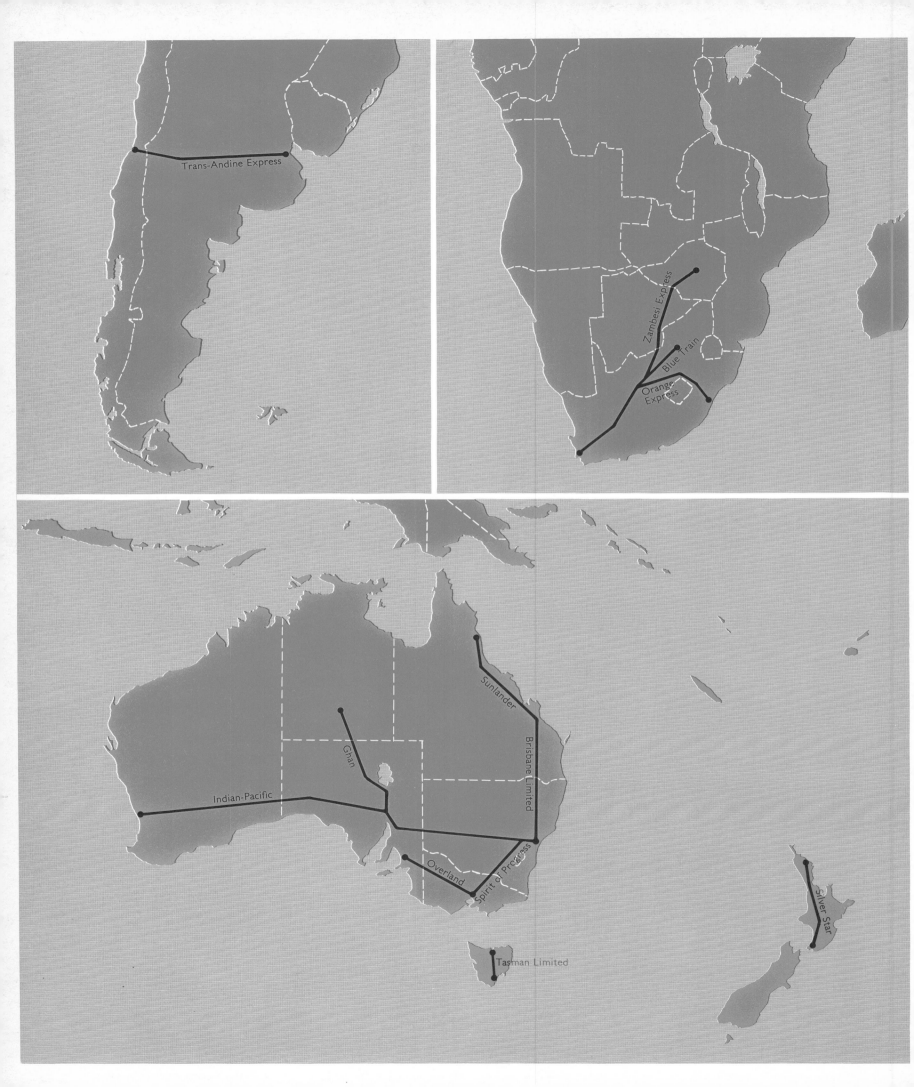

Trans-Andine Express

Zambesi Express

Blue Train

Orange Express

Sunlander

Brisbane Limited

Ghan

Indian-Pacific

Overland

Spirit of Progress

Tasman Limited

Silver Star

Contents

Invocation

After the first powerful plain manifesto
The black statement of pistons, without more fuss
But gliding like a queen, she leaves the station.
Without bowing and with restrained unconcern
She passes the houses which humbly crowd outside,
The gasworks and at last the heavy page
Of death, printed by gravestones in the cemetery.
Beyond the town there lies the open country
Where, gathering speed, she acquires mystery,
The luminous self-possession of ships on ocean.
It is now she begins to sing—at first quite low
Then loud, and at last with a jazzy madness—
The song of her whistle screaming at curves.
Of deafening tunnels, brakes, innumerable bolts.
And always light, aerial, underneath
Goes the elate metre of her wheels.
Steaming through metal landscape on her lines
She plunges new eras of wild happiness
Where speed throws up strange shapes, broad curves
And parallels clean like the steel of guns.
At last, further than Edinburgh or Rome,
Beyond the crest of the world, she reaches night
Where only a low streamline brightness
Of phosphorus on the tossing hills is white.
Ah, like a comet through flame she moves entranced
Wrapt in her music no bird song, no, nor bough
Breaking with honey buds, shall ever equal.

' *The Express* ': Stephen Spender

* * *

Prête-moi ton grand bruit, ta grande allure si douce,
Ton glissement nocturne à travers l'Europe illuminée,
O train de luxe! et l'angoissante musique
Qui bruit le long de tes couloirs de cuir doré,
Tandis que derrière les portes laquées, aux loquets de cuivre lourd,
Dorment les millionnaires.
Je parcours en chantonnant tes couloirs
Et je suis ta course vers Vienne et Budapest,
Mêlant ma voix à tes cent mille voix,
O Harmonika-Zug!

' *Poème* ': Valéry Larbaud

. . . Thy black cylindric body, golden brass and silvery steel,
Thy ponderous side-bars, parallel and connecting rods, gyrating,
shuttling at thy sides,
Thy metrical, now swelling pant and roar, now tapering in the
distance,
Thy great protruding head-light fix'd in front,
Thy long, pale, floating vapor-pennants, tinged with delicate purple,
Thy dense and murky clouds out-belching from thy smoke-stack,
Thy knitted frame, thy springs and valves, the tremulous twinkle
of thy wheels,
Thy train of cars behind, obedient, merrily following,
Through gale or calm, now swift, now slack, yet steadily careering;
Type of the modern—emblem of motion and power—pulse of
the continent,
For once come serve the Muse and merge in verse, even as here
I see thee,
With storm and buffeting gusts of wind and falling snow,
By day thy warning ringing bell to sound its notes,
By night thy silent signal lamps to swing. . . .
Fierce-throated beauty!
Roll through my chant with all thy lawless music . . .
Law of thyself complete, thine own track firmly holding . . .
Thy trills of shrieks by rocks and hills return'd,
Launch'd o'er the prairies wide, across the lakes,
To the free skies unpent and glad and strong.

' *To a Locomotive in Winter* ': Walt Whitman

Foreword

There could not be a more appropriate time for the appearance of this commemoration of the romance of *de luxe* railway travel in all parts of the world. Contrary to the gloomy prophecies of the total disappearance of express trains in the face of competition, an ever-growing network of high-speed trains today offers the weary business executive worn out by air hazards, and the holiday-maker frustrated by the congestion and danger of travel by car, an altogether new standard of comfort and relaxation by day and night.

I well remember, back in 1924 when I joined the Southern Railway (of England), being told by friends that I was foolish to waste my time in a rapidly dying way of life; if it was as a budding transport manager that I saw myself, then surely it must be obvious that only on the roads or in the air was there any future for a young man of spirit. As it turned out, I have never had any reason to regret going my own way.

During my forty years on the railways it was my good fortune to be intimately concerned with the planning and introduction of new trains where comfort and speed together were the objective, from the famous *Golden Arrow* Pullman service linking London and Paris in the late 1920s to the expansive network of TEE diesel and electric flyers which today criss-cross Europe. I also had a hand, as assistant to that unique railway administrator Sir Harold Clapp, in the early studies of the standardisation — now practically completed — of Australia's rail gauges. Today the splendid and highly successful *Indian-Pacific Express* between Sydney and Perth, giving air-conditioned all-sleeping (and *de luxe* dining-car) service over thousands of miles of the Australian continent, is the crowning glory of an outstanding railway engineering and operating achievement.

This surprising reversal of railway fortunes in the face of the keenest competition from the aeroplane, the express road coach of comfort and high performance, and the private car, has caught the public's imagination and revived an interest, which never really died, in those colourful expresses of the past as well as the present whose names are part of the social history of the last hundred years. The *Trans-Siberian*, the various *Orients*, the *Rome Express*, the *Flying Hamburger*, the *Train Bleu*, the *Flying Scotsman*, the *Cornish Riviera* and many more on this side of the world; the *20th Century Limited*, the *Broadway Limited*, the *Overland Express*, the *Santa Fe's*, the *Chief* and the *Canadian* on the North American continent, and South Africa's superb new *Blue Train* between Cape Town and Johannesburg — these are among the aristocrats of rail travel. This book tells their stories — and also something of the men of imagination and courage who first dreamed of them, planned and financed them, and set them on their way to make communication easier and more comfortable than ever before.

Two men in particular pioneered *de luxe* travel by rail. One was George Pullman in America, whose first true sleeping car was to make his name the synonym for luxury of every sort. A few years later, Georges Nagelmackers, a Belgian, formed a small company which became the famous International Sleeping Car company whose *wagons-lits* are still pre-eminent in Europe. If these two had not lived, other men of vision would have done what they did; but as it is, millions of travellers everywhere owe a debt of gratitude to these pioneers, a debt which this book gratefully acknowledges.

What of the years to come? For what it may be worth, I will commit myself to the prediction that fifty years from now people and freight will still be moved, all over the world, by railways. Track and traction techniques, of course, will be even more sophisticated and automated than today, and perhaps another book of Great Trains will supersede this one. Meanwhile, though, the wealth of facts and photographs about those of an earlier age contained in this volume will surely satisfy the enthusiasts of today and inform the historians of the future.

JOHN ELLIOT 1973

Sir John Elliot and the *Golden Arrow*.

Introduction

Ours is an age of retrospect and nostalgia, and hence of anniversaries and jubilees. And though this present book, this word-and-picture commemoration and praise of the world's great passenger expresses, is not conceived as a centenary history (for how can one set a formal *terminus ex quo?*), a backward glance as well as the forward one cast by Sir John Elliot suggests that it appears at an appropriate moment in time. For the 1870s — and in particular, perhaps, the middle of that decade — saw the appearance of a whole series of mile-posts along the track which witnessed the evolution of the train from a crude and none-too-speedy means of conveyance to a swift provider of comfort and even luxury. It is true that in the USA George Pullman had taken his first steps towards new standards well before 1870, and true too that for regular speeds much above 40 mph travellers in both America and Europe would have to wait another decade. But enough historic dates cluster around the central 1870s (the foundation of a predecessor to the Wagons-Lits company in 1872 and that company's coming into independent existence in 1876, the appearance of Europe's first sleepers at the start of the decade and of its earliest dining cars at the end of it, the opening of the first Alpine tunnel in 1871 and the construction of an increasing number of transcontinental routes in America, the revivification of interest in the Channel tunnel in 1874...) to suggest the mid-1970s as a fitting date for the publication of a *festschrift* for all the great trains of the world.

* * *

In presenting any assembly of railway writing there is the temptation to compare the editor's function to that of the marshalling of a train. But in fact the chapters which follow are grouped (in another simile beloved of the writers of introductory notes) more after the fashion of a meal — though, perhaps, one enjoyed in a Pullman or *wagon-restaurant* whilst varied and splendid landscapes slide past. Since the editor has frequently entered the kitchen to prepare his own dishes, it is not for him to commend the quality of the cuisine. But at least he can suggest that the menu offers variety, that the world's trains are here looked upon in many different aspects.

The dinner to which the reader is invited, then, follows the custom of today rather than of the opulent past in being divided into three courses. To whet the appetite, the *brigade* presents a range of *hors d'oeuvres* which represent those very varied techniques which needed to coalesce before the age of the great expresses could itself open — the advances in civil engineering, in locomotion, and most characteristically in the appointments of passenger rolling stock. To conclude the feast (for one can hardly equate the index with a *demi-tasse*, let alone with the presentation of the bill) there will be no heavy Edwardian pudding but rather what — it is hoped — will prove a savoury *bonne bouche* in the form of a taste of the way the world's named trains have provided themes for its authors and composers. And between comes the meat of the book — six substantial chapters in which as many writers serve up their selections of classic trains.

Each of these writers, furthermore, has chosen not merely his own ingredients but his own form of presentation, so that one has used a chronological framework and another taken a regional view, some have relied on personal memories and others adopted a more exhaustive approach, some have ended on a nostalgic note and others preferred the forward glance, and one — the editor — has thrown away the recipe-book and simply written of what appealed to him. Not every reader, therefore, will unreservedly approve of all the inclusions and exclusions in these central chapters. ('Why,' one can hear voices raised, 'is there not more on Scandinavia or the Near East, on such internal European trains as the *Conca d'Oro*, on China, on comparisons of speeds, on railway hotels...?') There are answers to all such objections: for instance, these pages *are* designed to offer an informed selection rather than a catalogue, and the comparison of speeds between different countries and ages is largely meaningless without a host of qualifications. But perhaps it is enough to say that there should be something here for every palate and digestion. And to wash it all down, bottles of vintage wine are uncorked between these courses which the art staff have lavishly garnished.

These bottles are provided by three British authors who looked about them in the classic years before the phylloxera of competition from road and air struck the world's railways, and who provide almost the only words not specially written for this book. The Gallatly is perhaps only light if amusing stuff; but Foxwell and Farrer, the earliest writers to appreciate the social effects of the coming of express trains, have the status of shippers of a domaine-bottled burgundy. The Château Pearson (which, the seeker after original sources should be warned, comes from his merchant only in the jeroboam size) is the steeliest of clarets, and a few large glasses such as are offered here will probably suffice all but the glutton: but it too is a classic for any who would savour the great years of rail travel just before the First World War.

*
* *

Or *were* these the great years after all? When the team responsible for assembling this book embarked on their task it was perhaps with the feeling that (as Hamilton Ellis put it) 'Brief years, from the death of Queen Victoria to the outbreak of war in 1914, were proud years. In many respects they made up the railways' golden era ... handsome expresses rushed about ... locomotives were often painted in gorgeous colours.' And with this image of the trains of sixty and seventy years ago was blended a vision of parasols at Biarritz, of huge portmanteaux at the Gare de l'Est bound for Baden-Baden, of winter-gardens and Fabergé jewels, of pink-shaded lights gleaming on the mahogany of the *wagon-restaurant*, of German bands and of garden-parties graced by boaters, blazers and picture-hats, of skies cloudless and untroubled save for the pioneering balloon, of 'summer journeys to Niagara' (and winter ones to Miami) in glistening green open-vestibuled Pullmans, of nabobs' and viceroys' private saloons on the *Poona Mail*, of Baedeker in its prime with the going easy...

In many ways this picture is not too misleading, for the first dozen or so years of the present century were not only socially gilded: they were, in a purely railway context, technically influential in some respects and glamorous in most. But a deeper examination suggests that the years just before the First World War were flanked by periods still more illustrious for the passenger express. The first of these great ages began with the acceptance of new standards in the 1880s and continued until (at least in Europe and North America) those standards became widespread shortly before the close of the century. After that the Edwardian or *belle époque* era appears one of capitalising on past achievement, perhaps more picturesque than enterprising, whilst the immediate post-war years seem almost years of anti-climax. Not until the later 1930s was there another great burst of creative energy — and one which, with the mists of nearly forty years softening the excesses of 'art deco' styling, has now acquired its own period appeal.

It may be that the stimulus of external competition which fired the great trains of the 'thirties is the same as that which (with every promise of success) today activates the TEEs and the Amtraks. But nowadays glamour is harder to find. And — as a first glance through its pages will show — it is to glamour and glory, rather than to brute efficiency, that this work is dedicated.

*
*   *

For this is not merely a book about expresses: it is, to a degree, a book about them in their social context and one with an eye frankly cast on their more luminous aspects — a celebration of high living as well as of high technical performance. From the years when former slaves from the southern states of America rode the rods northwards up to the present age of Russian Jews seeking a new life in Israel (and, for that matter, of blue-jeaned students passing the long night watches with their guitars and their Coke), such of the world's named trains as acknowledge a second, 'hard' or 'coach' class have carried their quota of the impoverished and sometimes the desperate: and they have also witnessed wars, labour disputes, accidents and grim deportations. All this should not be forgotten, any more than it should be forgotten that the passenger express itself represents only a small part of the world's railway activities; but when history makes an appearance in these pages it will often be when distinguished names have been concerned.

For it is a quality of the long-distance train that — even today, and whether by plan or by chance — it is associated with moments of not merely personal but national drama. Challenged to produce an historic image from the domain of air transport, for instance, the memory may perhaps provide that of President Johnson swearing his inaugural oath in 'USAF One' with Jacqueline Kennedy an exclipsed loveliness in the background. But a still more vivid picture from the past is that of Sir Winston Churchill being taken to his last rest behind the locomotive which bore his name — even if the Pullman goods-van which carried his coffin was so freshly repainted that the date of its overhaul, two days *before* that of the great knight's death, still gleamed from the underframes. One recalls the emissary of General de Gaulle, bearing vital news from unoccupied France, hiding in the locomotive tender of Laval's own Pullman special as it rushed north from Vichy. And whilst there may be some moral to be drawn from the glimpse of the recluse aircraft-millionaire, Howard Hughes, approaching the fastness of his desert hide-out in Nevada by way of a private railway carriage running into a private siding, there most certainly is one in the fact that Britain's first delegates to the Common Market had to be rescued from a fog-bound plane by rail. . .

*   *   *

At the far extreme from the luxury express which forms the paradigm of this book there is — or there once was — a very lowly type of train known as a pick-up goods, whose task was essentially a mopping-up operation. Similarly, the editor of a work such as this has the duty — or liberty — of following along metals covered by distinguished trains and of clearing them of the freight-vans of miscellaneous explanation. And this must serve as excuse for the apparently random nature of this introduction.

However, there is only one more comment which need be made before this book departs on its course — that, as a glance at its contents page will show, all save one of its contributors have 'British' stamped on those passports which (so far as western Europe is concerned) are again mercifully becoming as disregarded as in the years when the railways first opened up frontiers. Even the exception, who is America's premier railway historian, writes in the English language. For a work which sets out to be fully international in its approach — and in which a real effort has been made to minimise local bias — such a selection may appear chauvinistic: but the publishers and editor have not been led to such an arrangement through over-rating the admittedly large part played by Britain in railway technology across the world or even by the distinguished tradition of railway- and travel-writing in the English language. It is simply, solely and sincerely, that to attempt to assemble a work of the quality aimed at here from the words of a dozen writers who did not share the same native tongue — and of whom the majority were not within easy reach of one city — would be to invite unnecessary logistic problems.

If the editor is permitted a last metaphor, let it be one which, perhaps, conflicts with the prevailing note of nostalgia which must dominate these pages, and which suggests that not *all* change, even in public service, is for the worse. A century ago the railway passenger in certain countries on the continent of Europe was still kept penned in his waiting-room until summoned by an imperious bell. Today an international express may be sped on its way from the Gare de Lyon by a charming *mezzo* voice over the public-address system which wishes one a pleasant journey and is splendidly synchronised with the train's departure. Changing his hat yet again, and appearing in the last of all those avatars (yardmaster, chef, freight-train driver . . .) which he has adopted in this informal introduction, the editor now becomes station announcer, picks up the microphone, and adds his own 'Attention au départ — et bon voyage.'

B.M.

London/Lausanne - 1973

1889 Contemporary Viewpoint

In 1889 — the year after the classic railway race to Scotland — E. Foxwell and T.C. Farrer introduced with a quotation from *The Odyssey* their *Express Trains, English and Foreign, being a Statistical Account of All the Express Trains of the World...*; and although noting that speeds were everywhere on the increase, they went on to cover their subject in some 160 pages largely devoted to timetables. Furthermore, they adopted a very relaxed definition of an 'express', for in order to qualify a British or American train had to average only 40 mph whilst elsewhere 29 mph or less was acceptable. These figures, the authors pointed out, were not arbitrary but had emerged naturally from the current timetables.

Foxwell and Farrer's 'pamphlet' has become a classic of railway literature, not only for its thorough documentation of the world's 'fast' passenger trains towards the end of the last century but for its forcefully-expressed *obiter dicta*: though eschewing 'gluttonous patriotism', for instance, the authors left their readers in no doubt as to the superiority of the British system of competitive companies over the Continental practice of forming regional or even national monopolies. (Thus, they noted that one English company had a freight train faster than the French Riviera expresses and that on another goods travelled faster than did passengers on Italy's 30 mph 'lightning' passenger trains.) They also held strong views on the iniquity of charging supplements on fast trains and of banning these to third-class passengers.

In Britain itself, the companies operating north of London came in for general praise. The Great Northern, for instance, had 'worked like an inspiring leaven', the 'innovating energy' of the Midland was 'shown in its early efforts to introduce Pullman cars, glasses of milk *en route* [and] cheaper cups of tea', North-Western staff were seen to 'do their work with military precision [and] finished nonchalance', and even the Great Eastern, despite an 'unparalleled history of robbery and general misfortune' had 'set an example of sensible liberal behaviour'; only the North-Eastern suffered from 'an unexcitable executive and the consciousness of a safe monopoly'. But in the west the Great Western showed a 'timorous hand' and 'meanness in the matter of quick trains', and its South-Western rival showed up little better. The South-Eastern was 'audaciously unpunctual', and even the Brighton company not beyond reproach.

Further afield, things usually worsened still further. Of the Welsh network, the Cambrian, the best one could say was that 'refreshment bars are very frequent... and as the shunting operations... involve long delays, a journey over this system recalls memories of the old coaching days when inns were the leading features of the route'. In Scotland the traveller must 'leave behind English notions of railway discipline, and come upon a very sorry state of affairs as regards punctuality and intelligent organisation.' At Edinburgh, one could see 'every evening in summer a scene of confusion so chaotic that a sober description of it is incredible... Trains of caravan length come in portentously late from Perth, so that each is mistaken for its successor... while bewildered crowds of tourists sway up and down amongst equally bewildered porters [and] higher officials stand lost in subtle thought, returning now and then to repeated enquiries some masterpiece of reply couched in the cautious conditional'.

After noting the lack of speeds exceeding 30 mph in either South America or India, and praising 'the Australian colonies' for their much greater enterprise, the authors measured Ireland against both English and continental norms: that 'extraordinary island' naturally came out better by the second of these levels, for Foxwell and Farrer found standards dispiriting in most parts of Europe. In Holland (blessed with British locomotives) there was certainly little 'tendency to official hysterics when emergencies disturbed the prescribed routine', comfort was 'everywhere more prominent than red tape', and speeds too were better than in Belgium. After this, France showed a few trains approaching averages of 43 mph and so had 'the best set of expresses on the continent'; it was also punctual, but there was much to deplore such as the artificially high fares, the 'wonderfully few' expresses on the Nord system, and the lamentable standards of the great Paris-Lyon-Marseille line. In Germany 35 mph was very rare and state intervention had reduced the service to Berlin to 'simply an international disgrace', whilst for Austria the authors quoted: '*Immer langsam voran, dass die österreichische Südbahn nachfolgen kann*'.

In Italy, only one day express linked Milan to Venice — and for the passenger from London that implied a six-hour wait at Milan. Services in Sweden were 'very poor', and Russia, Spain and Portugal — perhaps not surprisingly — went without comment. Hungary, though, was praised for handling the *Orient Express* at nearly 32 mph, more smartly than her western neighbours, and Denmark attracted the odd comment that its 'educated aristocracy' insisted on 'being treated in a reasonable way'.

In the United States, however, the authors felt themselves at home again with British criteria of express speeds — as the last of the following excerpts shows. The first of them provides a rather imaginative justification of express running in general, whilst the second throws a contemporary light on one aspect of British habits. Unfortunately, there is no comparable passage in Foxwell and Farrer's book summarising European practice in general at the dawn of the age of the great expresses.

SOME EFFECTS OF EXPRESS SPEED

We have only room for a thumb-nail sketch, but we should not dismiss our statistics without a word as to the influence exerted on a country by the constant air of cheap and rapid locomotion.

The number and speed of the express trains of a country is not an unimportant circumstance. It is quite as pregnant as many smaller facts which compel the reader's respect because they are called 'phenomena'.

Like any other phenomenon, the remarkable one of English railway speed must have a parentage. It shows national 'grit' to maintain such a host of trains exceeding 'forty miles an hour inclusive', and every extra mile of speed above the 'forty' indicates extra good stuff in the composition of the natives. Just as rods of iron scarcely feel a strain up to a certain point, after which they quickly break, so in foreign countries 'forty miles an hour inclusive' marks the 'breaking-point' of the management. But the summer of 1888 saw *added* to the existing English total 5,000 miles of new 'exp.' mileage of a quality so high that the entire Continent does not produce so large a total absolutely... As it is our own country where these tense speeds are commonplace, we will not pursue the topic further.

Many, if not most, of the distinctive phenomena that constitute 'the nineteenth century' are directly due to railway speed; that is, we can scarcely imagine the possibility of their development in the absence of railways. As shrewd Mr. Edward Pease said seventy years ago, 'Let the country but make the railroads, and the railroads will make the country'; and they *have* made the country, for better or worse, moulded the leading features of its national life. Let us glance at a few haphazard instances.

First, for people who are nothing if not Socialistic, consider the unexampled *diffusion of wealth* in the last forty years; an unexampled *diffusion*, however striking may be the contrast still between the very rich and the very poor. This is shown by the wonderful approach towards uniformity of *prices* in different parts; goods instantly move from where they are most plentiful, and this quicksilver action could never have occurred before railways. Railways have made everything *common*.

And the people of different localities are getting to vary almost as little as the prices; there is a uniformity of 'common' manners, it is said. The immediate effect does seem to be this. Still, railways have introduced *freedom*, and from this will, later on, develop unimagined *individuality*. When 'a penny a mile' came in all feudal links with the past were snapped, including the traditional deference to surroundings from which one saw no means of escape; the abrupt freedom has produced an 'independence' of manners which is no doubt 'commoner', but perhaps not more unsatisfactory, than the laboured insincerity of former times. The railway has made the poor 'stand up' to the rich much as Luther stirred the nations to defy the Church.

This modern freedom must be held responsible for a great deal of our 'realistic' tendency in art and behaviour; people demand the genuine and true rather than the picturesque or sentimental.

Then the unprecedented growth of *population*. Free Trade has stepped in here and played Jacob with the birthright of railways. However 'free' trade had been made, to what extent could it have expanded without the launching impetus of railways? Previous to 1830 the roads leading from Manchester to Liverpool were blocked, not by tariff, but by want of carrying power. At least three-fourths of the enormous increase in our commerce since 1850 — by which date most of our trunk lines were in operation — should be credited to railways; but 'Free Trade' was contemporaneous, and since it was a Government stroke, dramatic and visible to all, it eclipsed the influence of its humdrum though mightier rival. Free Trade without steam would not have stirred the pool very much.

Inseparably connected with the growth of population is *the astounding cheapness of most necessaries*. The materials of *food* and *clothing*, being bulky, and rural products, depend entirely on cheap transit for a practical price; and our imports of these coming chiefly from regions where railways are making great strides, are arriving more profusely...

We might refer to the universal and sometimes frenzied spirit of *competition* — which of itself would separate this century from its predecessors — as another familiar instance of what railways do. How much competition would be left if railways went? Again, cheap *books* and *newspapers* depend on population and on railways for a sale sufficiently large to enable them to be sold so cheap. This prevalence of print conduces to *claptrap*, because the large audience is more hungry than nice; and from living in an age of print many of our most ordinary habits or acts assume a theatrical rouge, by passing under the yoke of the 'reporter'. Every small boy expects to see his half-holiday score at cricket duly figure (or cypher, as the case may be) in the columns of his local paper.

There are bigger things left. Who can help being struck by the *tolerance* of our age, a tolerance astounding when contrasted with the mental brutality of sixty years ago? The incessant shuttle of railway speed, the myriad daily encounters of all sorts and conditions of men owing to this cheap expedition, the resulting flux and murkiness in place of definite conviction, the unambitious content as long as one can find some *modus vivendi* amongst such heterogeneous diversity — this peculiar characteristic of the time (its weakness and its strength) is the special outcome of express trains. Bismarckism would have no chance in England...

From this restless diffusion of men arises a growing *complexity* of social problems; no more of the simple parish under despotic paternal government. Now all our various programmes interact — we are no longer autocrats on our own instrument, but have to observe *orchestral* behaviour; and any difficulty becomes more and more an orchestral disaster.

Then there is hope in the air, a new optimism, fed chiefly by perpetual motion. Constant change of place and circumstance, instead of the old local monotony, has infused new blood into the race; there had been repeated crossbreeding with the 'infinite variety' of the world, and a tonic is at work within. Partly from this better modern 'temper', and partly because of the tolerant mood before mentioned, the present generation is accused of no deep feeling. The fact is they will not be crushed, and they resent the worship of Tragedy, because the *new hopefulness* makes them think

that many belong to the class of preventible accidents. This healthy tone has been bred not only by the daily influence of railways, but by the annual practice of 'going to the seaside', or making a tour, a practice undreamt of before railways, and now endemic. From these same yearly tours have been developed the instinct for 'scenery', an article for which there was no general demand before George Stephenson...

We must not pass by our two latest and most fashionable phenomena. First, the 'emancipation of Woman'. Without claiming that this movement arose directly from the opening of railways, we may firmly maintain that it has been greatly strengthened by the mere fact of railway travel. Women are so tightly moored by Nature that if locomotion is also for them an impossibility they must indeed feel slaves. Compare the portentousness of a hundred miles journey for a girl last century with the ridiculous ease of travel now, and we see how they cannot bask in the new freedom long without tingling to assert their own individuality.

Lastly, the present agitation for 'Bimetallism', whether as a medicine for low general prices or for low agricultural prices in particular, must be attributed to railways. Raw materials fall in price with every extension of railway mileage in the new countries, and manufactured goods are cheapened by the growth of the quantity exported, which depends largely on railways at home and abroad. Here again, as with Free Trade in 1846–50, the Franco-Prussian War has been credited with the work of other agents, because these others are familiar and continuous...

In such good company we cannot do better than leave our railways. But if it is true that they have these high social connections, if express trains are the efficient cause of some of the most distinctive features of nineteenth century civilisation, there must be more than ordinary interest in examining the relative strength of this factor in various parts of the world... People say Ireland is 'scarcely civilised'; it certainly has scarcely any express speed.

REMARKS ON THE SOUTHERN LINES

The naturalist is still compelled to maintain that our railways south of Thames are, from the public point of view, quite another species from those to the north of that narrow stream. The traveller who cabs across from Waterloo to Euston, from Victoria to St. Pancras, or from London Bridge to King's Cross, is in each case moving to a higher railway atmosphere, where the time-bills are meant to be taken in good faith, where the quality of the service is superb, and where we can rely on its being the rule, not the exception, to carry out what has been contracted for. We say adieu (or *au diable*) to the 'cheery stoicism' of that South-Western terminus, where incoming trains arrive at

their own sweet time and place, to the subtle irony of the Brighton with its 'fast' and very 'limited' style, to the South-Eastern with its fore-ordained chronic block in sight of port, to the Chatham with its hand-brakes; and we alight upon platforms of common sense, where efficiency is high, where only fares are low. Good-bye to the sportive tricks of Southern complexity; now we come to stern simplicity, which merely says and does. Only the deeds are first class, though most of the passengers are third.

The Southern lines form a group which must be called a different species if only because they are wanting in that essential characteristic *punctuality*. Of course there are good reasons — though bad excuses — for the fact, but the unpunctuality is none the less a monstrosity. Trains which never (well, hardly ever) throughout the year arrive decently near their time are maddening to everyone except the officials; there is no point in them, they have lost their savour, and are as different from the real article as a stale egg from a fresh one. Besides this lapse in regard to the crowning virtue, there are other reasons why the Southern companies are justly unpopular. They pay very good dividends, yet charge exorbitant fares — what a contrast to the Great Eastern! But the *South-Western* must be exempted from this particular reproach; it deserves peculiar respect for upholding universal and unconditional third class amid such demoralising companionship, though its first and second class fares are high. On the South-Eastern we seem to hear the old greeting of the highwayman, 'Your money or your life'; for unless the victim be prepared to empty his purse he must adjourn to the slow trains of that corporation, and life is not worth living there. Then there is a feeling that in this part of England the companies are leagued against the public, because here flourishes the un-English system of 'pooling' the receipts from traffic to competitive places. Compare the number of express trains run between *e.g.* *Cambridge* and London by Great Eastern and Great Northern with those enjoyed by Portsmouth or Dover; in the latter case each company takes from its rival part of its motive to exert itself, while the two northern companies, adopting the grosser form of competition pure and simple, do the very best they can. The result is that Cambridge has fifteen times as many third class 'express' journeys as either of the southern instances.

But we must not paint things blacker than they are. There is something to be set off against all this abuse. In some respects the southern companies put the northern ones to shame. Though their trains run shorter distances than any, they are provided with the best communication between passenger and guard — not with that satirical 'cord' which undulates so gracefully beneath the eaves of the carriages on our leading lines. Again, it is on a southern line — the Brighton — that we find the greatest advance in the lighting of carriages. Not only on the Pullman cars, but in the third class of its commonest suburban trains, the electric light is gradually spreading, so that the smallest print may be read with ease.

Where the southern lines however most excel the northern ones is in the matter of *Sunday* arrangements. They make the best of this terrible day, not the worst, and deal with conflicting interests in a sensible way. To a layman fond of fresh air there is great satisfaction in watching the volley of 'cheap seaside' trains fired off by the Brighton Company every Sunday morning (in summer), carrying thousands of the 'masses' out of London and alcohol to the healthier air of Littlehampton, Bognor, Worthing, Brighton, Eastbourne, or Hastings. These trains are practically express, and charge one-third the ordinary third class fare. The Brighton is the largest benefactor in this respect, but similar praise is due to the South-Eastern and Chatham for their corresponding facilities to Ramsgate, Margate, and the Kentish coast in general. The South-Western is very genial, for it starts a 'cheap' train at the pleasant hour of half-past nine, and, running at 35 miles an hour inclusive, gives seven hours at Bournemouth before the equally quick return home. On Sunday these four southern companies show in their best colours, and offer a happy contrast to that gloomy dog-in-the-manger policy with which the northern lines disfigure the day.

No doubt these distinguishing traits, both good and bad, owe their existence in some measure to the intimate relation in which our southern companies stand to the Continental lines; in daily working partnership with them they cannot help adopting some of their ways and points of view. Unfortunately our southerners have failed to imitate their Continental brethren in that one point where they are most admirable, punctuality. From Mentone to Calais is 875 miles, but the through carriage will almost invariably arrive at Calais at its schedule time, and then on the remaining section of 100 miles to London the passengers will lose a quarter of an hour or more. We prefer 'this direct simplicity of the French mind' to the pretentious promise which cannot be fulfilled. There are, of course, sufficient reasons why it is much harder for an ordinary English express to be punctual than for one on the Continent (*e.g.* third-class passengers, heaps of luggage, booking allowed at the last moment, the barbarity of the English custom-houses, and so on); at the same time unpunctuality is such a blot that wherever it occurs it obliterates all the good features of the service (for *finis coronat opus*), and disarms us of effective repartee.

Another good word may be thrown in for these unpopular companies, and that is to praise them for the plucky way in which they carry on their traffic during *fogs*. When an English railway is hard pressed it rises to the occasion and shows the stuff it is made of, and we are never so proud of our southern lines as during dense weather. Thus in the early weeks of last January (1889), when for eight or nine consecutive days the fog was so thick at times that a pedestrian could not see the curb of the pavement on which he walked, it was a truly English experience to stand on the platform of such a station as Norwood Junction, and hear the Brighton expresses thunder through with not so much as half the length of a single carriage visible at once. The pluck and endurance exhibited by obscure *employees* whenever 'fogging' is the order of the day are beyond words; an unappreciative public is whirled up to its office snug and warm, and prefers to expend its admiration on those scarlet-coated heroes who are lucky enough to receive a scratch in the Soudan and a paragraph in the London papers.

In dealing with the expresses of the United States it is somewhat difficult to know what standard to take. As, however, the best Eastern roads approximate very closely to those of our country in equipment, and also because with the data at our disposal it would have been extremely difficult to take a lower standard with any approach to accuracy, we have taken *40 miles an hour including stops*, as our definite express train, and have allowed nothing under this.

It must not, however, be supposed for a moment that we consider this test as absolute in any way. In fact, there are a very large number of trains in the Eastern States at 38–39 miles an hour, which are most creditable, and in the Western States there are vast quantities of runs at 35–38 miles an hour, which are really marvellous performances considering the character of the track (generally single) and the sparse population. Mr. Hadley has shown that the proportion of passenger train miles to population is greater in the States than anywhere else in the world, and, if we except Great Britain, the same would be easily the case with regard to *express miles*.

But it would be almost impossible for any foreigner to do justice to these, and so we have had to be content with just the top performances...

Even now we fear that, in the vast mass of confused and ill-arranged time-tables, we may have overlooked some performances which reach our ideal. It will be noticed that the Pennsylvania Road contributes 44 per cent of the total. The average American fare per mile was in 1884 1.17*d*. on the ordinary cars; but though professedly there is only one class, almost all the express trains contain Pullman or drawing-room cars at extra fares.

It may be said that as a rule American trains and engines are heavier than ours, while the rails are lighter. All cars and engines are on bogie trucks, and each car weighs from 55,000 to 60,000 lbs. while ours weigh from 18,000 to 45,000 only.

Of course, the question of the average weight of train is almost impossible to settle, but it may be said that in England it is the rarest thing to see any express train with more than 20 six-wheeled vehicles drawn by one engine (we believe the 8.45 from Brighton is the only one habitually exceeding this limit), while in America expresses with vehicles equivalent to 20 or 26 of ours are common.

It is rather difficult to assign to any one train the merit of 'the best express'. The long distance New York-Chicago trains of the Pennsylvania and the New York Central Companies are highly meritorious, and so is the Portland and Bangor express of the Maine Central. All these, however, are limited trains at extra fares. The fastest running is from Baltimore to Washington, 40 miles in 45 minutes,

53 ⅓ miles per hour. Besides these, distinctly the best running in the States is made between Jersey City and Philadelphia, and between Boston and Providence. Between the two rival lines from New York to Philadelphia the race is very even. Over this ground there are 26 expresses by the Pennsylvania averaging 42 miles per hour, and only 14 by the Bound Brook route averaging 41 ½, but, of course, the Pennsylvania has more population behind it than the other route. As regards the New York and Chicago express trains, though the Pennsylvania route is 60 miles shorter, both routes take the same time, and thus the finer performance is that of the New York Central. It should be noted that we have not got the official time of rest at stations of the latter, as it is put down to arrive and start at the same moment at intermediate stations — clearly an impossibility.

Both are heavy trains, weighing about 290,000 lbs, and on both extra fare is charged. The long duration of run without a stop, 3 to 3 ½ hours, is specially noticeable. From Penzance to Wick is our chance of a similar journey at home; 957 miles done at just about the same speed, excluding stops, but owing to the quantity of these taking six hours longer. But from London to Perth over similar hills it is 7 miles further than from Jersey City to Pittsburg or from New York to Buffalo, but we have 6 trains a day 60 minutes quicker than the 'Limiteds' of the States, all carrying third class passengers.

The long car of the United States, with every convenience on board, enables stops to be reduced to a minimum. The 'Limited' express of the Pennsylvania Road is said to be the most luxurious train in the world, and contains even a barber's shop on board. Even if in our small island such trains would prove useless, it is to be wished that the continental railways would provide them at fares as moderate as in the States, since for long distance travel they are undoubtedly more comfortable. The P.L.M. of France are said to be building a set of these cars to run between Paris and Geneva without extra charge...

The only two other expresses which shall be specially mentioned here are those between New York and Boston and between Washington and Baltimore.

That the speed [on the former *c*. 40 mph] is not higher seems to be due to the lack of competition, all these routes being virtually subject to the New York New Haven and Hartford line, which alone holds the entrance to New York... Baltimore and Washington there are two trains each way daily doing the 40 miles in 45 minutes without stop, or 53 ⅓ miles per hour, which we believe to be actually the fastest running in the States. They are, moreover, almost the only 'expresses' run at all by the powerful 'B. & O.'

Many lines where we should expect to find good speeds run no technical 'expresses'; for instance, the New York, Lake Erie and Western on its 'Chicago and St. Louis Limited' takes 12 ¾ hours from Jersey City to Buffalo 422 miles, speed inclusive only 31. Again, great as is the reputation of the Boston and Albany, we have to be very indulgent to find an 'express' at all; there is none between the two terminal points Boston and Albany, and only one (one way) between Worcester and Springfield. It must, however, not be forgotten that the entrance to many American towns has to be traversed at very low speeds, as the railways are unfenced, running indeed in many cases along the public roads, while intermediately speed has often to be reduced where a railway is crossed on the level, so that the running speeds may be first rate, although the 'throughout' speeds *look* poor on paper. Still, our object is to show how quickly a train, and by it a passenger, gets from one point to another so that we do not take this into account.

A good deal of amusement may be got out of the American time-tables. We find, for instance, the high sounding title, 'Staten Island Rapid Transit Railway'. But its fastest train — New York to Perth Amboy — takes one hour fifteen minutes to do the 20 miles, just 16 miles an hour, which is almost an Italian speed.

Then an announcement of the Oregon Railway and Navigation Company runs thus: 'Mixed trains have accommodation for passengers, who wish to assume the additional risk of accident' — clearly implying the terrors of such a journey.

In the Western States there is not much to note, but the Union Pacific's 'Overland Flyer' is quite first rate. It does the 1,031 miles from Omaha (1,000 feet above sea-level) to Ogden (4,301 feet) over two summits of 8,247 and 7,395 feet respectively (sinking to 6,007 feet between) at 29 miles per hour inclusive, and 31 ¼ exclusive of stops. Against this creditable performance, which on the Continent of Europe would deserve a laurel crown, we have to put the boast of the advertisement of the Chicago and Alton line, 'the fastest train run by any road between Chicago and the Missouri River in either direction'. Now from Kansas City to Chicago, 488 miles, their speed is only 33 ⅓ including, 34 ⅓ excluding stops, and of this only 44 miles — Jacksonville to Mason City — is done at real express speed, viz. 42 miles per hour.

Another admirable run in the Western States is that of the Denver to Rio Grande, narrow gauge, through 771 miles of mountains and gorges at 23 miles per hour inclusive from Denver to Ogden; a better performance than the broad gauge Northern Pacific, which does the 1,699 miles from St. Paul to Wallula, allowing for two hours difference of time, at 26 ½ miles per hour. Any of these runs, however, seems to show the energy of these wild Western roads as compared to the slowness of Continental Europe, [for] even this last train runs quicker by 1 mile per hour than the Berlin-London express...

It may be of interest here to give the distance and time necessary for crossing from Atlantic to Pacific Coasts in the United States and Canada respectively, and the speed, allowing for difference of time... The new Canadian Pacific, which has the great advantage of being in the same hands throughout, averages just over 21 miles per hour, a very creditable performance for so enormous a distance, and and with no population west of Toronto to speak of, while the American line serves large towns throughout. The American run is spoilt by the extraordinary badness of the connections at Chicago (wait of 10½ hours) and Council Bluffs (3½ hours). To a foreigner, moreover, there are some very inexplicable facts. Thus though the Chicago, Milwaukee and St. Paul is 3 miles shorter from Chicago to Council Bluffs, it seems to make no effort to compete for the traffic. The same is the case with the Chicago, Burlington and Quincy. But as all the through traffic is practically controlled by the monopoly of the Union Pacific, perhaps these roads may intend to get across the mountains by some independent route in future. Under any circumstances we are promised shortly by the Union Pacific a 'Golden Gate Special, which is to render travel between the Missouri River and San Francisco luxurious and salubrious' and 8 hours quicker than the above. (*Note.* — This is now, Jan. 1889, an accomplished fact — at any rate as far as the increased speed goes.)

As regards gradients, the Canadian Pacific has much the best of it, its two big summits being the Rockies at Mount Stephen 5,296 feet (an ascent of 4,700 feet in 1,400 miles) descending thence nearly 3,000 feet to mount to Rogers Pass, 4,506 feet on the Selkirk range, and after that descending steadily to the Pacific, while the Union and Central Pacific start with a climb up the Rockies from Omaha (965 feet) to Sherman 8,240 feet (7,300 feet in 550 miles), and go on to Aspen 7,835 feet, descending 4,000 feet only to mount up again to the Humboldt Mountains 6,150 feet, then descending another 2,000 feet to mount again the Sierra Nevadas at 7,017 feet, dropping to ocean level in less than 100 miles. Considering the character of American traffic, viz., heavily loaded goods trains for long distances at moderate speeds, these better gradients of the Canadian Pacific must tell far more than in our impatient little island.

In the Southern States, as might be expected, speeds are very poor, with one or two exceptions, viz. the Atlantic Coast Line and a railway called the Central Railroad of South Carolina, which latter, if our figures are accurate, runs 40 miles from Sumter to Lane's with three stops in 56 minutes, about 43 inclusive or 47 exclusive of stops. We end by the company next in our time-book, which probably may aspire to the proud position of the slowest in the civilised world (excluding, perhaps, Wurtemberg): *Scotland Neck Br. W. and W Railroad.* — Weldon to Scotland Neck — 27 miles — in 3 hours 35 minutes, just 7 miles per hour.

Passenger Discomforts

Luxury in rail travel — except for a very few, and those few often of royal blood — was not to be bought by any traveller in any land much before the 1870s; and even if the sights are lowered from luxury to mere comfort it was to be found, at least in Europe, only in the first class. For the Old World's social system had made itself manifest on its railways right from the start, and however slow the train three classes were usually represented on it. Discomfort was more the word for the second or third class passengers in their small-windowed wagons, or in the open trucks in which they were exposed to tempests and tunnels until legislation compelled the companies to provide a minimal shelter.

So let us see what the railways had to offer in their first four decades to the man who could afford a first-class ticket in the country where railways began. Somebody once described an Englishman's idea of heaven as an empty first-class compartment — though railway history suggests that the French were just as jealous of their privacy — and, then as now, money bought solitude. The grand could have their own carriages chained on to wagons in anticipation of the modern car-sleeper system — though unlike the patrons of that service they sat in their vehicles, rather as the drivers of cars in Switzerland and Austria can sit in them while they are loaded on to flat-cars and hauled through Alpine tunnels — once the aristocracy had accustomed itself to the railways' habit of departing on schedule. This practice indeed continued until the 1890s, when a Mrs Caroline Giacometti Prodgers (who anyway regarded trains as a vulgar method of locomotion) was observed sitting in an open barouche at the end of an English express, 'a large red-faced woman covered with dust from head to foot'.

The normal European first-class carriage (which was usually marshalled at the front of the train, considered the safest from accidents) was however a four-wheeled vehicle, mounted on two sprung axles, with chain couplings, spring buffers and the bodywork which, with its quarter-light windows, looked not far removed from that of the stage-coach which it had so swiftly superseded. It had three separate compartments, in each of which were six well-upholstered seats with elbow-rests. A tall man could not stand up — but he *could* hang his equally tall hat from a pair of cords strung over his seat. Heavy luggage was strapped on the roof, in charge of the 'guard' (also inherited from stage-coach practice) who sat on top of the coach.

A first impression in looking at prints of the trains of the early railway period — at least in Britain, which for long set the pace in technical innovation — is that they seem curiously compressed within the gauge of the rails, as though the designers were afraid that rolling stock made too wide would topple over. But one line provi-

An elegant royal saloon, built for Queen Maria Pia of Portugal, which shows the horse-coach ancestry of early luxury stock.

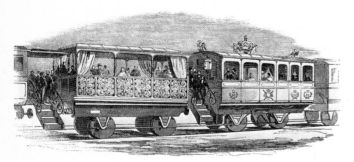

The exterior of Napoleon III's private train on the Paris-Orleans railway.

The interior of the saloon shown above, with the Emperor, the Empress Eugènie and the young Prince Imperial. After the fall of the Empire the coaches were sold to the Tsar of Russia, armour-plated, and converted to the broad Russian gauge.

The silver coffee-pot which (it is believed) produced the fluid which led to such bitter complaints from Brunel as to the quality of the refreshments supplied at Swindon on the Great Western railway.

ded a different experience. Isambard Kingdom Brunel's Great Western railway was built on a noble scale; and though full advantage was never taken of its anomalous seven-foot gauge, passengers were able to appreciate at least that amount of extra elbow-room conferred today by the broad metals of Iberia. These early GWR carriages were six-wheelers with bodies 24 ft long; and there were four compartments on each frame, each holding eight passengers. For speed and smooth riding broad-gauge travel was in a class of its own, as became clear when the passenger had to transfer to a standard-gauge line.

In the 'fifties and 'sixties — in Britain and elsewhere — the distances covered became greater, non-stop runs became longer, and speeds were somewhat higher. The former advances raised two domestic problems for the passengers — one of input, and one of output. In other words, how was one to get something to eat and drink and where was one to go to the lavatory? To the first problem there were again two solutions. The passenger could take his sustenance with him (perhaps as one of the pre-packed meals which the railways were early to offer), or he could use refreshment rooms — especially the larger ones at junctions or other stations where trains made a statutory stop of ten minutes or so for the purpose. The most famous, or infamous, British example was that at Swindon, where the Great Western railway unwisely let the catering contract to a hotel-owner from Cheltenham. The apalling food and drink he provided has gone down into history, if only as a result of an often-quoted letter, written by one not without influence on this line:

'*Dear Sir,*

I assure you Mr. Player was wrong in supposing that I thought you purchased inferior coffee. I thought I said to him that I was surprised you should buy such bad roasted corn. I did not believe you had such a thing as coffee in the place; I am certain that I never tasted any. I have long ceased to make complaints at Swindon. I avoid taking anything there when I can help it.
    Yours faithfully,

                    I.K. Brunel.'

A better example was Normanton in Yorkshire with its six-course meals for 2s 6d, whilst at Wolverton on the London & Birmingham railway a woman supervisor and 'seven very young ladies', helped by a staff of eighteen behind the scenes, refreshed the traveller with pork pies (made from their own pigs), cake, lemonade, stout, beer, gin and brandy. Wolverton, indeed, has been credited with the introduction to Europe of the bar, the barmaid and the whole principle of counter-service: it soon had its *haute cuisine* equivalents in the USA such as Poughkeepsie, NY.

As for that other problem, the first known lavatory fitting was on a train provided for Queen Victoria in 1850 by the Great Western: this emptied of course, in the usual proletarian way. Soon afterwards the South Eastern railway too fitted a w.c. into a royal saloon — though in Scotland it was to be some while before the sovereign and her ladies-in-waiting were spared the need for their specials to pull up at a station specially equipped for their comfort.

As for the ordinary European passenger, even the first-class one, he or she could not hope to find a convenience on his train until the 1870s, when some early LNWR sleeping cars were fitted with florally-decorated plumbing. The day traveller unprovided with his own utensil had to run for it at a station stop, or on branch lines take a chance on lineside relief when the train was held up by signals.

In Britain there was no real need for sleeping cars themselves until the night Anglo-Scottish services were running, but the Grand Junction railway between Birmingham and Manchester provided a 'bed carriage' as early as 1838. This was an invalid's coach rather than a true sleeper, wherein the passenger could lie stretched along the length of the train as in some present-day European stock: his middle was supported by stiff cushions while his feet projected into a cubby-hole in the opposite partition. Heat from the engine was non-existent: heavy cloaks and cans of hot water hired at the start of the journey were the only sources of warmth, and until the ingenious locomotive engineer Francis Webb took advantage of the heat of solidification of sodium acetate to produce an improved foot-warmer night passengers tended to awake to find either their boots glued on by their rubber soles or their stockinged feet attached with a film of ice. Lighting was just as miserable, whether provided by candle-power or by the oil-lamps hung in holes in the roofs through which their fumes were supposed to rise — though the changing of these lanterns at termini was carried out with great agility by porters running along the carriage roofs. The Argand lamp brought some improvement, and was favoured by a few companies in the supposed interests of safety even after gas illumination became practical; but reading a small-print Dickens or Balzac novel on a train before 1880 called for dedication and excellent eyesight.

While our first-class man was making the best of his lot, his royal betters (plus a few aristocrats such as the railway-minded Duke of Sutherland) were having a foretaste of the comforts which a later generation of commoners would be able to command at a price. For splendid is the word for some of the royal coaches that the British companies built to tempt Her Majesty on to their lines. If we exclude the eight-wheeled ceremonial vehicle, looking like Cleopatra's barge on wheels, that was built for the Duke of Wellington to use on the opening day of the Liverpool & Manchester railway, the earliest state carriage of note was constructed in 1840 for Queen Victoria's first railway journey from Slough to Paddington in 1842: this also was a rigid eight-wheeler. In the same year the dowager Queen Adelaide had a special carriage built for her: a variant on the normal London & Birmingham first-class coach, this had the sleeping arrangements referred to earlier, and apart from its finer upholstery and its being designed for one distinguished traveller and maybe two ladies-in-waiting was not far different from a standard vehicle. In 1843 the same company equipped its royal saloon with a heating system which was the brain-child of an inventor otherwise remembered mainly for his experiments with a steam gun. But the coach used for Louis Philippe's disastrous return from London in 1844 was a real improvement and was described by *The Times* as a:

The European class structure was reflected by the provision of several classes on the railways. Here a British first-class carriage is being filled with elegant travellers on their way to the Derby race at Epsom in 1846.

Second class travel could be distinctly less comfortable even on trains less congested than this same excursion to the Epsom races. Smaller windows and less elbow-room persuaded many to do what the railway companies intended they should — to spend a little extra and 'travel first'.

Third class travel was mainly for the hardy and the indigent: it was indeed often made deliberately uncomfortable, and the straw-covered floors led some to describe it as 'pig class'. Most carriages *did* boast a roof even if they were window-less, but for excursions such as that to the Derby open wagons were pressed into service. In good weather they could provide pleasures of their own.

'. . . beautiful structure, externally plain but light and elegant; the interior fitted up with much taste, lined with a light drab silk damask richly trimmed with crimson and white silk lace, the ceiling formed of white watered silk, exquisitely embroidered with crimson velvet and silver in relief, forming the national emblems of the rose, shamrock and thistle, with the Royal Crown at each corner. The carriage was entirely surrounded by light and tasteful draperies of crimson and white satin damask and lined with crimson satin richly trimmed with fringes, etc. The blinds are of a delicate peach colour, with silver tassels. The carpet is of Axminster manufacture, in colours to harmonize with the rest of the interior decorations, which reflect credit on Mr. Herring, the upholsterer of Fleet Street by whom they were executed.'

Soon afterwards, similar vehicles made their appearance on the continent. But for another three decades most passengers went on rattling around Europe in four-wheeled, and later six-wheeled, carriages. The improvements which led to the luxury travel of a later era came from across the Atlantic, where railroad practice had from the start developed on different lines.

The American companies had huge distances to cover: they were pushing their lines fast into a West that was full of promise: they had no money for grand stations or splendidly permanent engineering works. They could afford to tunnel through mountains only where there was no alternative: otherwise they had to go round them, so that lightly-laid single tracks with alarming curves and hair-raising gradients became the rule. The rigid-based European engines and coaches would have plunged off these crazy curves at any speed above a walking pace even if they had not smashed the trestle bridges with their heavy axle-loadings. And so in North America (as, later, in other lands of similar geography) the bogie carriage — a long vehicle supported at either end on a swivelling four-wheel truck — became standard well before 1860.

The length of these vehicles and their slow journeys also led to a different layout within the American car. A day in a typical European compartment, however well upholstered, would have been insupportable in America — where in any case the more generous loading gauge allowed for a wider and taller body. So America introduced the clerestory roof (giving better ventilation), hanging oil lamps, reversible seats and so on; and above all it democratised classes and did away with separate compartments, so that any passenger could have the freedom of the whole carriage to walk in — or of the whole train if he cared to step from the end platform or open vestibule of one coach to the next. A lavatory, probably segregated by sex, was early installed at the end of each car.

America also led the way with another essential for express travel, an efficient train-braking system; for in 1869 George Westinghouse successfully demonstrated his continuous compressed-air brake on the Pennsylvania railroad. Until the 1880s, though, most European (and particularly British) trains were stopped by the engine only, and considering the equally-primitive communication-cord systems it was a miracle that there were not more accidents

The history of state journeys by rail began disasterously when, in 1844, Louis Philippe of France departed from Windsor for Gosport and the yacht which was to take him to France. The story is recalled in this series of contemporary lithographs. The King of the French, accompanied by Queen Victoria and Prince Albert, set off in the royal saloon of the London & South Western railway; on the footplate was Joseph Locke, the engineer of this (and of France's first trunk) railway. But at Gosport the sea proved so stormy that it was decided that Louis Philippe had best return by the regular Dover packet. A high-speed journey back to London was hence made — only to discover that at New Cross, the then terminus of the Dover line, a fire had just broken out and the place was a shambles of railwaymen, firemen and a hastily-summoned guard of honour. (With Gallic realism the King remarked that he hoped the company was well-insured.) But London was in a Francophile and royalist mood, and eventually a substitute state train was got away — with another great railway builder, Lewis Cubitt, at the controls — and the journey completed without further crises.

28

A smoking carriage — and almost, one feels, a 'divan' — provided by Britain's Eastern Counties line in 1846. Note the lamps available to enable passengers to light their cigars.

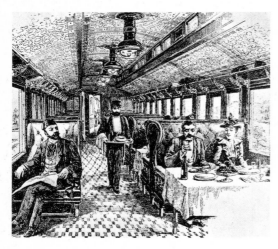

When eventually 'meals on wheels' reached Europe, a pioneer was Britain's Midland Railway which provided this very comfortable accomodation even for its third-class passengers. The gentleman on the left has affected a travelling cap typical of the times.

A Belgian first-class carriage, with a smoking saloon across the gallery, exhibited at the International Exhibition in London in 1862.

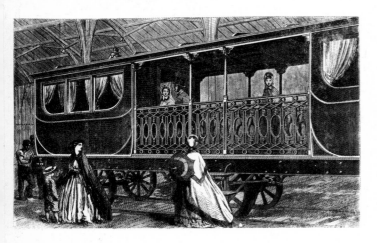

caused by lack of stopping-power on densely-worked lines. There were various early experiments with continuous chain brakes, but not until the Armagh (Ireland) accident of 1889, in which an excursion train was divided on a hill, and half of it rolled back down a gradient to collide with a following train, was an Act passed which compelled Britain's railways to fit 'fail-safe' braking to all passenger trains. Most companies then adopted a vacuum-line system; but the European continent (where, earlier, an accident in France had led to the abandonment of the obnoxious practice of locking passengers into their cars) favoured the Westinghouse method.

The introduction of such American ideas into Europe in the 1870s ushered in the era of luxury travel which forms the theme of this book. The name of George Mortimer Pullman is the key here, for it was Pullman who first converted two day-cars of the Chicago & Alton railroad to provide upper and lower sleeping-berths and then designed the first of the true sleepers which were to spread all over the USA. In these an upper berth hinged above window level folded up against the roof during the day to provide storage-space for bedding: at night it was swung down and the day seats were flattened to form the lower berth — an arrangement perpetuated in today's *couchettes* on the European continent, except in that Europe berths normally run crosswise of the compartment. Finally, in 1867, the first dining car appeared on the remote Great Western railroad of Canada. Steam heating and electric lighting (the latter being first introduced in England in 1885) were available on main lines everywhere by the end of the century, though proper air-conditioning had to wait until the 1930s.

Many of these improvements reached Europe by way of the familiar British royal route, for 1869 saw the building of the first state carriage of a new era by the London & North Western company. In this magnificent set, two six-wheeled vehicles were joined together by a flexible gangway or 'bellows connection' which seems to have been the world's first such — though later the two vehicles were united and mounted on one twelve-wheel bogie frame, and complete 'vestibule' connection had to await Pullman's patent of 1887. But commoners were not for long left behind in the new trend, for in 1873 a Scottish company put on a 'family' sleeping car, and all the time there had been improvements in such unregarded devices as buffers, couplings and springs.

In 1873 too James Allport of England's Midland railway negotiated an arrangement with George Pullman by which the latter was to build cars for Midland expresses at his own expense, receiving the supplementary fares but paying a fee to the company. Long, mounted on bogies, with end platforms, clerestory roofs, oil-fired heaters and American-style sleeping berths (or occasionally armchairs in 'parlour car' style), these eight-wheelers offered the comfort that the well-to-do American passenger had come to accept on *his* long journeys. Now, like his Queen, the first-class Englishman could travel in regal comfort; and with Georges Nagelmackers of Belgium also in touch across the Atlantic, the great days of railway luxury were about to begin.

First-class travel in Victorian times. The painting, one of a pair which suggested that the way to success lay through joining the Queen's Navy, is entitled 'The Return' and faithfully reproduces the interior of a typical compartment. The buttoned seat-backs, the tapes across the roof to hang up a top hat and the tapestry grab-handles by the windows are all evocative of Victorian travel.

Another well-known painting — 'The Journey' by Augustus Egg. Even in 1860 the carriage shows traces of its coaching ancestry in the curved 'quarter-lights'. Although the artist never visited Italy his backgrounds were often trans-Alpine, and here the rather overclad young ladies are travelling with their basket of fruit along the Riviera.

Two Pioneers

It is given to few to join the Earl of Sandwich in having their names adopted into at least twenty languages in thanks for some benefit conferred on mankind. For so many fewer do such names carry an overtone of supreme luxury that this class may contain only two members, César Ritz and George Pullman. But whereas the great hotelier could have originated from any one of a dozen countries, Pullman needed the particular challenge of American travelling conditions to lead him towards immortality, and without that challenge might well be recalled only as the father of such railroad improvements as his improbable-sounding cardboard wheel.

George Mortimer Pullman had been born in New York state in 1831, the first year to see railways in full operation in both Britain and America. He was *not* the first man to supply inland travellers with some form of recumbency, for in addition to the primitive *couchette* arrangements provided for invalids in the very earliest days of Britain's Grand Junction railway there was a proto-sleeper introduced on Pennsylvania's Cumberland Valley line in 1837 which antedated Queen Adelaide's famous vehicle with its 'boot' to accommodate the royal feet. Furthermore, enterprising proprietors had provided convertible beds on canal boats and even stage-coaches well before the railway age. But it is Pullman who will forever be associated with the custom-built sleeping-car with its adequate upholstery, bed-linen and toilet facilities — and in particular with the classic American pattern using two tiers of bunks running lengthwise of the train.

Legend says that he was inspired towards his invention as a result of nights spent in mining prospectors' shacks: the fact is that it arose from his work as a builder and carpenter by trade and as an overnight traveller by necessity. For in the mid-1850s, when Pullman was living in the new and expanding city of Chicago, one travelled overnight *only* from pressing need. From the earliest days of America's railroads, journeys implying one or more nights *en route* had been a part of business life and not the rare hazards which they appeared in Europe: this, of course, was an outcome primarily of the much greater scale of the New World and secondarily of the low speeds imposed by those uneven and sharply-radiused tracks so often referred to in these pages. But so little had been done to improve the lot of even the most affluent passenger that when some type of dossing-down accommodation *was* provided its effect was (in the words of one English traveller) 'like sleeping on a runaway horse'. In general, conditions were even worse than those experienced by R.L. Stevenson when, towards the end of the century, he crossed America in an immigrants' special with as many passengers

George Mortimer Pullman explains the advantages of his compressed-paper wheels as fitted to the Pullman Palace car 'President'.

to each coach as Pullman considered the fitting complement for an entire train — all of them sharing an ill-heated, ill-lit, ill-padded and suspectly-infected fetor.

In 1858 George Pullman resolved to change this, and began by redesigning the two cars for the Chicago & Alton Railroad referred to in the previous chapter. These rebuilds were only a small improvement on their predecessors, though, and passengers needed some persuasion before they thought it incumbent even to remove their boots on retiring. Then came civil war; and it was not until 1864, when Pullman introduced a car specially built at a price which represented virtually all his capital, that the sleeper could be said to have arrived in the shape of the largest, costliest, grandest, most luxurious — and also *safest* — vehicle yet seen on the railways of the world. So large was this 16-wheeled 'Pioneer', indeed, that at first few systems even in America could accommodate it. But after it had been prestigiously chartered for President Lincoln's funeral train line after line was rebuilt to accept it, and even today Pullman's first specially-built sleeper remains the determinant of the main-line loading-gauge throughout the US.

Other such 'elegant and homey' cars soon followed, for the public were more than willing to pay $2 or $3 for Pullman luxury as against $1.50 for its primitive rivals. Soon most of America's long-distance railroads had conceded their arrangements for overnight accommodation to the Pullman Palace Car company, which was established in 1867 with a stock of 48 carriages. To the same year belongs Pullman's other great innovation — that of the 'hotel car', which was essentially a sleeper with a kitchen incorporated and had as its prototype the Canadian 'President'. Then 1868 saw the appearance of 'Delmonico', the world's first specialised restaurant car; and by 1870 the Pullmans were rolling westward on the week-long way between New York and San Francisco.

Yet it was not only on scheduled expresses that Pullman placed his imprint, for between the 'seventies and the end of the century the ownership (or, at a pinch, the hiring) of a *private* Pullman coach, set, or entire train became as much a status-symbol as that of the steam-yachts from which so much of their architecture derived. Presidential candidates, barons of steel and oil, brewing magnates, theatrical impresarios, newspaper proprietors and the mining millionaires who were responsible for introducing narrow-gauge Pullmans to Colorado — all had their 'private varnish'. So large, indeed, did this fleet become that it eventually ran into many hundred cars, and money-no-object hotels from Newport to Florida were equipped not merely with private sidings (such as existed, for example, at Gleneagles in Scotland) but with private sidings reserved for private coaches. And whether presenting Adam, 'Louis the Who', gothic, rococo or more free-lance styles, these products of the Pullman carriage-shops often displayed a perfection of craftsmanship which even the 'royals' of Europe could not eclipse.

They were, in fact and in the late Lucius Beebe's words, 'mansions on rails', costing up to half a million dollars, over 90 ft long and weighing nearly a hundred tons apiece. Perhaps none was ever

Georges Nagelmackers, founder of the Wagons-Lits company.

equipped with a swimming-bath like that featured in Kipling's short story (though in the 1920s a train in public service could offer a shallow pool); but this was almost the only luxury which *was* missing, and various 'private varnish' vehicles or trains boasted such conveniences and inconveniences as open grates, harmoniums, portable mushrooms farms, printing presses and Jersey cattle to provide fresh milk, as well as the inevitable potted plants, acres of inlaid hardwoods, bevelled glass and bobbled plush, epergnes and winecoolers by the dozen, and legions of servants in full fig. Whether out on their own or included in the 'consists' of regular trains, such cars rolled across the plains of the *post-bellum* states and into Mexico and Canada, often affording the only approach to civilised — let alone luxurious — living for many hundreds of miles about them.

And inevitably they attracted their own folk-lore — of 'Diamond Jim' Brady who silver-plated his car's coupling gear and of the lady who thought *gold* plate more practical for bath-taps since it never tarnished: of the gambler's bet of a million dollars on which of two rain-drops ran down a window first: of Brigham Young, with the ceiling of his own bedroom painted with angels and the two attendant carriages of which one was reserved for his bishops and the other for his wives: of Adelina Patti's gowns overflowing into the bath: and, not least, of the Hungarian princess whose saloon was accidentally left accessible to the ordinary travellers who innocently invaded it — a situation saved by her *major domo*'s presence of mind in presenting each voyager by name to Her Highness... It is easy to dismiss all this as belonging to the trivia of social history rather than to the development of railroading, but in the breeding of rolling stock — as of animals and even automobiles — improvements start at the top end of the market. And it was the demands of the very rich for better-lit, better-heated, better-upholstered and better-riding carriages which led to improvements which eventually percolated through to the benefit of the common traveller.

In Britain and on the European continent, for example, a few cars built before 1870 for emperors, kings, queens and dukes had embodied such revolutionary innovations as lavatories and proper beds. But these luxuries were now drawing in sight of the general public; for in 1873 George Pullman cemented an agreement, mentioned in the previous chapter, with that dynamic Midland railway of England whose chief had visited America a few years earlier. Soon full-blooded 'American cars' were running on a number of other British lines; and in 1879 there came a further innovation with the introduction of Europe's first dining cars intended for the general public. Owing to the oddities of Britain's drinking laws and the inability of the authorities to find a precedent it originally appeared that these would have to run with at least the passengers unlubricated, but a way was soon found round the restriction. Orders were taken as the train left London, and a manifest was thrown out at a handy signal-box: this was then telegraphed down to the first stop, where the liquid refreshment was ready as the express drew in. Since this counted as buying drinks at the refreshment room rather than *en route*, it was apparently as legal as con-

suming one's own wine in an unlicensed restaurant. And today, of course, a train is one of the few places in Britain which is *not* regulated by restrictive laws — in contrast to America's 'dry' zones, or to Belgium where no spirits may be sold within the national frontiers.

The rail-borne drinker has cause to thank Pullman and the 1870s for another innovation — the luxurious day-saloon, most probably with light refreshments available. It was this which became particularly associated with the name of 'Pullman' in Britain; for the imported sleepers themselves did not survive for long, the last being withdrawn in 1908 after the long-distance companies had proved quick to learn their lesson and were operating their own carriages equipped with typical Pullman improvements. After 1890, too, company-owned diners became normal, though they did not displace Pullman restaurant cars from British metals. Indeed, an express could be observed in 1922 which not only offered a choice of Pullman and Great Eastern diners but provided each in two classes, so as to offer a choice of four independent restaurants on one train.

The Pullman saloon in fact lasted for more than sixty years after 1907 — the year in which, ten years after the founder's death, the British company severed its connections with the headquarters in Chicago and the model factory built in Pullman, Illinois, and set up on its own. The backer of this enterprise was the future Lord Dalziel, a former journalist and taxi-owner who had turned his talents to railway matters and had become — for example — god-father to a 50 mph predecessor of the *Brighton Belle*. As a decided improvement on both the rather drab olive paintwork (politely known as 'Brewster green') adopted by the American company in 1900 and the overall brown hitherto used on British Pullman stock, Dalziel's company adopted a splendid livery of umber and cream adorned with a royal-looking heraldic device; but it retained its parent's pleasant custom of christening individual cars, and together with such touches as scented soap tablets and white-gloved attendants this endured even after its nationalisation in 1962 and right up to the final withdrawal of those traditional saloons which at their peak had approached two hundred in number. And here it is left to the connoisseur to choose his favourite name from a list which runs from 'Audrey' to 'Vivienne' by way of the royal 'Phoenix'.

On the European continent the concern's influence was at first still more tenuous; for even before 1876, when the Pullman company appeared in Turin, a mighty rival was shaping-up on that scene. But in its homeland George Pullman's enterprise continued to expand. The introduction of through bookings and unified standards throughout America, for instance, owed much to Pullman's need to work his stock over various systems; and beyond that, perhaps, the typical image of the American train — immensely long and heavy by European standards, trailing for days without re-marshalling across the plains and the mountains — derives as much from Pullman as from any man.

In the late nineteenth and early twentieth centuries the American Pullman company survived many business vicissitudes. But

In Britain, the name of Pullman became a synonym for luxury travel by day rather than night — a fact of which the Birmingham Railway Carriage & Wagon Company was well aware. Deeply-upholstered individual seats, lamps casting a soft pink glow on the tables, beautifully-inlaid woodwork and attentive service of food and drink to every seat, together created the Pullman image.

Below: One of the most magnificent railway sights in Britain was the distinctive Pullman livery. Here the London Brighton & South Coast's *Southern Belle*, forerunner of a long line of 'Belles' on the Southern system, races down to Brighton with its matching rake of Pullman stock hauled by one of the Brighton Atlantics.

standards of service were usually so immaculate that one staff booklet could devote two pages to setting out the twelve essential stages in pouring out a glass of beer, and the name 'Pullman' hence became associated with luxury. By 1930, the company operated nearly 10,000 cars, had a travelling staff of the same magnitude, and with its accommodation of over 100,000 travellers every night could claim to be 'the world's largest hotel'. It consumed, for instance, four million cakes of soap and nearly a hundred million drinking cups a year, and its annual laundry bill exceeded three million dollars.

It survived too into the age of the streamliners, an age characterised by those 'roomettes' and 'duplex rooms' which — if the Hollywood films of the period are to be believed — provided such delicious opportunities for farcical confusions and near-seductions, and by the replacement of the grand piano of old by the cinema-car and the dancing-car. (These also made an appearance on European trains, with mobile ballrooms proving popular in Germany though they were excluded as vulgarities from the Côte d'Azur expresses of the period). And it even survives in today's uneasy era of the rail-borne telephone for business and the rail-borne TV set for relaxation, though what remains of the American company has now ceased to own or even operate stock and become a unit in a general engineering consortium and (at least outside the United States), the very name 'Pullman' has become a mere synonym for comfort and is abrogated by trades ranging from furniture design through cinema proprietorship and road-coach operation to — most ironically of all — aircraft construction.

George Pullman had certainly never been alone in his field; for instance, before his company absorbed its half-dozen or more major rivals (including one named Rip Van Winkel) he had suffered sharp competition from the Vanderbilt-backed Webster Wagner enterprise. Yet in the event it was neither of these but rather Colonel William d'Alton Mann's 'boudoir cars' which were destined to make perhaps the greatest impact of all on the world's railways, and this despite the fact that the colonel was best known as a newspaper columnist whose extravagant tastes were financed by the proceeds of a type of blackmail which admittedly was taken fairly light-heartedly in the New York of the 1870s. One of his few mistakes, for example, had been to approach the actress Lily Langtry for some $200,000 in return for silence concerning details of her private life gleaned while building her private coach. Mann soon learned that the 'Jersey Lily', mistress of the future Edward VII and of others only slightly less luminous, was sharper in business (as well as having a shaplier person) than a man whose idea of a modest breakfast was three chops and two bottles of champagne.

But he was lucky in two ways. One stroke of chance was that his promotional activities attracted the attention of the young Belgian engineer, Georges Nagelmackers, who in 1868 crossed the Atlantic to see if American methods could make long-distance travel in Europe less depressing despite the jealousies between nations and their railway administrations. Mann's other fortunate break was

The Great Northern railway was one of the earliest of British companies to experiment with American-type Pullman cars. Here the cook, exposed to wind, smuts and rain on the open verandah, prepares the food...

... which was served to elegant passengers in the ornate restaurant car. Padded seats and much *boiserie* distinguished Pullman cars in Britain as in their homeland, but the loading gauge could restrict elbow-room and enforce one-a-side seating.

that George Pullman's own sleeping cars — which, as has been seen, were introduced to Europe a little later — were to prove a comparative failure there. The French in particular did not like being surrounded by strangers in the open-planned early Pullman sleepers, whereas Mann could offer — and under that seductive name of *boudoir* car too — the more private arrangement of a sleeping carriage divided into compartments, with a side-corridor and berths running transversely.

Already Nagelmackers was operating a few primitive sleepers built in Austria to his own specification. But the little Mann cars were more comfortable than these — and also appeared more suited to European conditions and tastes than did Pullman's sleepers. And so the Belgian asked Mann to supply some to the company which he had founded with royal approval in 1872 and whose title was to become engraved on every European traveller's heart — though it was to take another decade, and some ponderous thought, before to the words *Compagnie internationale des wagons-lits* was added the resounding termination *et des grands express européens*, and for the first few years it was in any case the name of Mann which was given prominence.

A few months earlier — and despite the Franco-Prussian war — Nagelmackers had seen his first sleeping car run from Ostend to Brindisi as part of the important Indian mail service; now routes from Paris to Berlin and Calais followed. The reception of the new idea by the various railway administrations was mixed, and in particular the Pullman and Wagons-Lits companies were to be at loggerheads until 35 years later, after the deaths of both the American and the Belgian, Lord Dalziel acquired a controlling interest in the CIWL and so cemented that British involvement with it which had been visible from the start. But there was less doubt of the public appeal of such services; and by 1876, when Nagelmackers acquired the Mann interest, he had more than fifty sleepers (distinguished, like Britain's Pullmans, by the name of the owning company being lettered in American fashion above the windows) running as far afield as Vienna and Breslau. Mark Twain's comment in *The Innocents Abroad* that not in all France could one find 'that culmination of all charity and human kindness, a sleeping car' was hence out of date before it was published.

Six years later, with his services now operating in Italy, Nagelmackers took a further if inevitable step and introduced the dining car to continental Europe, after having overcome such problems as customs regulations regarding the sealing of wine-lockers at frontiers. Then, on 5 June 1883, came the first all-CIWL international train, when after negotiations between Nagelmackers and eight mistrustful railway administrations the Gare de l'Est in Paris witnessed the departure via Germany of the three teak bogie cars which composed the earliest of all trains to bear the name *Orient Express*. Though 1,800 miles to the east, Constantinople or Istanbul was not everybody's idea of the orient, and in any case the lower Danube was not yet bridged and the journey had to be completed by steamers. But the route captured the imagination of Europe and the world —

Nagelmackers was a visionary who dreamt of linking all Europe with a system of through trains. One of the most famous was the *Nord Express* shown here in Imperial Russia in 1901. Its original route was Paris-Berlin-St Petersburg.

The Trans-Siberian express — one of the most romantic trains of the world, whose name conjures up the vast hinterland of Russia, wolves and snow, samovars and furry hats. It is here shown in about 1906, soon after its inception. This was one of the Wagons-Lits company's most ambitious projects, entailing much staff work and worry to see the train on its fortnight-long journey across the width of Russia and through Manchuria to Vladivostok.

Another of the world's legendary trains, the *Orient Express*, was created in 1883. It was the first international train to be composed solely of the Wagons-Lits company's cars, and was for long the only way to cross Europe's frontiers without change of carriage. A heroine of literature, stage and screen, the train still runs today.

A Wagons-Lits dinner menu for 1884.

as, despite all political impediments, it continues to capture it. Two contemporary accounts of this historic run (which neared its end with an impromptu invasion of the express by a party of Romanian *tziganes*, after whose 2½ hour performance of song and dance the Burgundian chef left his galley to oblige with the 'Marseillaise') are mentioned later in this book. But neither there nor here is there space to follow out all those complexities of re-namings and re-routings — for instance, the concentration on the Simplon route after the First World War and the opening of the Athens connection — which surround the history of the fleet as it penetrated nations sensitive to banditry and to inter-administration wars in its earlier days and to political upheavals throughout the present century. For a loving and detailed presentation of the story, fortunately, the books of George Behrend are available.

One point, however, should be stressed here — that the inaugural 'Orient' consisted of only two sleepers and a diner bracketed between its baggage vans. (Initially, too, the service was of a single departure a week). This miniaturised quality remained typical of the continental luxury express until the present century, when as locomotive power kept pace with passenger demand frequent full-length trains could be run. After the Second World War, however, the need for such services contracted again, bringing a tendency to include the ordinary day cars and even goods vans of various national railways into the rakes of such trains as the *Orient Express*. And today, it must be confessed, the sight of the typical European ultra-long-distance express, with its line of ill-matched cars broken only by a few *wagons-lits* bearing an illustrious name in rather slovenly lettering, is not such as to impress a visitor used to the long consists of matching stock characteristic of the streamliners of the USA and similar lands. Such a visitor may, in fact, find more external elegance as well as much higher speeds in the internal *rapides* of such countries as France and Italy.

After the first flurry of journalistic attention the 'Orient' settled down to the transporting of diplomats and exporters, of health-seekers, and above all (and particularly after the passenger's comforts had been improved, through-running became possible from the Channel ports to Istanbul) of grand-tourists. More exotic characters there were and still are: the spy and the man on the run (who is hinted at in a mysterious early illustration which seems to introduce Sherlock Holmes to the train a decade before he was created): the drug-smuggler secreting his contraband behind the toilet and the refugee clinging to the underframes until smelt out by trained dogs at some frontier; the actress for whose poodles the chef prepared a special *Wiener Schnitzel* and the salesman who was 'arrested' at a Balkan frontier and, after anxious moments, found he was needed only because the border-guard had seen his passport and wanted to drink champagne with one who shared the same birthday; a king on the footplate who fulfilled the secret ambition of many by taking control when the regular driver was injured, and the members of Britain's 500-year-old-corps of royal messengers who wear the silver greyhound and who have only recently (for the most part) deserted the rail for the air: these are from fact rather than fiction. But only once has the 'Orient' been connected with even a suspected murder, and only once has true drama struck it — in 1891 when, with the Turkish extension only two years old, partisans in Macedonia kidnapped four Germans and held them to ransom. It appears true that the express was snowed-up for nearly a fortnight beyond Sofia in the winter of 1929; but though the story is attested by a King's Messenger there are maddening gaps in it, and such details as a wolf-menaced crew hacking down trees to save the passengers from dying of cold appear picturesque accretions.

For the most part, indeed, all such *grands express européens* fail — like life itself — to live up to the expectations of the novelists. There may be tales of the 'Orient' and its sisters still to be told, but if they go for ever unrecorded it will not be through a lack of journalistic diligence but rather because of the remarkable loyalty which the CIWL inspires in its staff. The present writer, for example, recalls how a retired *conducteur* was about to relate a promising anecdote concerning an Orthodox bishop and his favourite (if platonic) travelling-companion — who was a *poule de luxe*, and not one of those peasant girls for whose services the station masters would telegraph down the line when a traveller bored with the Balkan plains felt the need for sentimental diversion. Just as the tale was ripening the official remembered his duty to a prelate dead for three decades, and shrugged. 'Il faut être discret, monsieur...'

Yet discretion was only one of the qualities demanded of Nagelmackers' corps of sleeping-car attendants and waiters. Members of what was virtually a new profession, they had to be masters of half a dozen languages, able to carry out mental arithmetic in even more currencies, experts on frontier formalities and diplomats in all things. Some were qualified as barbers and others as nurses; and all, of course, were immaculately attired even when they had had to spend their nights on hammocks slung in dining cars. (On some of the great expresses, indeed, the waiters were dressed in blue silk breeches and buckled shoes, and on state occasions even the locomotive crews wore white coats.) But their passengers too dressed the part, a change into evening dress being regarded as *de rigueur* before one settled down to one's seven-course dinner; and this was itself probably shared with an old acquaintance re-encountered, for whereas the term 'jet set' became outdated in a decade the CIWL remained synonymous with European luxury travel for seventy years and irresistably attracted its regular patrons.

Finally there was the matter of accommodation for baggage and the mail. The company owned its own *fourgons* (in experimental days one of these was combined with a bathroom, which introduced the hazard of a lady stepping from her tub to discover that the van had been detached in Italy whilst all her clothes and her passport sped on to France), and in some early literature these appear almost as important as the passenger cars. For in those years there was no travelling light, no air-weight valises: Edward VII, for example, went around Europe equipped with up to seventy pieces of luggage.

The *Anatolia Express* was inaugurated in 1925 to provide a sleeping-car service from Haydarpasa, on the far side of the Bosphorus from Istanbul, to Ankara. The train runs through the wild spaces of the Taurus mountains. This photograph, taken in 1930, shows the original wooden rolling stock.

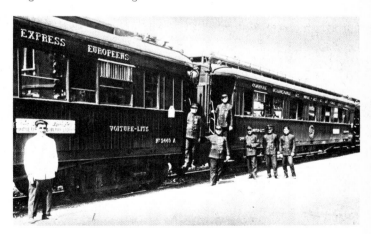

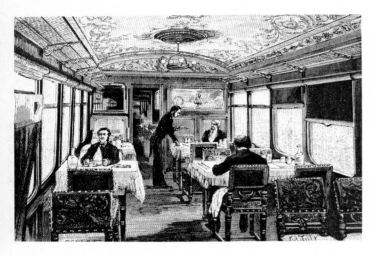

A restaurant car designed in 1883 for use on the luxury expresses of the Wagons-Lits company.

The original caption to this 1905 drawing of a scene in Germany reads: 'Nowhere's Christmas: A Movable Feast. On the continental railways Christmas is kept as far as possible as if the passengers were at home. Not even the Christmas tree is omitted from the celebration...'

The provision of all this new equipment and all these novel services called for immense organising ability. But it was in this direction — plus his persuasiveness — that Nagelmackers' strength lay, and he was not long content with the 'Orient' alone. Throughout the '80s and '90s the *grands express européens* were introduced until there was barely a land where the name of the company could not be seen in proud brass letters standing out from varnished teak. By 1887, looking for new worlds to conquer, the company was represented in Russia (whose railways had also been early to introduce their own sleepers) and two years later it appeared in north Africa, so that strange Cyrillic and Arabic blazons were added to the languages of a company which had long known that 'Do not lean out of the window' was *kihajolni veszelyes* in Hungarian. A few day-saloons were to be seen on boat-trains in Britain too. And in 1898 — as a theme which again is developed later in these pages — the CIWL introduced what was then the most luxurious train in the Old World and remains perhaps the most famous anywhere — the *Trans-Siberian Express*, some cars from which were displayed at the Paris Exhibition of 1900 in such a fashion that diners could enjoy a typical menu whilst a panorama of the route unrolled past the windows. Only the plan to unite St. Petersburg directly to Lisbon by a *Nord-Sud Express* which should link seven capital cities, overcome two changes of gauge, and still cover more than 3,000 miles in under four days, eventually defeated Georges Nagelmackers.

By the turn of the century, then, the empire of the CIWL was beginning to look much as it appears on that great cast-bronze map which dominates its operational headquarters in Paris, and which shows the company active in twenty-four lands. Nagelmackers, too, had already expanded into property development and general tourism; and despite the warning of a close colleague who rightly considered that 'un bon restaurant ne se fabrique pas en série' a host of Palace Hotels arose in Europe, Asia and Africa to accommodate grand-tourists in the style which they expected. Their spiritual needs, too, were catered for by the company's building of Roman and Anglican churches in heathen parts.

But the CIWL did not have things entirely its own way, for after 1900 an increasing number of European railway companies decided to operate their own diners and saloons even if they conceded to the CIWL a sleeping-car monopoly. To take only one such example, the Paris-Orleans company was in 1909 running a *rapide* to Bordeaux which, in addition to providing the usual luxury facilities such as news bulletins and a 'dainty little boudoir' for the ladies, made imaginative use of electricity for more than lighting purposes. The electric-razor point might lie nearly half a century in the future; but this train provided electric cigar lighters for the gentlemen and electric curling-irons for their travelling companions.

But then, France has always been proud of its electrical gadgetry: a recent pattern of French buffet car, for instance, proudly displays to the public not only a dozen meters indicating the state of five types of supply but also a wiring diagram suggesting considerably greater complexity than the simple 110v DC devices whose massive brassware was not long ago shown off in old carriages on Britain's LNER. And to revert to the last years of the *Belle Epoque*, a greater challenge to the CIWL than that presented by the P-O was being planned in the same year of 1909, if far away beyond the Alps in Vienna.

Although the earliest opposition to the CIWL's operations had come from France, the Germanic countries were now feeling that (perhaps because of the death of Nagelmackers, who as a Belgian had been able to maintain a neutral stance) the company was unduly orientated towards Latin lands. In particular, the 'imperial and royal' railways of Franz Josef's domains considered that they were losing much-needed tourist revenue through the CIWL's failure to exploit the scenic routes of Austria — or even to run comfortable boat-trains to their port of Trieste.

So the Austrians called in a company which could provide something which even the CIWL could not — observation cars. This concern, amazingly enough, was the Canadian Pacific, which had already made a name for itself as a world-ranging tourist agency as well as a railway operator. And so in 1912 there began the CPR's short-lived 'Austrian adventure', an adventure which took the form of operating transatlantic-type carriages (including eight specially-built and admirably-designed observation cars) between Vienna, Zurich and Trieste.

So transatlantic *were* these, indeed, that they were even lettered with the Canadian Pacific name. Perhaps the CPR overplayed its hand, for it gave some Germans — who were worried at the loss of their shipping traffic to the Mediterranean port — an excuse to start a smear campaign and even use physical violence against the Canadians. But before the matter could be resolved the First World War broke out.

As has been noted, Germany had its own quarrels with the CIWL — though these would have been much fiercer had the Kaiser foreseen the coming humiliation of a surrender which was to be signed in the most famous of all *wagons-restaurants*, an event which so haunted Hitler that he was to turn the tables in the same car 22 years later. But back in 1914 the fatherland could at least seize the chance to confiscate all Wagons-Lits stock on German or allied territory. And this stock provided the nucleus for the CIWL's only serious competitor, 'Mitropa' — a company which operated widely until after the Second World War, following which it served mainly East Germany whilst a new German sleeping- and dining-car company, the DSG, took over its services in the West.

Despite German gestures southward, however, the only territory where the CIWL and Mitropa were ever in direct competition after 1920 was Switzerland; and even there the federal railways remained loyal to a CIWL subsidiary, leaving only the private systems to be contended for. So it was that Mitropa provided the red-dining-saloons of the metre-gauge Rhaetian railways (one of the partners which operate the spectacular *Glacier Express* route, linking the Rhine and Rhone valleys, which crowned the age of Swiss mountain railway construction) and the great CIWL felt

The Montreux-Oberland Bernois *Golden Mountain Express* passing through typical mountain scenery.

The *Glacier Express*, operated by three Swiss companies, runs through spectacular mountain scenery along the valleys of the Rhône and Rhine as it spans the width of Switzerland.

Even the narrow-gauge railways of Switzerland were anxious that British and American tourists should find the luxury of the main line on their mountain routes. One such venture was that of the Montreux-Oberland Bernois railway, which arranged with the Wagons-Lits company to operate a Pullman train on its Montreux-Interlaken route. Although they have a grand title — the *Golden Mountain Express* — the cars only ran as far as Zweisimmen, where the passengers had to change to the standard gauge for the rest of their journey, and the experiment proved uneconomic. Some of the cars — pictured below in their present state — are, however, still in service for private excursions.

bound to reply with its elegant — and equally narrow-gauge — *Golden Mountain Pullman* on the dramatic little Montreux-Oberland line. This latter train ran for only a single season, in 1931, but its stock is still frequently used for excursions.

The mention of the name of Pullman above is a reminder of the harmony which now existed between the CIWL and the British Pullman company. This accord was symbolised by at least two facts — that Nagelmackers' son had in 1903 obligingly married Dalziel's daughter, and that the lower panels of some continental Pullmans were painted in the same royal blue as distinguished the steel bodied CIWL stock which was first introduced in 1922. Dalziel had acquired his CIWL shares as a private individual rather than on behalf of his company, and the event had little direct effect on railway operation before 1914; but the years from 1925 onwards saw the establishment of that fleet of such part-Pullman and all-Pullman trains as the *Oiseau Bleu* which characterised European luxury travel up to the Second World War — and which were not quite extinct even at the date of the nationalisation of the British company. Another component in this international jigsaw was the Thos. Cook agency, which was acquired by the CIWL in 1928 and operated as a subsidiary of it until the post-war changes.

One disappointment of this era was the failure for political reasons to link-up the CIWL's new services in the Near East with those in north Africa, so providing a through service from the Channel to Cairo and beyond. But for the rest the empire founded by Georges Nagelmackers — by that 'nail-maker' whose nails of steel helped fasten the nations together — endured through the depression, the Second World War, the political and social upheavals of the 1950s and the increasing challenge from the air and the road. And so in essence it endures today, when international civil servants have taken the place of archdukes and when migrant workers and package-deal tourists follow the routes pioneered for those of infinite leisure and credit.

For, just over a century since Mann's boudoir cars first ran in Europe, the CIWL survives as an independent company. It has lost Asia and (apart from some hotel interests) Africa, eastern Europe has gone the way which Russia went at its revolution, and most Scandinavian countries now operate their own sleepers. The glorious but impractical coats of arms of former days are being replaced by the squiggles and scrawls of 'industrial design'. More countries than in former years undertake their own catering, and the CIWL itself serves fewer four-course meals than of old and relies far more on the self-service *ventes ambulantes* and *à la carte* snacks which now account for most of its catering revenue. And above all today's practice is for the CIWL (and, for that matter, the DSG) to leave the ownership of both dining and sleeping cars to individual countries or an international 'pool' and to concern itself with service. To balance these losses, the CIWL has over the last decades become more and more deeply — and, for lovers of the past, saddeningly — involved with motorways and even with airline catering.

The *Mediterranéen Express* at Vintimillia in 1910. Unusually, the Wagons-Lits coaches were painted blue and cream; another feature is the very pronounced 'bird-cage' lookout on the baggage wagon.

The *Riviera Express* at Beaulieu in 1907, with the more usual teak-sided Wagons-Lits stock of the period and the PLM *coupe-vent* locomotive which represents one of the earliest attempts at streamlining.

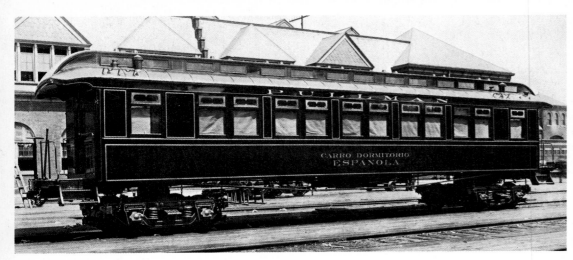

Top left: A special lounge-sleeping car, named 'George M. Pullman', built of aluminium for the 1933 World's Fair in Chicago. This car marked the transition from steel rolling stock towards the light weight streamliners.

Above: A narrow-gauge Pullman sleeping car, 'Española', originally built in 1880 for service in Colorado. It was renovated in 1900 for operation on the Interoceanic Railway of Mexico.

The Pullman sleeping car 'Atlantic' under construction at the company's Detroit works. The enormous amount of painstaking handwork that went into the decoration of these cars is apparent. The two men are applying gold-leaf decorations.

The enclosed passageway between cars, called a 'vestibule' in America and a 'concertina' or 'bellows' connection in Britain was patented by the Pullman company though in fact first used on a British royal train. It was employed on the *Pennsylvania Limited* of 1887. A supremely high standard of finish was displayed by these cars, extending down even to their names being lettered on the bogie frames.

As a blazon of ownership, the proud and time-honoured gold legend on the blue cars is hence nowadays misleading. It is also anachronistic in itself, for in 1967 it seemed realistic (but is the pursuit of realism always even the most *profitable* course?) that, after those comparatively uneventful decades either side of the Second World War, the company should amend its name again. . . . *Et des grands express européens* vanished from the multilingual letter-heads, and it is now the *Compagnie internationale des wagons-lits et du tourisme.*

Yet amid all this diversification the traditional operations of supplying meals and beds to railway travellers prosper, thanks not least to the popularity of overnight car-sleeper services. From Stockholm to Madrid and from London to Istanbul nearly a thousand royal-blue cars still network Europe, not merely providing their admittedly costly amenities but trailing all the romance of a hundred years of railway history.

Compagnie Internationale des Wagons-Lits

INDIAN MAIL TRAIN
CALAIS-BOLOGNA (BRINDISI)
in connection with the train

LEAVING LONDON EVERY FRIDAY NIGHT
THROUGH SERVICE WITH
SLEEPING CARS
MOST COMFORTABLY APPOINTED. GREAT SAVING OF TIME

LIMITED NUMBER OF PASSENGERS

No other carriages in this train but the well known BELGIAN SLEEPING CARS with separate compartments.

Places can be retained at the London office of the P. & O. STEAMSHIP COMPANY or by applying to the steward on board the steamers between Alexandria & Brindisi.

This poster advertises the first sleeping-car service on the *Indian Mail* in 1879. This train was much patronised by passengers to India who wished to avoid the sea journey from the Channel to the Mediterranean, since they were met by P. & O. steamers at Brindisi for the journey through the Suez Canal.

THE KEY DATES

Before 1840:	Primitive sleepers exist in US and Britain.	
During 1850s:	Sleepers used by royalty, etc., in Europe.	
During 1860s:	Sleepers available for privileged travellers in India, possibly Russia, etc.	
1864:	World's first true sleeper for general booking built by George Pullman in USA.	
1867:	AMERICAN PULLMAN CO. FOUNDED.	
1868:	World's first public diner used in Canada.	
1869:	First 'bellows' connection (on royal coaches in Britain).	
1872:	NAGELMACKERS' FIRST COMPANY FOUNDED. First publicly-available sleepers on western European continent.	
1874:	Britain introduces its first 'public' sleeper.	
1876:	NAGELMACKERS' COMPANY REFOUNDED AS CIWL.	
1879:	Britain introduces its first true diner.	
1882:	First regular diners on European continent.	
1887:	First fully 'bellows'-connected train (USA).	
1907:	BRITISH PULLMAN CO. BECOMES ENTIRELY BRITISH-OWNED: ITS CHAIRMAN ACQUIRES CONTROL OF CIWL	
1916:	'MITROPA' FOUNDED, USING CIWL STOCK	
1928:	CIWL ACQUIRES THOS. COOK & SON LTD.	
1947:	AMERICAN PULLMAN CO. CEASES TO OPERATE CARS	
1962:	BRITISH PULLMAN CO. NATIONALISED	
1968:	AMERICAN PULLMAN CO. CEASES TO OWN CARS	

The Golden Age of Steam

It has often been remarked that the steam locomotive is one of the few things which man has created that seems to have a life of its own. Without fire in its belly it is a lifeless object — cold, greasy, and dank. But when the fire is kindled it wakes and starts to breathe. Its limbs are naked, and one can see the sources of its strength and the manner in which it moves. As it prepares to shift a load it audibly tenses itself; as its starts, it labours; as it masters its task it exults; and as it slows again it relaxes. It always tells you what it is doing, how fast it is going, how steep a hill it climbs, how much it hauls. If it is in good health it sounds tight and sure-footed, but if it is run-down it limps, clanks, and wheezes. It needs rest and occasional coaxing. It is, in fact, exactly what it was so often called: an iron horse.

Yet fundamentally the steam engine is an extremely simple machine, and that has always been its major virtue. It is indeed so simple that remarkably few variations have ever been successfully made on its basic layout. A few early experiments were needed to settle the question as to whether smooth iron wheels could grip smooth iron rails firmly enough to haul a useful load. A few more were needed to establish that the boiler ought to take the form of a horizontal barrel containing a firebox, with heat and smoke drawn through tubes along the rest of the barrel by the exhaust steam from the cylinders. The final decision of where best to place the cylinders took almost twenty years to resolve; but Robert Stephenson settled it in 1830, his answer being — at the front, in line with the wheels, and set either level or slightly inclined. So, well before a hundred locomotives had been built the world over, they had already reached an approximation of their final form and the rest was to be largely a matter of growth and improvement of detail.

Even in the earliest years, however, several national schools of locomotive design had become established. First, by right of seniority, came the British tradition. The fundamental requirement which British builders had tried to meet was economy, not just in capital cost but in running. The early British main lines had been extremely soundly built: their tracks were well-aligned and substantial, immense sums had been expended to make them as straight and level as possible, and considerable tunnels, viaducts and cuttings had been built so that trains could be worked with the least possible power. The engines were substantially built also, if small; but the requirement of cheapness meant that they should burn as little fuel as possible. The cost of repairs was, possibly mistakenly, regarded as of less importance.

Cheapness also demanded that engines should have the minimum possible number of wheels — at first four but later, for reasons

One of the primary *desiderata* for a railway is a firm and easily-graded track-bed, and in this the British excelled. Below: The formation for the Great Central line — the last trunk railway to be built in Britain — cuts its swathe through the midland shires.

A rather posed portrait of the 'Lison', 0–4–2, taken in 1860 on the Paris–Cherbourg line. Evidently no standardisation of rolling stock had yet taken place.

Above: The 'Outrance' type of French locomotives which did sterling service on many of the routes of France. This machine, Nord No 2836, was converted in 1890 from a 2-4-0 to a 4-4-0 by enlarging the smoke box, extending the frames, and adding a front bogie.

With an outline typical of the cluttered French design (which, by exposing all ancillary gear, made for ease of maintenance), Nord engine No. 2874 hauls a mixed-stock train in 1910.

A powerful 4-cylinder compound locomotive, built in 1908 for hauling heavy expresses over the steeply-graded Gotthard tunnel route, which was the original North-South route through Switzerland.

of safety, six — fixed rigidly in a plain frame for simplicity's sake. A single pair of driving wheels was long preferred for fast passenger work, since with the inconsistent nature of the wrought iron used for tyres and connecting-rods before 1870 it was not easy to produce engines with coupled wheels capable of running at speeds over about 40 mph. Cylinders were more often set inside the frame than outside it, since though this practice exacted a cost-of-maintenance penalty through their inaccessibility it simplified construction and gave better protection from cold air. British locomotive designers, who had to face a somewhat less rigorous climate than most others, were long reluctant to provide fully-enclosed cabs and were content with plain weatherboards, though by the 1870s this spartan approach had begun to disappear.

American practice differed in several important ways, fundamentally because American railroads themselves followed a contrasting plan. Almost always the object had been to lay tracks as quickly as possible, regardless of difficult curves and gradients. Earthworks and structures were cut to the minimum, and to provide a smooth track was an objective secondary to getting one laid in a hurry. The initial result of this was that the English engines exported to America were always falling off the rails since their rigidity of framing meant that they could not follow the track's irregularities. This was at first disconcerting; but it was soon found that if a little flexibility was introduced into the wheel-base all would be well. This involved using either a leading 'pony truck' — a two-wheeled sub-frame set under the front of a locomotive with spring-controlled side-play which allowed it to steer the machine into a curve — or, more often and under rolling stock as well as engines, a full bogie or four-wheeled sub-frame able to swivel about a central pin.

So one difference in locomotive practice between Britain and America appeared early: in America, suspension had to be more complex. Another important difference followed from the steep US gradients. Power was needed, and brute haulage capacity had to take precedence over economising on the last few pounds of coal. Rapidly American locomotives became considerably bigger than British ones — a move made possible because the 'loading gauge' or all-round clearance of American railroads, thanks to the rarity of tunnels and over-bridges, was far more generous than the European tolerances. Single drivers were almost unknown and even in the 1840s locomotives with six coupled wheels were not uncommon, whilst some with eight had begun to be experimented with. Finally, in a new and growing country where skilled manpower was scarce and expensive, it was important to reduce the effort required to build and maintain machinery, so that cylinders and auxiliary equipment tended to be placed where they were easily accessible.

Between the extremes of American and British practice most other railway countries found some intermediate course. In many European states British engineers built the first railways and supplied the first machines, so that British ideas led; but local conditions soon produced changes. In France, for instance, most early lines

As passenger train weights increased, a need was felt for more powerful locomotives. Here a 4–6–0 of the Paris-Orleans railway is under test coupled to a dynamometer carriage.

had been built to Stephensonian standards of perfection. But the greater distances soon made it more profitable to run fewer and heavier trains, so that locomotive size and power moved towards almost American values. British ideas of the importance of economic performance still prevailed, however, even though Frenchmen early abandoned the British concern for an elegantly uncluttered exterior, showed a distaste for crawling under the machine to get at its vitals, and so preferred — like the Americans — to expose all accessories such as pumps and sand-boxes for easy access.

Germany and Austria, on the other hand, had taken much notice of American thinking from the 1840s onwards, and in general the further east one moved the cheaper and rougher railways became and the more American-influenced were the locomotives and rolling stock. Russia and China still show clear marks of this tradition; but in much of Africa, South America, Australasia and (above all) India, British ideas often led for reasons of history.

Such was the world situation around 1870, when locomotive practice seemed to have reached a plateau of development with few innovations to be expected except for a general if gentle trend to 'build bigger'. But before the turn of the century several developments had begun to force the cycle of progress into a new age, and of these the most important was a considerable increase in train weights. In part this was due to a move — inaugurated for reasons of safety following a series of unpleasant and incandescent accidents — towards replacing wood by steel in carriage construction. Partly too (at least in America) it followed the invention of strong automatic coupling gear; and all the time passengers were demanding more comfortable, and hence heavier, rolling stock. But perhaps the main reason behind the increase in train weights was the invention during the late 1880s of satisfactory systems of power brakes operating the whole length of a train. One, Westinghouse's, depended on compressed air and the rest (due to Smith and others) on reduced pressures; but all gave the driver a means of instantly applying brakes to virtually every wheel on the train and thus made heavy loads safe to run at speed.

The consequence of all this was a comparatively sudden growth in the demands made on motive power. The first reaction of turn-of-the-century designers was simply to increase size, even if this meant articulating the locomotive: but such juggernauts as resulted were usually disappointing in performance, and the alternative of double-heading was a costly one. Soon, however, two new inventions changed the picture. The first — less successful in the long run in all countries except France — was the development of the 'compounding' which had already been tried in Britain, with high- and low-pressure cylinders using the same steam in succession: this combined an increase in power with reasonable fuel-saving. The second, and more important, innovation was superheating. Several engineers had sought for a means of re-heating and drying the steam before it entered the cylinders, a practice which would have the effect of increasing power and general 'liveliness'; but the first successful system was that developed by Schmidt on the Prussian state railways and used in a class of passenger 4–6–os introduced in 1906. The device swept the world, and by 1914 few railways were still using non-superheated locomotives for main-line duties.

So by 1910 the stage was set for the final main phase of development of the locomotive, and thanks to the inventiveness of such men as Goldsdorf in Austria, and Walschaerts in Belgium the golden age of steam was about to dawn. Despite the English elegance of Patrick Stirling's huge-wheeled 'singles' for the Great Northern railway and of other fabled beauties of Victorian times, despite maintenance standards so exacting that only pure olive oil from Lucca was permitted to lubricate the locomotives used in the rail races to Scotland, despite the nostalgic charm of the typical diamond-smokestacked, cow-catchered and timber-clad American engine with its great headlamp and bell, despite the free-wheeling glamour of the last of Europe's ubiquitous Cramptons and the achievements of the first of de Glehn's four-cylinder compounds in France, one cannot date this dawn much earlier. Romance and interest there had been in plenty in the nineteenth century, but from the engineer's point of view locomotive practice had then laboured under too many restrictions of lack of communication between rival schools of design, and incomplete theory, for anything like the full development of the potential of Stephenson's ideas to have been possible.

Before following these developments, though, it is worth taking a backward glance. Everywhere in the world just after 1900, in local and branch-line working, much was still being done by thousands of elderly and unimproved machines ranging from small tank engines up to the fleets of 2–6–os and 2–8–os that had proliferated in the American tradition, or to the 0–6–os and 0–8–os of the European line, since the 1860s. But the most demanding work had begun to be tackled by ten coupled engines, or here and there by machines articulated on Mallet's or Garratt's principles. All these behemoths were built for the shifting of the greatest possible load, never mind how slowly; for speed, in freight service, was still unimportant. So while tractive effort (measured in pull at the drawbar) was high, horsepower (or drawbar pull multiplied by speed) was not always very impressive.

In passenger service, though, the scene was more exciting. During the latter part of the nineteenth century most of the world's passenger trains of all types had been hauled by 4–4–os. This pattern had first appeared in America, (where between the 1850s and 1880s it outnumbered all other varieties put together) in the 1840s, and had spread across the world. But although the type still abounded in 1910, the day of the 4–4–0 was done even in Europe. For all its virtues it could no longer produce the needed horsepower, and in passenger service it was horsepower that counted. Even the heavy new steel coaches and luxury stock did not send train weights up to the levels attained in freight service, so that tractive effort was not too important; but speed *was*, and the demand for power and steam grew proportionately.

To provide these, boilers and fireboxes had to be made larger. The first move in this direction had been taken in the 1860s in

Speeds too rose, and the turn of the century saw the introduction of the Atlantic with its 4-4-2 wheel arrangement. Superheating was also introduced in this period, as in this Atlantic seen in 1913 on the Nord railway of France.

Left, above: German designs were typified by gadgetry rather than grace. This massive 2-8-2 has two cabs, one in the usual place, and another on the tender for easy reversal in shunting and tender-first running.

Above: For many years the typical American locomotive was the 4-4-0 whose wheel arrangement gave the optimum performance on lightly-laid and heavily-graded tracks. This example is seen on a New York to Philadelphia express near Jersey City about 1870.

Left, below: At the start of the twentieth century America introduced the 'Pacific' or 4-6-2 wheel arrangement, which allowed high power to be united to good track-holding facilities in high-speed running. An Illinois Central railroad 'Pacific', built by the Brooks Locomotive works is seen here hauling the *Panama Limited* in 1916.

Below: A typical American style in the pre-streamline era is represented here by a Baldwin 'Pacific' rolling out of Little Rock, Arkansas, with bell tolling, at the head of the *Sunshine Special* which ran between St. Louis and Mexico City.

By contrast, the classic British look which concealed most of a locomotive's ancillary gear is demonstrated by this 4-4-0 of the Great Central railway seen heading a north-bound cross-country express out of Leicester.

America with the introduction of the 4–6–0, whose extra length could support a bigger boiler; and although this type was slow to find favour it was by 1900 the commonest of all in US main line express service. But it had two challengers.

The first of these was the 4–4–2 or 'Atlantic', which developed through a need to enlarge the firebox more than the boiler and so get adequate steam production even from mediocre coal. Atlantics could be built much larger than 4–4–0s — indeed, some were larger than most 4–6–0s — and they had an advantage in fast running. The type got its name from its first conspicuous use on the competing high-speed flyers of the Pennsylvania and the Reading railroads from Philadelphia to Atlantic City, which during the 1890s were the first in the world regularly to attain overall booked speeds of a mile a minute.

The other challenger was the 4–6–2 or 'Pacific' type. The Atlantic's limitation was that it had only four driving wheels, which meant that it was hampered on a hilly or difficult route and unable anywhere to deal with trains of more than moderate weight. The 4–6–0 avoided these drawbacks, but unless given first-rate coal lacked the steam-raising capacity and hence power potential of the 4–4–2 with its large firebox. The 4–6–2, however, combined the advantages of both types. Whether it got its name because it was bigger than the Atlantic, because the earliest production order was delivered from America to New Zealand, or because its first major American use was on the Missouri Pacific road, is in doubt; but certainly the 4–6–2 was to prove the most successful twentieth-century type of passenger locomotive, even if it never had the unchallenged supremacy that the 4–4–0 attained in the nineteenth once it had ousted the 4–2–2 or 4–2–0 singles. Arguably, too, the Pacific was the most graceful of all locomotives, as well as being highly functional with good track-holding qualities added to its other virtues. In appearance it seemed well-balanced about its six large coupled wheels, with the big power-producing cylinders at the front given just the right amount of emphasis over the big power-supplying firebox at the rear by being supported on one more pair of small carrying wheels. Its proportions were *right*.

After 1918 locomotive development, especially in Europe, began to be more affected by economics, as with the growth of road transport the financial position of railways started to deteriorate. This set-back affected locomotive design in several ways. Firstly, the railway organizations themselves tended to combine — pooling their strengths, accepting various degrees of state control and making economies in overheads: one of these savings was, of course, in the elimination of rival schools of locomotive design. There was also the start of a search for new technical devices designed to increase efficiency or to save labour. For as world standards of living rose so did wages, and the provision of large staffs of men for railway maintenance work, whether skilled or menial, became more and more impractical. The passenger locomotive of the years after the First World War might be a far more powerful and effective animal than its predecessors; but unless it was earmarked for a prestige express it was unlikely to be as immaculately tended, and it certainly did not wear so elaborate a livery.

During the 1920s, however, these effects were only just beginning to be felt, and there was certainly no sense of crisis. The emphasis was still on improved performances and lowered running costs, and it was the superheater that was to prove the key to the last phase of design improvements aimed at these objectives. In itself, by raising the temperature and thus the power-producing properties of the steam being fed into the cylinders, the superheater gave a fuel economy of around 10 per cent. But this led to another consideration; for, to take advantage of this more 'expansive' steam, valves and cylinders had to be further improved. And so in this period designers began to rethink the whole rule-of-thumb traditions which had hitherto ruled the proportions of the locomotive's front end.

Thus, larger piston valves with longer travel gave wider port openings, getting steam in and out of the cylinders more quickly and with less pressure drop so that fuel consumption fell yet again. G. J. Churchward of the Great Western had been the first British engineer to work systematically along these lines, but he had developed his ideas only after a close on-the-spot study of the best usage in America — where, it is worth noting, design was generally in the hands of outside engineering companies rather than of the railroad organizations themselves. Then, after 1920, a series of comparative trials demonstrated the superiority in Britain of his practice. The man who learnt most from these trials was Nigel Gresley of the London & North Eastern; but designers in other European countries, such as Chapelon of the French Paris-Orleans company, were working on similar lines. There were also important metallurgical advances in this era.

The result of all this was that, quite suddenly in the late 1920s, there came into existence a number of passenger-express classes which could as a matter of course reach maximum speeds of the order of 100 mph and maintain an economic 80 mph on reasonably level track. *This had never been possible before.* There are a legion of legends about speeds over the 100 mph mark reached on special occasions before 1930 in Britain, America and elsewhere, but in the author's opinion not one of them stands up to meticulous examination. If we say that no train anywhere in the world had before the late 1920s maintained 100 mph we will be much nearer the truth. But by the early 1930s Gresley's 'A3' Pacifics were doing so under such rigorous checks as dynamometer-car readings. So were German locomotives — and so, before long, American ones.

In 1935 the LNER's A3 No. 2750, 'Papyrus' — one of a class which for the first time in Britain combined the free-steaming and powerful Pacific layout with the improved GWR valve design — worked a 217 ton test train from London to Newcastle and back, averaging 80 mph over 300 miles and reaching a maximum of 108 mph. At about the same time, with a 130 ton test train on a virtually level road, the German state railways' 4–6–4 No. 05.001 — the first of a series of three-cylinder engines — reached a speed of 125 mph.

When the 'Pacific' type crossed the Atlantic it was adopted by many railway companies as their standard express engine. The example above worked on the Nord railway of France in 1923.

And this marked the beginning of the brief but brilliant era of ultra-high-speed steam working. The age demanded it, for in many parts of the world railways were feeling, for the first time, the pressure of rivalry for long-distance passenger services from the road and from the air. It was hence essential to compete — and in every way possible.

One such way, of course, was through publicity, and some would claim that the various forms of 'streamlining' which made their re-appearance at this period in America, Germany and Britain derived as much from advertising considerations as aerodynamic ones: certainly they often owed little to aesthetics. But at a more fundamental level three possible systems of traction existed. Electrification, then as now, offered the best long-term solution, and had been employed in special situations since the beginning of the century. But the initial cost of electrifying a mainline railway was enormous (it was, in fact, never faced by a company anywhere in the world not using government funds after the Milwaukee railroad's conversion of parts of its transcontinental track in the 1920s), and was feasible only when very heavy traffic would be handled by the fixed equipment or when (which was a major reason for early conversions) the extra power and freedom from smoke of electric locomotives was essential to work heavily-graded and tunnelled lines in such mountain areas as the Alps.

Diesel traction, too, had began to be regarded with interest in the 1920s. But it had many drawbacks and was unreliable in units above a certain small size, so that its early successes were in powering lightweight railcars. Within these limits, though, diesels were already running at lower overall cost than steam engines, and by the mid-1930s a few high-speed diesel train sets had been built in Germany and the USA. These performed quite well, but they suffered from the disavantage of a rigidly pre-determined formation to which coaches could not be added and, with their unfamiliar machinery, they could prove a vexation when out on the line.

The most practical proposition for most express trains in the 1930s was therefore still the steam locomotive. It could do the job: it needed no special equipment: it was cheap in first cost, it could haul any stock, and it was surrounded by public respect and affection. On running costs there was little to choose between steam and internal-combustion power; but the former was a tried, faithful and above all flexible servant, while the diesels were still much of an unknown quantity whose successes could be honestly rated as freakish. It seems fashionable today to suggest that the engineers of the 1930s made a mistake in staying with steam; but they had good reasons for so doing, and indeed it can be claimed that when the change-over to internal combustion did come in America and Britain it was so sudden and complete as to represent a waste of capital assets.

Hence a number of countries introduced extremely fast steam-powered trains at this time, generally streamlined. Britain and the USA led, and in the latter country inter-company rivalry caused a rapid spread of such trains, which sometimes used hastily-

Some classic preserved French locomotives.

One of the famous Nord 'Atlantics'. These, built between 1904 and 1912, gave impressive performances at the head of such trains as the *Oiseau Bleu* and the *Nord Express*. Working on the de Glehn-du Bousquet compound system, they saw service for some 35 years.

Left: Locomotive Nord 701, built in Mulhouse in 1885. This was the first class of locomotives to use the de Glehn-du Bousquet compounding system, which found favour all over France except on the PLM lines. The high- and low-pressure cylinders acted on different axles, which were not coupled.

Right: The PLM *coupe-vents* were among the best-loved engines of France. Their early 'streamlining', introduced before the First World War and supposedly to minimise effects of the Mistral blowing up the Rhône valley, added greatly to their individuality. Used on such trains as the *Côte d'Azur Express*, they were for long the pride of the PLM line. An interesting feature shown in the picture is the sealed speed register on the left frame just in front of the cab.

repainted and cased-in older equipment. But they were to be found also in France, Germany, Canada, Belgium and elsewhere. Often they ran at speeds which, through the intervention of war, were not to be matched for twenty years behind any means of traction.

Three railways operating such trains deserve special mention. All had one thing in common — that they were subject to pressures not purely economic — but this does not detract from the achievement of their engineers. Thus, the German state railways were under political pressure: if their trains were faster, it proved the superiority of the Nazi regime. But they still built a number of very fine high-speed locomotives of several types to run on routes including Berlin/Hamburg. Here they virtually matched the times of the better-known (but rather unreliable) diesel-powered *Fliegende Hamburger*, and with considerably heavier trains. It was doubtless for political reasons that the diesels received most of the publicity.

The pressures on the London & North Eastern and the Chicago, Milwaukee, St. Paul & Pacific companies were not political but competitive. Both concerns were not at all well off and were overshadowed by larger neighbours. The need to get themselves noticed, and to do something unmistakably better than their rivals, hence led them to make special efforts with their best passenger trains. Both decided to stay with steam power, and the LNER built the world's largest fleet of high-speed steam locomotives in Nigel Gresley's 'A4' class Pacifics. Of these, No. 4468 — christened 'Mallard', for until the end of steam Britain maintained the tradition of naming its best locomotives — hauling in 1938 a 240 ton special train on a 1-in-200 down-grade, reached a momentary top speed of 126 mph. Thus by a hair's-breadth it captured the speed record from the Germans and ran at a pace never equalled behind steam power since — or, for that matter, by any diesel-hauled train either, though France and other nations have shown the possibilities of electric traction to be almost limitless. As a technical achievement it was not perhaps quite as fine as the German run, made with a lighter train but without material help from gravity, especially as 'Mallard' suffered important mechanical derangements from its work. But both achievements were very remarkable.

The 'Milwaukee road' started with some very fine and handsome stream lined Atlantics in 1935, which at 140 (short American) tons without tender were by far the largest four coupled engines ever built. But the company soon found that the fast trains they hauled attracted more traffic than they could handle, and so in 1938 it enlarged its fleet with some yet more remarkable 207 ton 4-6-4s. Even after the war these continued for some years to reach speeds well over 100 mph in daily service, the last of all the dragonfly breed of high-speed steam locomotives to run anywhere in the world.

But these streamliners formed only a small group, and by 1939 the emphasis in the great majority of new steam designs was on simplicity, flexibility and the greatest possible ease of maintenance — plus, of course, power. Furthermore, the improved front-end design of valves and cylinders which enabled the high-flyers to go

Perhaps the ultimate in steam power before the Second World War was represented by Sir Nigel Gresley's 'A4' streamlined Pacific. Here the type heads the inaugural run of the *Silver Jubilee* express, hauled by the 'Silver Link' as it leaves London for Newcastle at the head of its streamlined train. Left: Interior of the cab of the record-breaking A4 'Mallard'.

Left: During the 1930s experiments with streamlining steam locomotives produced some unfortunate results. But this 4-8-4 built by the Lima Locomotive Works for the *Daylight* expresses of the Southern Pacific Railroad of America is a fine example of the engine builder's art.

Below: As in America, and Great Britain, so in France. The French also experimented with streamlined locomotives, with more or less happy results. This is a 4-4-2 of the PLM.

extremely fast also enabled engines that would earlier have been thought of as slow freight sloggers to run at express speeds. For the first time, high tractive effort or brute load-shifting could be combined with high speeds. Large fleets of standardised mixed-traffic locomotives thus came to be built, giving considerable economies through reductions in stock.

In a number of countries, too, long-overdue experiments were carried out on the basic economy of the steam locomotive: for example, aerodynamic discoveries were called in to secure improvements in draught induction in the smokebox. Often enough the use of new methods in the 1930s, 40s and 50s could halve and then quarter the cost of running a railway's motive power department, especially when it was combined with the allied savings won by faster transits, quicker turnrounds and heavier loads. The immense capacity for improvement of Stephenson's invention was an exciting discovery, ardently pursued in many countries.

Yet quite suddenly all this came to an end, and the glittering visions presented by the last giants of the steam age were forgotten. This was not directly a consequence of the Second World War. In the early 1940s the world's major railways fell under considerable stress; but their prime mover was still overwhelmingly steam, and in these years the steam engine demonstrated as never before its ability to slog on for a long time with minimum maintenance. After the war, too, the quest for improvements was resumed, and some of the locomotives built after 1940 greatly outclassed anything that had gone before in high mileage between servicings and in general performance. In America alone, for example, one thinks of the splendid 'Niagara' 4–8–4s of the New York Central, each of which on average ran nearly a quarter of a million miles a year; or the somewhat similar 4–8–4s of the Santa Fe, among whose regular jobs were working expresses the 1800 miles from Kansas City to Los Angeles without an engine change at an overall speed approaching a mile a minute; or the Union Pacific's 4–8–8–4 'Big Boys', weighing 386 tons without tender and (by a small margin, with many close behind) the largest locomotives ever built; or the Pennsylvania's 'TL' 4–4–4–4s, belting 1000-ton expresses along at 100 mph across the Illinois plains. Nor should the 'standard' engines of the French, German, Russian and British national railway administrations be forgotten here. But the post-1945 steam renaissance, as impressive in its way as the work of the pre-1939 flyers, proved almost equally short lived. What killed it was, basically, the rising cost of coal in comparison with oil.

Steam locomotives could, of course, burn oil, and obtain many advantages in cleanliness and dependability from doing so: but diesels could burn it more efficiently, and during the war years American engineers at last succeeded in designing reliable, flexible and powerful mass-produced diesel engines. Furthermore, men no longer queued for the heavy, generally dirty and relatively unskilled work of servicing and maintaining steam locomotives. After 1945 electrification too became more financially attractive, especially where governments were willing to make the huge capital invest-

A 'V1' 4-6-4 of the Nord railway, another variation on the streamline theme, running over an electrified part of the system.

ments involved. And, finally, fashion also played its imperious part. So the steam locomotive at last vanished from its proud position at the head of the world's great expresses. It was totally displaced first in North America (where for the most part the diesel held sway) and then, one by one, in the major European countries which with their dense populations offered more possibilities for main-line electrification. And with it there went those men who had passed their lives in an often skilled and always exacting trade, men who had spent years as firemen and freight drivers before they handled the controls of a passenger express, men who stood, responsible for more lives than any airline pilot, between an Alpine or Appallachian blizzard and the hell's mouth of the fire box whilst far behind them their passengers dozed in the pillowed comfort of *wagon-lits* or Pullman. By 1960 main-line steam was becoming a rarity: in the 1970s it was to be found only where labour and coal remained cheap and fashion uncompelling, as in India, South Africa and some of the Communist countries, notably China. After 150 years, an era distinguished in human achievement and fascinating in engineering detail was drawing to its close.

One of the classic designs of France, this Nord Pacific is an example of a class that was the backbone of passenger and freight services. Here it is burning up the soft smoky coal of France in the final years of steam power.

The great tunnels which pierced the Alps transformed the economy of Europe. Above, a group of workmen and engineers are seen in 1880 at one portal of the St Gotthard.

The earliest of the Alpine tunnels was the Mt Cenis which provided a direct route from Paris to Rome. Here a workmen's train takes the labourers up to the working face.

A north-bound train leaves the Simplon tunnel after the electrification and doubling of the line. (Note dates on the twin portals.)

Stations and Structures

Some time in the early 1860s an alert attendant in the office of a New York mining company noticed that the sample-case of a visiting salesman was emitting alarming brown fumes. Taking what seemed a reasonable precaution, he threw the valise out of the window — and watched it burst on the pavement below with a blinding flash, a shattering explosion but, fortunately, no casualties. For the case had been packed with bottles of 'Nobel's blasting oil', today more widely (if incorrectly) known as nitroglycerin.

This compound had been discovered as long before as 1846, but it had been left to the eccentric Swede to manufacture and market it in bulk. Almost immediately its use was banned in Europe; for it proved far too sensitive and temperamental for everyday use, despite the fact that Nobel himself remained convinced of its safety even after his own factory had been blown sky-high. In the more pioneering conditions of America, however, miners were prepared to handle the liquid, and Nobel believed that it could help there in civil engineering too.

Nitroglycerin was, in fact, soon used to hasten work on America's first great (if ill-planned) tunnel — the $4\frac{1}{2}$ mile Hoosac in Massachusetts, which was begun before 1851 and not fully opened until 1875. But for the most part American enterprise was at the time of Nobel's promotion eclipsed by the Civil War, the 'war between the states'. And in Europe there were other challenges to be met.

There the geography of a continent turned about the central massif of the Alps, which had dominated transport since long before the time of Hannibal and which, 40 years into the railway age, remained virtually undefeated. Either by following British models or by working out local techniques, national rail networks had over these decades grown up in one European country after another, and since there were no gauge problems outside Iberia and the extreme East these were soon cemented by international links wherever the terrain allowed. Lines from Mulhouse to (Swiss) Basle and from Zurich to Baden in Germany, for instance, were opened as early as 1847. But to travel between France and Austria or between Germany and Italy two decades later one had still to take somewhere to a jolting *diligence*, the only truly Alpine rail crossing being that afforded by the Brenner Pass.

Even between France and Italy the Alps pressed so close against the sea for a hundred miles or more that the obvious coastal route — which was not in fact opened until 1872 — implied a total of more tunnelling than was demanded by a single bore near Susa. This Mont Cenis route, which gave direct access from Paris to the rich

Lombardy plain, had been promoted by far-seeing Italians as long before as 1848; and by 1857 tunnelling had been put in hand with capital largely raised by that nation and with pneumatic drills which eased the problem of ventilation. But progress was slow, thanks largely to the limited blasting power of gunpowder; and so important was the route that in 1868 a temporary and unconventional narrow-gauge track was laid over the summit which for a few years carried the British mail for India through to Brindisi.

It was now that the Nobels came to the rescue with a new invention — dynamite. In essence a solidified form of the treacherous nitroglycerin, dynamite was almost as powerful as its parent but safe in use: measured against gunpowder, it was not only at least five times as strong but more shattering too. And so the introduction of dynamite after 1867 on the 8½ mile Mont Cenis or Fréjus tunnel meant that, despite the outbreak of the Franco-Prussian war, this was completed ten years ahead of schedule — perhaps a world record for any civil engineering work on such a scale.

The roar of high explosives in High Savoy, indeed, inaugurated a new phase of the railway age as surely as the crash of cannon at Liverpool had inaugurated all modern railways back in 1830. In Britain itself the main-line network was by 1870 virtually complete, for there had been no great mountains to impede progress there and the worst of what there *were* had been subdued when the original 4½ mile Woodhead tunnel was opened below the Pennines as long before as 1845. But in a world context railways could not economically be knit together without such safe power as dynamite deployed.

So in the wake of the Mont Cenis the great Alpine tunnels were opened up one by one. Each presented its own difficulties and generated its own tales of recklessness or heroism, but in length they were fairly consistent — the 9½ mile St. Gotthard, which marked a new era in international rail co-operation, in 1882 after eight years of work, the first bore of the 12½ mile Simplon (still the world's longest rail tunnel through mountains) in 1906, and the 9 mile Lötschberg, which is even today operated by an independent company, in 1913. Further afield were the Arlberg (1884), the Tauern (1909), Karawanken (1906) and tunnels in Austria, and the Apennine gallery in Italy of 1934 — a country which also added the Monte Santomarco to the table as recently as 1968 and so became the latest as well as the first European nation to construct a great mountain rail tunnel.

The cumulative effect of these works was to transform the transport map of Europe and the economy of at least one of its countries, Switzerland; for in a few decades the confederation of the cantons of Helvetia ceased to be the mountain-tracked impediment to international travel as which nature appeared to have designed it and instead became the turntable and marshalling-yard of a continent's railways. The Swiss naturally took advantage of this dispensation to develop their own industries as well as to expand as an international entrepot — and first among these industries was that of tourism and winter sports, with the British providing the keenest customers. This in time was to lead to a multiplication of mountain

The 'steam navvy' or excavating machine, an American invention, came too late to be of great benefit to the railways of Europe. Here, however, a Ruston excavator is seen at work on the Great Central line.

branch-lines; but even by 1900 this unpromising land was on the way to becoming one of the most densely-railwayed in the world, both for internal needs and because it was here that the great transcontinental routes met, the freight wagons were exchanged, and the sleepers and through-cars of the international expresses were re-marshalled. To and from Copenhagen, Amsterdam, Calais, the Pyrenees, Marseilles, Milan, Vienna, Prague and Berlin the long trains ran, in two senses, all round the clock-face.

But high explosives were not the only contribution of the later nineteenth century to the technology of railway building. Their development went hand-in-hand, for instance, with that of the rotary or reciprocating rock-drill as it was steadily perfected by men from many lands after Sommeiller had first put compressed air to use at Mont Cenis, and also improved was the boring machinery whose own history dates back to Marc Brunel's work on a Thames passenger tunnel in 1818. At the same period America began to introduce steam-powered digging, hoisting and similar machinery, so that for the first time civil engineers were freed from the limitations of man-power and animal-power. Not until Britain built its last main line at the very close of the century, for instance, were the methods of excavation used there far in advance of those known to the Stephensons — or, for that matter, to the Pharaohs.

Yet Britain itself witnessed one substantial achievement when, in 1886, the 4½ mile Severn tunnel was at last opened after many battles against treacherous waters — battles of which one hero was the diver whose pioneering use of self-contained underwater breathing apparatus to help him close a leak remains an outstanding example of cold-blooded courage: this will remain the world's longest under-water tunnel until Japan completes its immense 36 mile New Kammon bore. And at a higher level the homeland of railways made another — if indirect — contribution to their technology through its development of steel-making techniques from 1856 onwards.

In fact, it was not until well into the 1870s that cast and wrought iron — the materials on which the world's railways had hitherto been based — were supplanted by that cheap, tough product made possible by the Bessemer and Siemens processes which led to Andrew Carnegie exclaiming 'Farewell, age of iron, all hail, King Steel'. The new product did not always bring aesthetic improvement, as is witnessed by such works as the Forth bridge in Scotland — an edifice which was itself the key to one of those valuable 'cut-offs' typical of the later railway age in sophisticated lands. But there *were* designers who could turn steel to breath-taking use, as did the Alsatian engineer Gustave Eiffel with his spans in southern France.

Longer tunnels through the employment of high explosives, rock drills and improved boring shields; more ambitious bridges utilising structural steel: the introduction of powered aids and of precise calculations to supplement the older traditions of sweat and rule-of-thumb: all these helped to knit together the railways of Europe and provide the means and the incentive for fast, long-distance running. The movement, too, continued well into the

Even the application of power to railway building left many tasks to be performed only by hand. Here workmen are seen trimming the cutting edges of the new GC line.

Right: Two spiral tunnels between Hector and Field in the Canadian Rocky Mountains form a figure '8' in shape — the line doubles upon itself twice in 8.2 miles. Above: The *Empire Builder* enters the Cascade Tunnel, longest bore in the United States when it was completed at 7.79 miles.

One of the most famous scenes in railroad history — the celebrations at the completion of America's first transcontinental line in 1869.

present century with such achievements as the Little Belt bridge in Denmark of 1935 and major works of route improvement in Italy, whilst in the era from the First World War onwards great engineering works were also carried out in connection with electrification schemes. But outside Europe (though in conjunction, for the most part, with the almost-anonymous skills of European engineers) progress in civil engineering after 1870 did much more, and made substantial railway systems possible for the first time. In Russia and Japan, in Latin America and central Africa and throughout the whole British empire at its zenith, from Pernambuco to Peking and from Adelaide to the Arctic, the four or five decades before the First World War were those in which many countries realised a sense of nationhood through the comparative ease of communication across hundreds of often road-less miles which was brought by railways which could be constructed with reasonable ease and economy. For such lands it was the end of the nineteenth century, rather than its middle, which witnessed the most intensive period of railway construction.

Of no part of the world was this more true than of those States which, with the last battles fought and the years of the carpet-baggers being left behind, found themselves truly United at last. The task there now was to reinforce political with geographical union, for there remained unconquered the great continental divide of the Rockies which themselves formed part of a mountain chain running almost unbroken for 7,000 miles from Alaska to Cape Horn. And ever since the Baltimore & Ohio line had become operative in 1830 (and so challenged the Liverpool & Manchester for world precedence) the movement of American railroads, as of American civilisation, had been a westward one. Indeed, the story of colonisation beyond the Missouri or even the Great Lakes is largely one of cattle-lands and farm-lands being opened up around new railheads, a little nearer to the sunset every day.

Well before 1870 the railroads of the more easterly parts of the North American continent could show engineering works which were substantial in their dimensions, if flimsy by European standards with their timber viaducts and light roadbeds. ('No one worries much about choosing the shortest route ...' wrote Jules Verne, '... The line goes up hillsides, scrambles down into valleys, and runs along blindly and rarely in a straight line. It is not costly, nor in anyone's way, but the trains have a habit of running off the line and jolting most uncomfortably ...'). But though a line was operating from the Great Lakes to the Gulf of Mexico, the central plains remained a railway desert and the Rockies themselves *could* still be crossed only by the covered wagon and the pony express.

Thus it was in the United States and Canada that dynamite and the rock drill faced their most heroic tasks. While the Civil War was still in progress Abraham Lincoln had resolved that, for political reasons alone, the tracks must be laid, and soon a Union Pacific railroad was striking west from Omaha and following the route of the old Mormon trail into Utah whilst a Central Pacific line set out from Sacramento in California to join it by way of the Sierra Nevada

A painting of Austria's Semmering line around 1905 which captures the *gemütliche* atmosphere of a halt for refreshment.

The elaborate vernacular style of Kuala Lumpur station, Malaya, is a relic of British rule.

and Reno. So on 10 May 1869 — only six years later, six years sooner than had at first been planned, and in good time for what this book has taken as the start of the age of the great expresses — came that historic meeting of Promontory Point when, after a long wait by the western party, the driving at the third attempt of a golden spike between two locomotives facing cowcatcher-to-cowcatcher clinched one of the epoch-making achievements of civil engineering history and of human endurance. For the hazards faced by the building gangs had ranged from raids by Sioux and Cheyenne tribesmen (even the ornate directors' cars at the opening carried guns) to blinding heat and a cold that caused steel tools to shatter.

These gangs (who laid six, seven, eight and, once, in reply to a bet, *ten* miles of track in a day) were largely composed of Chinese, Irish and other recent immigrants; but there was a coherent enough core of longer-established Americans — black and white, and including many war veterans — for a genuine folk-culture to evolve within the groups of navvies and shot-firers, of 'trackwinders' and 'tiehacks'. This culture was reflected by such well-remembered songs as 'I've been Workin' on the Railroad' or 'Drill ye Tarriers, drill'. And above all the period — if not this particular project — is epitomised by the legend and ballad of John Henry, the man who, with his sledge-hammer and bits, fought against the mechanical drills.

In the decades which followed the building of the Union Pacific, route after route was opened between the Atlantic and Pacific oceans. Thus, the Santa Fe was completed in 1881, the Southern Pacific early in 1883, the Northern Pacific (with the promise that US army troops and the company's own armed 'outriders' would be present in each coach 'to protect passengers from raids by road agents') at the end of the same year, the Great Northern — which was constructed without government funds — in 1893, the 'Milwaukee road' in 1909, and the Western Pacific in 1910. By 1913 — when the nation's rail network reached its peak of over a quarter of a million miles or a third of the world's total — the east-coast system had also extended to Florida, where it pebble-hopped across the seas for 128 miles to end with a grand gesture on Key West; and another outstanding work of this period was the bridging of the Great Salt Lake. These were the great years of American railroading, years for ever evoked by that most nostalgic of all sounds, the cry of a chime whistle in the lonely night — and years which made more than one man into a millionaire.

Meanwhile, although Canada's first rails had been laid in 1836 and no less a contractor than Thomas Brassey had been active there, that underpopulated country had been slow to develop and only a few miles of track were open as late as 1860. But a connection with the US network was completed in 1864, and in 1880, when the young dominion was threatened by the secession of British Columbia unless it received better communications with the eastern states, its government backed the construction of the great Canadian Pacific line and witnessed its completion within five years. The routes which were to be incorporated into the Canadian National system followed from 1915 onwards.

A London Brighton & South Coast train pulls into Victoria station, London. Note the head-code distinctive to the company. The station itself was opened in 1860 and is still many visitors' first contact with Britain.

Amsterdam Central station displays a fine example of the arched and glazed train-shed roof.

Below: Rawalpindi station, Pakistan is an example of the large through stations built in vernacular style by the British in India.

Whether in Canada or the USA, though, speed in construction was bought at a price, and it is significant that America produced almost as few great railway-builders as it did great individual locomotive designers. For, for the most part, even these huge undertakings which were each some two or three times the length of any railroad built elsewhere in the world before 1900 were still constructed with the aim of forming *some* kind of link as swiftly as possible. It was left to the present century to smooth-out their routes with more substantial engineering works employing such techniques (well-tried on the railways of the Old World) as spiral and S-bend approaches to the crests; and even so the longest tunnel in the Americas, the Cascade of 1929, was at less than 8 miles no mammoth by Alpine standards and even a class below Japan's Hokuriku tunnel of 1962.

Thus it was that, with all the civil engineer's repertory of techniques, the railways of five continents were extended, united and improved from 1870 onwards. But inevitably the casual traveller anywhere in the world barely lifted his head from his newspaper as his express flashed, in far less time than it took him to smoke a cigar in the small saloon which was usually the only place where such indulgence was then permitted, through a tunnel which had taken a decade and many million solid nineteenth-century pounds to construct, or over a bridge which had cost a hundred lives. For him, the point of contact with any railway system was its passenger station.

The atmosphere of the late nineteenth century is often found most vividly embodied in such middle-sized provincial stations as Châtel-Guyon in central France; but for importance one must look to the great city terminals. As late as 1860 Britain itself had still been groping towards the most workable arrangement of arrival and departure platforms, of facilities for handling passengers and their monstrous luggage, and of all the support systems necessary for what was commonly a city's most important building. But these problems were solved by the time of the completion of the archetypal 700 ft by 250 ft train-shed by Barlow and Ordish, and of Gilbert Scott's exuberantly gothic hotel, at London, St. Pancras, in the mid-70s — the whole of which formed a striking unity of architecture and engineering. To the same period belonged the rather more modest Liverpool Street. And thenceafter the initiative was to pass to the continent of Europe, where even 'through' stations tended to be situated nearer to the centres of large cities — and hence to be more closely integrated into their lives — than in Britain. At York, for example, the 1877 station with its elegant train-shed but unimpressive buildings was exiled without the mediaeval walls.

So they arose, those monumental structures nurtured by state funds and national pride which were to witness the comings and goings of royalty and statesmen as well as the partings and reunions of millions of ordinary mortals — and which in times of war were to be thronged with bemused conscripts and forlorn refugees. So far as public expressions of the importance of the railway in civilisation went, Britain was left behind after 1880, as in France, Germany, Italy and elsewhere, architect and engineer toiled to achieve ever greater grandeur, and reached far beyond the requirements of necessity with their huge masses and spaces. Beside such giants, the modestly-spacious rebuildings at Edinburgh, Waverley, (1898) and London, Waterloo, (1921) seemed almost puny.

In Germany and Italy the new wave of construction was associated with the achievement of nationhood and the development of unified railway systems; state control facilitated the expression of national and civic pride. Thus, Berlin's Stettiner and Anhalter termini (1876 and 1880), though presentable enough, were soon surpassed by the great Cologne station of Frentzen and Jacobsthal (1894), by Eggert and Franz's Frankfurt of 1888, and by Müller's Dresden of 1898. Below the towering spires of the cathedral of the three kings Cologne's typically German through train-shed brooded, 815 ft long and 80 high, its romanesque street building dominated by a 132 ft clock tower. Passing through the domed entrance hall here, passengers climbed stairs to reach fourteen platforms serving tracks raised to cross the Rhine. Despite substantial alteration in 1912–14 and the making-good of war damage in the 1950s, some of this magnificence still survives.

At Dresden, a complex of raised through tracks was surmounted by four linked train-sheds served by a modern-renaissance street building. Carroll Meeks has described Frankfurt's terminal station as the most significant of the latter part of the nineteenth century, and even Baedeker awarded it a single star. Between the platform heads and the frontage building was a concourse with room for a small army. The exterior of the massive gothic front block, with its central entrance-hall protruding out of the multi-arched train-shed, was adorned with allegorical sculptures including the Genius of Steam and the Miracle of Electricity.

Paris, like London, had acquired most of its railway structures before 1870; but the closing years of the century saw the reconstruction of St. Lazare, the largest of the city's termini, with the triangular trussed roof immortalised by Manet sheltering behind a huge new hotel by Lisch. This work was followed, under the stimulus of the World Exhibition of 1900, by the rebuilding of the Gare de Lyon and the opening of the Gare d'Orsay. Victor Laloux's building for the latter straddled all-electric platforms below street level, and in monumentality and elegance matched its situation amid some of the city's finest architecture. Marius Toudoire's neo-baroque Gare de Lyon was dominated by a huge-dialled clock tower added at the behest of the municipality, and this station had a sumptuous and picturesque grandeur which extended to the buffet and which befitted the metropolitan terminus of *la ligne impériale*, the departure point of the *Rome Express*, the *Simplon Express* and the *Train Bleu*.

In Italy the nineteenth century produced little of note after Carlo Ceppi's superbly-sited Turin, Porta Nuova, of 1868. More interesting than the highly-decorated old stations at Rome (1872) and Milan (1878) was Belgium's Antwerp, Centrale, of 1900, a cathedral-like structure by Louis de la Censerie with a great glass and iron dome and overtones of Paxton, the designer of London's Crystal Palace, amid the *art nouveau*. Absorbed in his efforts to

Chicago Union station, termed the 'Cross roads of the nation', was completed in 1925 at a cost of $90 million.

The splendid hall of Grand Central Terminal, the New York City station of the New York Central and the New Haven lines.

One of the most striking features on the railways in Britain is the Forth bridge opened in 1890. This fitted into the second of the 'cut-offs' to northern Scotland, the first passing over the ill-fated Tay bridge.

The *Glacier Express* crossing over the spectacular Landwasser viaduct above one of the branches of the Rhine in eastern Switzerland.

segregate departure and arrival flows and to use nothing but Belgian materials, the architect forgot to provide any lavatories.

Outside Europe and America, the strange Anglo-Indian gothic extravagance of Bombay, Victoria, was probably the most impressive building erected before the new century. Then Tokyo acquired a huge through station in 1914, with a frontage building in French-renaissance style which emerged still recognisable from the worst ravages of the 1923 earthquake and the bombings of the Second World War. Set elegantly above Belmore Park, Sydney's Central station with its 211 ft clock tower was started in 1920; eventually it was to have 23 platforms, but the luxury of a train-shed was foregone.

Germany's own era of great stations moved towards its apogee in parallel with the imperial tumescence. At Hamburg in 1906 Reinhardt and Sössenguth thrust a huge pointed-arch train-shed over tracks running below street level, placing a handsome structure at one end in the form of a clock-towered bridge. Fine stations were also built at Karlsruhe (1913) and Nuremberg (1911); but the summit of imperial Teutonic railway majesty was reached with the elephantine Leipzig, Hauptbahnhof, completed in 1915. A symmetry of metallic tracery in the form of 8 linked train-sheds sheltered 26 tracks abutting on a sandstone front block of almost overwhelming size, 984 ft wide and sufficiently high to obscure the arches of the sheds. This building contained equally huge vestibules for the Saxon and Prussian railways, both leading to an arch-roofed concourse. Though Leipzig was truly a 'Leviathan among termini' with halls recalling the 'vast bare temples of the Nile', its traffic never matched its size; even at its opening it handled fewer trains daily than Liverpool Street or St. Lazare.

The other outstanding European exercise in pretentious grandeur was Milan, started in 1908 but not completed until 1931. Ulisse Stacchini's polished marble and rose-granite halls, oppressive in their size and monumentality, were reminiscent of sets for a Hollywood epic. The frontage was guarded by angry stone beasts; but when intimidated and tired by the pomposity, the vast spaces and the changes of level between street and train, the passenger was able to enjoy an excellent 'day hotel' secure in the knowledge that his luggage was handled by some of the best-organised arrangements ever devised. And balancing the quaint ugliness of the architecture there were magnificent quintuple high-arched train-sheds, the last (and possibly the finest) ever built on the grand scale.

Yet Milan and Leipzig were out of date before they were finished, for a simpler, cleaner style was already apparent in Eliel Saarinen's boldly-formed Helsinki terminal of 1914. This, for reasons which are not entirely clear, had no shelter at all over the platforms; but in any case the high-arched train-shed was now going out. At Florence the very elegant Santa Maria Novella, designed by Michelucci and other young Tuscan architects in 1936, had only simple canopies over the platforms. The forms and profiles of this building, spurning the pomposity of most earlier Italian work, were to contribute to the best of all modern stations — Mazzoni and Montuori's spacious and stylish Rome, Termini, completed in 1951.

North America contributed little of note until the era of Chicago, Grand Central (1890), Reading and Philadelphia, Broad Street (both 1893), the vast St. Louis, Union (1894), Coolidge's Boston, South (1899), and above all the Illinois Central station of New Orleans which was an early work by Louis Sullivan and Frank Lloyd Wright.

But some majestic stations were built in the US after 1900, rivalling in splendour the best that Europe could show and huge in relation to their traffic by English standards. Two of the most princely were to be found in the business area of New York, both being all-electric from the start: these were the opulent yet practical multi-level Grand Central terminal (Reed & Stem and Warren & Wetmore, 1903–13) with its cathedral-like concourse and McKim, Meade and White's Pennsylvania station (1906–10), built over through tracks, with its 150 ft high concourse of masonry, glass and steel and its equally-magnificent waiting-room inspired by the Thermae of Caracalla. Only the first survives, in somewhat mutilated form and with the busiest ticket windows now those converted to take off-course racing bets.

Washington's impressive but unimaginative Union station was contemporary with those of New York, and between the wars lavish stations were provided at Philadelphia, 30th Street, Buffalo, Cleveland, Cincinnati and Los Angeles. Canada too produced some fine architecture at Toronto, Union (1914–28), with its classical façade and well-planned flows, and finally at John Schofield's Montreal, Central (1938–43), noteworthy for a careful attempt to reduce the horizontal distance between street and train but today quite hidden by a huge hotel and office complex.

Yet before even the earliest of these North American stations was complete the world was feeling the effects of the greatest of all revolutions in architectural and civil-engineering practice. Up to the First World War, virtually every railway structure had depended on the materials which had served civilisation from its start. Stone (or brick) and timber had remained man's staples, and the main developments hitherto had been the introduction of first iron and then steel. But the late nineteenth century had seen the rediscovery of a material known to the Romans.

As far back as the 1860s a few minor railway structures had employed concrete, and at the turn of the century this material was used for the bridges and viaducts of a branch-line in Scotland. But in all such cases it was merely poured into traditional forms, and it was left to the engineers of Scandinavia, Switzerland and France to develop the new forms which it made possible.

After the First World War, concrete steadily took the lead: after the Second it was accepted as the normal material for a man building a station or viaduct anywhere in the world. The forms which it imposed could have a beauty of their own; but it was a beauty bearing no reference to its environment. And today the new railway structures and stations of the world, like the trains they serve, are distinguished by their technological efficiency, their fitness for purpose, their occasional elegance — and their almost total anonymity.

A Bordeaux — Geneva express crossing the Neuvial viaduct in the central mountains of France.

Left: Calais — the most prestigious of continental cross-Channel ports, in the heyday of the packet-boats from Britain before the First World War. From its Maritime station rail routes radiated across the continent, so that it became a starting point for many famous expresses.

Below: Boulogne, too, was developed as a railway port. Here a very open-decked paddle-steamer leaves the old harbour, which existed in this form before extensive damage in the Second World War led to substantial rebuilding.

Railways Afloat

As railways were extended during the first half of the nineteenth century they reached many points where an arm of the sea, a wide river or an estuary blocked their path. Some of these gaps — such as were created by sections of the Baltic, the firths of Forth and Tay in Scotland and huge rivers like the Danube and the Mississippi — were later spanned by bridges, but initially passengers had to be ferred across the water. And frequently the crossing was made in considerable discomfort as passengers and luggage were turned out of one train, put on a fairly crude vessel, and entrained on the further shore.

Even before 1870, though, some of the more enterprising railways had evolved primitive train-ferries, laid with a line of rails, upon which passenger carriages or goods trucks could be shunted and transported bodily over the water. Thus, Charles Dickens has this poignant description of American train-ferries on the 'Shore line' route between New York and Boston: 'Two rivers have to be crossed and each time the whole train is banged aboard a big steamer. The steamer rises and falls with the tide which the railroad can't do, and the train is banged uphill or banged downhill. In coming off the steamer at one of these crossings yesterday, we were banged up such a height that the ropes broke and the carriage rushed back with a run down-hill into the boat again...' Another pioneering company (which had earlier introduced the bogie carriage into Europe) was rather unexpectedly the Würtemberg state railway, with its twin-track ferry on Lake Constance.

Such experiments were, however, in advance of their age: the main stream of development is represented by the railway steamer, and perhaps most typically by those plying the English Channel. Even in 1821, or well before the new era opened, a little wooden paddle steamer of ninety tons (named the 'Rob Roy' and built by Denny of Dumbarton, a firm which became the principal supplier of railway ships for Britain) was working between Dover and Calais. Then, as lines reached the Channel coast from London before the middle of the century, sea traffic intensified and design and engines improved rapidly: the ships of the 1840s and 1850s were still paddle-driven but soon iron was challenging wood, an early iron ship being the 'South Western' of 1843 built for the Channel Islands service. An important stimulus to traffic between continental countries and Britain was the Great Exhibition of 1851, for passengers landing at Dover that year averaged 2,000 a week with many of the ships making the crossing from Calais in 1½ hours — a timing which scarcely varied for the next fifty years.

Though the sight of paddle wheels churning the soapy foam and of the great steel fists of cranks punching round may have thrilled our grandfathers, the scanty amount of covered passenger accommodation meant spartan conditions for the average traveller. Yet

British enthusiasm for contact with the continent, both for business and pleasure, was such that by 1914 no fewer than five of the railway companies of England operated major cross-Channel routes. (There were as many again more minor ones, until eventually even the LNWR joined the battle; and in addition Holland was served by the comfortable night crossings of the Dutch ships of the Zeeland company.) For instance, the London, Chatham & Dover railway held the 22 mile Dover/Calais route, whilst its one-time rival, the South Eastern, ran the Folkestone/Boulogne service. Spurred on by the Thos. Cook agency which did so much for pioneer tourists, the London, Brighton & South Coast company connected Newhaven with Dieppe in 1862, offering the shortest (and cheapest) route in mileage between London and Paris though it involved a sea passage of some seventy miles. Further to the west the London & South Western railway had the Southampton/Havre route as well as that to the Channel Islands, while the Great Western squeezed into the competition with ships from Weymouth to the islands and, briefly, to Cherbourg too.

Despite keen commercial competition, vessels on all these routes developed on similar lines. First came the wooden paddle steamer making about 12 knots and next the iron ship with a speed nearer 15 knots: ten years later, still with paddles, 20 knots was achieved with craft of around 500 tons. The occasional single-screw ship had been tried earlier; but — fittingly, considering Brunel's enterprises — it was the Great Western which was the pioneer screw user on any scale, this company having three twin-screw steamers serving its Channel Islands crossing in 1889. The LSWR followed a year later with 1,000-ton twin-screw craft. It was, however, the French Etat railway which first used such a ship between England and France. This was the 'Seine', of 900 tons and 19 knots, for the Dieppe/Newhaven route.

A new century brought the first twin-screw turbine steamer, 'Queen', with the impressive tonnage of 1,650 and a speed of $21\frac{3}{4}$ knots. This set a new standard for the Dover/Calais run in 1902 and established a pattern for all Channel services for the next twenty years. (Originally such ships were coal-burning, but a trend towards oil firing developed strongly in the 1920s.) The Belgian Marine company which linked Dover and Ostend went one better in 1905 with its triple-screw turbine 'Princess Elizabeth' of 1,747 tons and 24 knots, and the French followed with a similar vessel of 1,882 tons for the Newhaven/Dieppe service.

But these miniature 'blue riband' challenges brought little real saving in time, and though standards of comfort had slowly risen it was not until well into the 1920s that ships were built with sufficient seating under cover to enable a fully-laden one to offer reasonable conditions to all its passengers; when Evelyn Waugh wrote his *Vile Bodies* a rough crossing on a crowded boat was still regarded as a most unpleasant ordeal for all but the hardiest. One could choose a deck-chair in the open, good enough on a fine calm day but cold and cheerless at other times and virtually impossible in rough weather; or there was the stuffy saloon where,

Until the strategic rivers and inlets of the USA were bridged — often at formidable cost — many routes relied upon the train-ferry. Thus, the Southern Pacific system operated the ferry 'Solano', which transported expresses of the *Overland* and *Shasta* routes across the Benicia Straits (northeast of Oakland, Calif.) until it was replaced by a giant bridge as late as 1931.

before the age of stabilizers and sea-sickness remedies, there could be horrid scenes of helplessly vomiting people falling about while stewards hurried to and fro in a vain attempt to maintain a supply of basins. As late as 1930 a rough January crossing was made on a Calais boat with only canvas protection from cold wind and spray if one wanted to avoid the squalor below.

But as the size of the typical railway steamer grew to 2,000 tons (and then, in the 1930s, to nearer 3,000), a higher superstructure made it possible to provide a fully-enclosed deck with ample seating for those who could not afford private cabins. By 1939 the average cross-Channel ferry approached a small liner in its standard of comfort; and this was particularly noticeable on the Hook-of-Holland route, where ships of over 4,000 tons had a generous provision of cabins for the night crossing.

After the First World War, steam turbine propulsion largely gave place in its turn to the motor ship with its space-saving diesel engine: here the Belgian service from Ostend had made a start with its 'Prince Baudoin' as early as 1934. Then in the 1950s came the rapid growth of the drive-on car ferry. Though some independent operators entered the field, most of these car ferries were owned by the now-nationalised railways.

Before leaving the Channel and Britain, reference should be made to the scores of pretty little railway paddle steamers which, for nearly a century, connected the Isle of Wight to the mainland and which also served the islands and west coast of Scotland: easily manoeuvrable in shallow tidal waters, some of these were built as late as 1947 and are still in service. And, lastly, traffic across the Irish Sea engaged the ships of no fewer than five of the pre-1923 railway companies. On all these routes, and those to the Isle of Man too, mechanical development largely kept pace with that of the ships used on the continental crossings.

Although the British, French and Belgian companies set the pace with ordinary steamers, it is necessary to look northwards to the Baltic and its limited tides to pick up the idea of conveying railway vehicles themselves on a ship. There Denmark in particular was divided by several channels too wide to be bridged or tunnelled economically, and so in the 1870s this became the pioneer of successful train-ferries. At one period, indeed, there were eight such links working, the busiest being that over the 16 mile Great Belt from Korsoe to Nyborg. The first ferries here were paddlers, with four funnels belching out smoke as they made a speed of around 11 knots: originally they carried a single set of rails, but later vessels had three tracks. Wooden piles connected to the stone pier by spring buffers ensured that as the ferry nosed its way into the U-shaped dock it was gently eased from one side to the other until it was firmly up against the end piles. Thus could sleeping-car passengers be transhipped at night blissfully unaware of their change of situation, with the whole operation from ship to shore carried out in as little as six minutes even in the nineteenth century.

The twentieth has, of course, brought typical improvements to those vital links between Scandinavia and Germany, some of them

Italy, too, had from an early date a train ferry across the Straits of Messina, running from Villa San Giovanni on the mainland to Sicily. Originally, it was served by an early single-track, paddle-wheel ferry seen crossing the Straits of Messina just before the disastrous earthquake of 1908.

It is still active today with modern equipment, and below a Rome-Palermo express is seen leaving its ship.

imposed by the descent of the 'iron curtain': thus, the main north-south route has been switched from Warnemünde to the Lübeck area. Typical of all such Baltic terminals are the three-way points installed to facilitate marshalling. Even earlier developments, though, did not go un-noticed by authorities further south, so that after a wartime experiment from Richborough in Kent the Harwich-Zeebrugge train ferry began to carry freight in 1924. And 1936 brought something quite new — the luxury *wagons-lits* services operating directly from London to Paris and later Brussels, with the high Channel tides defeated by locks and massive pontoons.

Two other train ferries to be especially noted in the Old World are, first, that on Lake Baikal on the route of the Trans-Siberian railway, where in Tsarist days a large ship was designed successfully to carry three lines of rails and also cut its way when needed through three inches of ice. The other was the first Italian service across the straits of Messina from Reggio. Here comparatively small paddle ships carrying a single set of rails enabled passenger carriages, including sleepers, to work through from Paris to Sicily.

At the turn of the century there were also many train ferries in North America, though only a few served major passenger routes and there were not many train-connecting *ships* of note. New York City then relied heavily on ferries, for example, and a busy service operated on Chesapeake bay between Cape Charles and Norfolk. Another ran from Oakland across San Francisco bay until 1931, and several transcontinental lines used ferries across the Mississippi into the 1930s. Pre-revolutionary Cuba, too, saw the arrival of many ship-borne railway cars. On Lake Michigan, ferries fitted with four tracks and able to convey up to thirty-four large freight cars at a time still operate: these are built to withstand ice and, it is said, rougher weather than could be encountered even in the English Channel. And a train ferry connects Detroit and Canada.

South America offers a rarity in Peru, where the railway runs from Cuzco to Puno on the shore of Lake Titicaca (where Kon Tiki was defeated before his escape by raft across the Pacific). Here a steamer takes one overnight to Guaqui, whence the journey to La Paz is continued by train. And whilst in Latin America, mention must be made of a service which appears elsewhere in this book — the fifty-mile-long run up and across the river Plate. Here the train is parked on the craft so that the ordinary coaches are on the central track and the firsts and the diners (which also serve as the ship's saloon) on the outside ones, affording a view of the passing scenery; and once a week through-cars continue into Paraguay, a journey which involves another ferry — across the Parana — which is approached by a cable-hauled incline.

A few other ferries are mentioned elsewhere in these pages, and there are also important train-connecting ships such as those which cross the Bosphorus. Indeed, were this chapter to attempt a world-wide coverage it would have to sweep from Tasmania to Newfoundland by way of the river-crossings of China, always asking the question as to whether the railway existed to serve the ships or the ships the railway since the two transport media are so closely linked

Left: The English packet at Boulogne in Edwardian times. This picture demonstrates how much of the accommodation for passengers was on open decks, which led to many miserable crossings in bad weather.

Right: Britain's Great Eastern railway moved into the continental carrying trade with a service which is maintained today for the *Rheingold* and other expresses leaving Holland.

Below: Belgium was also not neglected. As well as the Ostend services for Vienna, a train ferry took freight wagons to Zeebrugge.

CHEMINS DE FER DE L'OUEST & DU LONDON BRIGHTON.

PARIS à LONDRES
par Rouen, Dieppe et Newhaven

ROUTE PITTORESQUE & ÉCONOMIQUE
Départs tous les jours de la
GARE St-LAZARE
à 10ʰ du matin et 9ʰ du soir

Les trains du Service de jour entre Paris et Dieppe et vice-versa comportent des voitures de 1ʳᵉ et 2ᵉ classe à couloir avec W.-C. et toilette, ainsi qu'un Wagon-Restaurant; ceux du Service de nuit comportent des voitures à couloir des trois classes avec W.-C. et toilette.

VOIR LES CROQUIS CI-DESSUS

ENVOI FRANCO D'UN BULLETIN DU SERVICE DE LONDRES
sur demande affranchie adressée au Bureau de la Publicité, 20, rue de Rome à Paris, (VIIIᵉ).

Britain's beefeaters were used to advertise low-cost Channel service operated by the French Ouest company via Dieppe and Newhaven in conjunction with the LBSCR.

historically. But this book is about *trains*, and from a railway viewpoint the water-break is at best a nuisance and at times a hazard. It is hence not surprising that ever since engineers began to conceive themselves capable of almost any enterprise they became haunted by perhaps the greatest railway challenge of all — that of burrowing *below* the Channel. For in these twenty or thirty miles nature seemed to present the situation of a Suez or Panama in reverse, and the sea to form a barrier which would not present such difficulties.

The idea of a tunnel between England and France, then, had been in men's minds since the very start of the nineteenth century. As early as 1802 a French mining engineer named Mathieu put forward a plan to Napoleon, who was impressed and said to the British ambassador in France, 'This is one of the great things which we ought to do together'. The ensuing wars pushed the scheme far into the background, but some form of link — whether as a vast bridge, an iron tube on the sea bed or a massive causeway — still haunted engineers. Thus, in 1859, plans for a tunnel to run from Folkestone to Cap Gris Nez were supported by the two railway giants I.K. Brunel and Robert Stephenson.

The greatest step towards realisation, however, was that taken in 1874 by an expansion-minded railwayman who appears more than once in these pages — Edward Watkin, who then added to his many chairmanships that of the Submarine Continental railway company. Seven years later an exploratory bore was begun, using a machine with a head 7 ft in diameter worked by compressed air which cut 40 ft every 18 hours through the 'impervious flintless chalk'; when recently examined this experimental section was found to be still smooth and clean, and though it was unlined there were very few places in which water had entered. Shafts sunk at Sangatte near Calais and at the Shakespeare cliff west of Dover enabled successful trial borings to be made for over a mile under the sea and there seemed every chance that such daring nineteenth-century engineers as had successfully tunnelled the Alps and the broad estuary of the Severn would triumph with *la Manche* also.

Unfortunately, though, the dynamic Watkin had an opponent in J. Staats Forbes who represented a bitter rival of Watkin's South Eastern concern. Fearing that the South Eastern might capture traffic if the tunnel plans matured (it was said), Forbes fostered the objections which were voiced for the first time in 1880 and were to be raised frequently in years to come. At all events, the Board of Trade stopped the experimental work in 1882.

The Channel Tunnel company which had been formed to take over the assets of the earlier 'Submarine' concern sought fresh authority to continue the work, however, and the matter was referred to a parliamentary committee. Over five thousand questions were put down, and among the opponents there emerged the Adjutant-General of the British army who appeared to visualize 6,000 enemy soldiers arriving in Dover before an adequate alarm could be given to the defending garrisons. Even in pre-telephone days this seems unlikely — but such views discouraged further work for nearly eighty years, despite the suggestion that trains might emerge *via* a helical tunnel passing under the guns of Dover. Three times the project was debated, in 1906, 1913 and in 1929. But despite (or, perhaps, because of) enthusiasm on the French side the results were always negative, and the channel tunnel seemed as much of a lost cause as the Bosphorus tunnel.

Such short-sighted isolationism was by no means new, for the Duke of Wellington had for military reasons opposed the building of the railway from Folkestone to London and Lord Palmerston thought the cutting of the Suez canal would lead to the loss of Britain's Indian empire. Nor did it end with the First World War, for as late as 1930 Lord Balfour urged the view that 'so long as the ocean remains [Britain's] friend, do not let us deliberately destroy its power to help us'. But today, a round century after the enterprise of Edward Watkin and with Britain an acknowledged part of Europe, the 'chunnel' is again a live issue. And it is much to the credit of the pioneers that their ideas appear very close to those likely to be adopted by that Channel Tunnel company which (with shares held by private investors as well as by both national railway authorities) had kept itself alive throughout all vicissitudes. For present plans for a scheme estimated at nearly £1,000 million are for what should be in essence a system of twin railway tunnels, with all road vehicles being transferred to transporter-cars.

Traction is to be on a 25,000 Volt system, and traffic potential is expected to support at first one train every half-hour and eventually one every three minutes. The installation of such a tightly-used link between railways systems with their own traditions of signalling, trackwork and the like obviously raises unique tactical problems: the continuation of the French loading-gauge to a new London terminal, for instance, would involve engineering work more complex than that demanded by the 'chunnel' itself. But behind these problems in turn lie the strategic ones bound up with the concept of uniting the great cities of northern Europe with a network designed for speeds of some 200 mph. Even with a maximum through the actual 'chunnel' section of 90 mph, this would give timings of only $2\frac{1}{3}$ hours London/Brussels, $2\frac{3}{4}$ hours London/Paris and $3\frac{1}{2}$ hours London/Cologne — all highly competitive with aircraft speeds.

But what of railway individuality? Would such developments bring the titled expresses of Europe (whether of traditional or TEE type) into a more intimate contact with Britain than was afforded by the *Golden Arrow* in its most prosperous years? Would there be an express traversing the industrial 'golden belt' of Europe named the 'Sir Edward Watkin'? Or would the great trains be lost in a 'clock-face' shuttle-service of startling speeds but saddening and almost suburban anonymity? And what, in the age of the 'chunnel', of those old retainers of the railways the Channel packets? Perhaps all that can be said here is that the signs are that for many years to come the Channel and North Sea will continue busy with railway shipping — the last home, as they were the first, of those faithful servants of the great trains of Europe.

Many projects for a Channel tunnel between England and France have been put forward since the time of Napoleon. In 1884, under Sir Edward Watkin it seemed well on the way to realization, but war scares produced a Government embargo on the operations after some preliminary work had been carried out, and this celebratory poster was issued at least a century too soon.

The preparatory 'chunnel' works on the French side, at Sangatte near Calais. On the English side, about a mile of pilot tunnel and headings were driven under the sea.

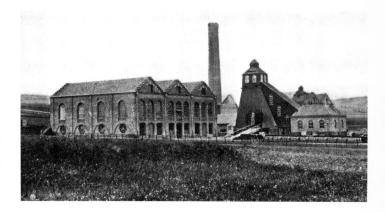

1910 Contemporary Viewpoint

In June 1910, the *Railway Magazine* of London published an article by J. M. Gallatly on 'Railways as a Mirror of National Character'. Brief, light-hearted and grammatically eccentric as this was, it made some interesting points — such as that the German railways then exercised the degree of surveillance today associated with Spain and with Communist countries. And so it is here rescued from near-oblivion.

'That railways reflect the characteristics of a nation is a fact so obvious as to be often overlooked. Everyone is conscious of the enormous difference in travelling in Italy or America, in England or Finland, but it does not at first occur to us that the differences largely coincide with the differences in the characters of the nations.

'The Italian railways, for instance, exhibit a cheerful irresponsibility, and a happy venality that is entirely in keeping with the country. Punctuality would be so out of keeping with the atmosphere as to be positively painful, and would convey to the bewildered traveller the idea that he was being cheated, and that this was not Italy after all. The precautions necessary, too, to prevent your baggage being plundered, give a pleasant suggestion of that picturesque brigandage which is so often associated with the Italians.

'The German railroad has so long been the butt of the humorous writer, that there is little fresh to be said about it. Method has been carried so far, that it is almost a crime for a passenger to want to know. At the proper time he will be told by the proper person just what he has to do, and somebody will see that he does it. For the system is red-tape ridden to a degree that makes the wild uncertainty of Italy positively refreshing. You take your ticket to be allowed to travel, another ticket to be allowed to use this particular train, and a further ticket to be allowed to sit down in it! How entirely German!

'Then, as befits a martial nation, everything connected with the railroad is essentially military. The guard salutes when he comes for your ticket, the stationmaster salutes as the train leaves the station, and at every intermediate station, whether the train stops or not, there is a red-capped official standing severely to attention to verify that the train is all that it pretends to be. I do not know whether a driver is courtmartialled for bringing in his train behind time, but I have always imagined it.

'The American railroads, on the other hand, though every whit as regular and precise as befits a business nation, are, in keeping with the democratic principles, quite free from the fetters of officialdom. No one, not even the foreigner, needs to be told or shown anything. Everyone in the station can see quite clearly where every train is going to, and when it is going; and knowing that it will start just then, no sooner and no later, he arrives at the station one minute before the time. I have often seen a local train quite empty until the last minute, and yet, when it started, there was not even standing room.

'This overcrowding is very characteristic, as it represents very vividly the national passion for saving time. Five electric cars I have seen leaving Philadelphia all bound for the same suburb, with barely 100 yards between them. Yet while people were hanging on to the first three by their eyelashes, the last two were quite empty. For one minute is infinitely more precious to the American than "oodles" of comfort.

'The railroads, like the country generally, bear the brand of newness. They lack the safety and solidity of the English lines, and the rails are lighter and not so well laid. Open grade crossings are frequent, and corners are sharper. So sharp sometimes as to necessitate banking to a most uncomfortable degree as a fast train rolls like a steamer.

'Typical of America, too, is the one-class system, and the absence of compartments, and also, in a country of violent contrasts, the presence of parlour and private cars decorated with a lavishness only to be dreamt of by a nation newly come to its wealth.

'In violent antithesis to such a system as the American, we have the State-controlled railways of Finland. The trains are very safe, very comfortable, and very punctual — as they may well be. For the big express from Helsingfors to Bjorneborg covers the 150 miles in ten hours!

'Not that the train runs 15 miles an hour. For true to the Finnish character, which exhibits a series of outbursts of excitement from an almost bovine placidity, the engine driver will often, in moments of enthusiasm, run as fast as 45 miles an hour. But this means waiting 20 minutes at the next station, to promenade one's self and purchase wild strawberries from the grave-eyed children who line the platform.

'Ten minutes before the train starts — here speaks Russian officialdom — a bell is rung; again at five minutes before the hour. And at the exact second a third bell is rung, the guard blows his whistle, the porter his horn, the engine gives a prolonged shriek, and starts ringing its bell, and — we are off.

'As long as you are of patient temperament, this is a delightful method of travelling, and one thoroughly calculated to imbue you with the national placidity. Anyone however, who is in a hurry, would be wise to avoid the country altogether.'

Great Trains of Britain

In a book which knows no frontiers from the Urals to the Rockies or from the Arctic to the Capes of Horn and Good Hope, it seems almost impertinent to devote an entire chapter to one small group of islands set off-shore of north-western Europe. And yet for historical reasons alone Britain, which even at its peak boasted a mere 25,000 miles of track, must be granted a unique position. The deepest roots of the concept of a railway may be found in central Europe in the sixteenth century or even in the Egypt of the Pharaohs. But in its modern form it was the creation of a group of engineers, financiers and men of vision who worked in England in the first quarter of the nineteenth century — Blackett, Rastrick, Pearse, Murray, Trevithick, George Stephenson and their fellow pioneers.

Furthermore, Britain's pre-eminence did not end as the world's first full-blooded train departed on its way from Liverpool to Manchester in 1830, nor with the development after 1845 of home-grown railway techniques in Europe and elsewhere, nor even as — three quarters of the way through the century — signs appeared that to be the leader in any industrial field might bring its own dangers of complacency. It is true that, almost from the start, the USA had charted its own course and that by 1870 Europe had much to learn from that quarter in the direction of building stock which allowed long journeys to be made in comfort and even luxury. But *in* Europe Britain was still operating the fastest trains — as, with few exceptions, it was to continue to do for another thirty years. And even as the twentieth century progressed and there were increasing challenges from individual expresses in France and Germany as well as the USA, Britain continued to run by far the greatest number of fast trains per mile or per head.

Further, Britain was also a pioneer in the introduction from America of all that was newest and best in passenger rolling stock as 'bellows' connections, train toilets, the diner and the sleeper, continuous braking, gas and electric light were introduced first to supplement-paying passengers but eventually even in the third class. Actual speeds even in 1875 were unremarkable anywhere in the world, the 40 mph average which had been achieved in Liverpool & Manchester days being accepted as as fast as any gentleman should wish to travel. But in Britain more and more expresses were running at about this rate (according to Foxwell and Farrer, express travel there multiplied fourfold in the 1870s), and there was little remarkable in occasional sprints with special light-weight trains at 60 mph, 70 mph or above. Even 100 mph — a magical figure for Anglo-Saxons — seemed drawing in sight.

The Great Western railway drew a somewhat fanciful comparison between Italy and Cornwall in this advertisement with its theme of 'holidays at home'.

Opposite: A down boat express of the South Eastern & Chatham railway emerging from the Shakespeare Cliff Tunnel and approaching Dover. Note the original timber trestle. The engine is No. 740 of class 'D', built at Ashford in 1901 and this was her maiden run.

Opposite below: The London & North Western railway, with a down Manchester express passing over Bushey Troughs in 1899. The engine is one of the 'Teutonic' Class of 2-2, 2-0 three-cylinder compounds, built at Crewe in 1889 and 1890.

That Britain had played almost as great a part in the development of a network of passenger expresses as she had in the introduction of the railway itself was due to several factors as well as simple technical enterprise: of these factors, the competitively-minded Victorians themselves would certainly have laid greatest stress on their country's rash of rival companies and multiplicated routes. But another consideration was that (viewed simply from a geographical viewpoint, and neglecting the social considerations which after 1860 led to a demand for fast, comfortable travel by all classes) Britain is ideally designed for the operation of express trains.

For England's own great centres of population lay between 100 and 300 miles from London, a range wherein an acceleration from 25 to 50 mph (or, today, from 75 to 100 mph) produces a very real gain in convenience. Then, moving out to the Celtic extremities of Britain, there are journeys in the 250–500 mile bracket which fit conveniently into the sleeping-car range, and which remain within it even in an era of internal air transport. In a Belgium or a Switzerland — countries where the great trains are international trains — on the one hand, or in a Russia or Australia on the other, the whole demography is so different as to make fair comparison impossible.

However tiny on the world map, then, Britain has for the last century provided an exercise-ground for almost every type of thoroughbred train devised by man. For some fifty years, indeed, the British Isles have even been able to show a genuinely international service with the full paraphernalia of frontier inspections and customs formalities. For in 1921 the curtain of partition descended between Northern and Southern Ireland and so formally severed the Great Northern line between Dublin and Belfast.

If only because it is often forgotten that Ireland *is* geographically a part of the British Isles, the present selection of a handful of 'great' trains past and present can fairly begin with a mention of this 113 mile line whose best current timing is a respectable but unspectacular 130 minutes. Purely from the standpoint of the lover of railways of individuality the GN(I)R has many attractions — the broad gauge which, as the result of a typically Irish compromise, it shares with the rest of the lines of the green island, the fact that until the end of steam its locomotives displayed the brilliant blue livery of a company which, *as* a company, had long ceased to exist, the through-coaches to Cork which for a few years worked round the Dublin loop-line immortalised by James Joyce, and the brave gesture (made in 1947, at a time when there was a threat that Irish closures might go so far as to leave the two capitals without any rail connection at all) of inaugurating a name-train service, the *Enterprise*.

On this service customs examination is carried out at the termini, not the frontier; and customs examination between the two Irelands can have aspects of its own. During the Second World War, for instance, it was regarded as a matter almost of patriotism for fighting but ill-fed northerners to raid the neutral South for the means to keep up their strength, a trade to which the *douaniers* of

the 'six counties' were prepared to turn at least one blind eye. Those years are typified by the confession of the traveller who filled the lower part of his infant's pram with steaks and butter, announced to the officials that he had nothing to declare, and after a little questioning was able to congratulate himself on his dissimulation when the pram was adorned with a chalk scrawl. Only later did he see that this took the form, not of the usual meaningless cipher, but of the word 'LIAR'.

Yet inter-Irish smuggling has often had its darker side too. In comparatively peaceful days it was said that the communiqué 'A flying column of the Irish Republican Army has been despatched north' could be interpreted as meaning 'One man in a dirty rain-coat has got on the *Enterprise*, and pray God that gun of his works'; in Ireland laughter is rarely far over the rain-drenched horizon, and one of the most hilarious of border incidents was the confrontation of the southern revenuers by ladies who challenged them to search for contraceptive devices concealed about — or, indeed, within — their persons. But in still more recent days the Dublin-Belfast service has run in a climate close to that of open war, and it may well be that its full story would disclose more of danger and treachery than those of more illustrious railways.

For the rest, Eire is no country for the lover of luxury travel; for though both dining and sleeping cars made token appearances there they found the republic's fields as inhospitable to them as to the snakes which St Patrick banished. But in recent years the South has at least christened a handful of its less-slow trains, if in Gaelic terms as puzzling to the overseas visitor as are those patriotic names now attached to Dublin's terminal stations. *Slainte* and *Failte* may be almost international words — but what of *Seandun*, *Sairseal* and *Cu-Na-Mara*? And why *not* 'Deirdre of the Sorrows'...?

For the average British railway enthusiast, however, the word 'Irish' would inevitably be linked in a psychologist's test with 'Mail' — and rightly so, for the *Irish Mail* is the oldest of all the world's trains to be accorded a name, if at first an unofficial one. In fact a whole fleet leaving London at various hours of the day and night has carried this great title since soon after a rather leisurely service began in 1842, only a couple of years after Robert Stephenson's route from Chester was opened along the coast of North Wales and over the Menai Bridge to the traditional port of Holyhead; and quite early the transport of the Queen's mail took second place to a passenger service which included the running of what was then the best-provisioned as well as fastest dining-car on Britain's rails. But the classic has always been the down, night 'Mail' which left Euston around 2045 h. It still does so leave, though the rebuilding of London's premier station has destroyed — together with better things — the typically-British paradox of its greatest trains departing from its most obscure and murky bays.

More to be regretted is the loss since 1939 of a unique railway tradition — the solemn handing-over to the driver of the *Irish Mail* of a watch intended to carry Greenwich time to Dublin. The ritual, of course, lost all its usefulness with first the laying of cables and then

One of the Great Western's idiosyncracies was its use of slip coaches, detached from the rest of the train while it was in motion and brought to rest at some station *en route*. Here two *Ocean Mail* coaches are being slipped at Bedminster in 1906, the speed of the train at the time being reported at 69 mph.

One of the most romantic of all the named trains of Britain — the *Cornish Riviera Express*, here seen in the years when its nickname 'The Limited' had received official recognition. At various periods, its run from London to Penzance was claimed as the longest non-stop journey in Britain, Europe or the world.

The *Sunny South Special* was a service originated by the London & North Western railway to convey passengers from the north and midlands to the south coast. The trains by-passed London to arrive over LBSCR metals at Eastbourne and Brighton.

The 'Cheltenham Flyer' caught the public imagination when in the 1930s it became the world's fastest train in normal service. Running down non-stop from Paddington, London to Cheltenham Spa, it averaged 71 mph behind one of the Great Western Castles.

A down express leaving Teignmouth in the inter-war years. The elegant 'Ocean Mail' type carriages, Churchward's 'Castle' class locomotive, and Brunel's sea wall combine to produce the authentic Great Western atmosphere.

the coming of Irish independence, and the return of the timepieces must always have been somewhat of an anticlimax. Yet, by those who love the small ceremonies of life, the abolition of this rite was mourned as much as was the passing of those majestic top hats worn by the masters of Britain's larger terminals.

The Irish trade was not, however, a monopoly of the old LNW — and later LMS — railway. In the first decade of the present century the Great Western — having finally abandoned its broad gauge and built a number of those 'cut offs' whose lack had earned it the soubriquet of the 'Great Way Round' — had become so aggressive that it laid out vast sums to improve its link to Fishguard at the south-western tip of Wales. But though the route survives today as a way to Southern Ireland it was never competitive to Dublin, and the 'Fishguard Irish Mails' should rather be remembered as an example of the type of rivalry which, in this period before South-ampton became Britain's premier passenger port, set the GWR and the South Western at each other's throats for the trans-Atlantic mail contract from Plymouth. There are stirring — and tragic — tales to be told of that race. But the British traveller today, thinking of Plymouth in a railway context, thinks not of upholstered saloons and crashes at Salisbury but rather of the *Cornish Riviera Express*.

A non-stop run from London to Plymouth was inaugurated as long ago as 1904; and since this was two years before the building of the direct route to Taunton by way of those lonely marshes of Athelney where once King Alfred hid it implied a journey of over 245 miles, by far the longest such in the world at the time. With the opening of the present tracks and the introduction of the GWR's new corridor stock came that 1030 h. departure which was to continue for nearly seventy years; and with it too came a 4 hour timing, the provision of a valet to clean the gentlemen's boots and of a maid dressed in nurse's uniform to 'constantly patrol the train' and 'especially watch over ladies travelling without an escort' (both these for *third*-class passengers, since the thirty-six first-class travellers were expected to have their own servants), and the title of the *Cornish Riviera Limited*. The very existence of such a geographical feature seems to have been an inspiration of the railway's publicity department, which was struck by a similarity in shape if not in scale between Cornwall and Italy; but the train's own title was the outcome of a public competition.

Over the years the word 'Limited' has been replaced (at least officially) by 'Express': indeed, this term for an all-seats-to-be-booked train never became popular in Britain. The array of slip-coaches have slipped their last dramatic detachments, the immortal-seeming chocolate-and-cream which was the most distinguished and beloved of all Britain's dozen or more major coaching-stock liveries has vanished from the vales of the west, the long and legible name-boards have become at best tin posters, the great series of locomotives designed by Dean, Churchward and Collett have declined to soulless diesels, and even the hallowed departure time has now been tampered with. But today's 'Limited', it must be confessed, reaches Plymouth to a 3½ (and Penzance to 5½) hour schedule which Isambard Kingdom Brunel, the great engineer of the system, would have regarded as commendable even at the height of his dreams of atmospheric traction beside the estuary of the Exe.

The same glories never quite accompanied the 'Limited's rival, the *Atlantic Coast Express*. This was in any case a far younger train, for it did not begin life under that title until three years after the salmon-and-milk livery of the London & South Western company had given place to the green of the consortium which formed the Southern railway after the government-imposed amalgamations of 1923; and perhaps even 'rival' is too strong a word, for many years earlier the LSWR had conceded to the GWR the laurels for speed to the deep west. There was, in fact, a measure of co-operation between these two morning expresses to England's sub-tropical holiday-land: for in its hilly journey the South-Western train not only twice met the Great Western's route *going the other way* but once contrived (though leaving London a little later) to pick up one of the eight or nine sections of the 'Limited' itself.

The 'ACE', though, had distinctions other than that its name lent itself to an acronym long before such things became fashionable. It was, for instance, not only one of the most replicated of holiday trains (with up to seven reliefs running of a Saturday in the hot high summers of the 1930s), but was itself divided into so many sections at drowsy, bee-humming junctions in the west that at Wadebridge the young John Betjeman wondered: 'Can it really be / That this same carriage came from Waterloo?' The present writer's memory is a humbler one: it is of passing through Clapham Junction in 1946, and of seeing the stock of the 'ACE' being scrubbed and cleaned and fitted with its gold-on-green boards (though not yet the abomination of buffet-cars painted to resemble half-timbered inns), and of knowing that the war was *really* over.

'The emptying train, wind in the ventilators / Puffs out of Egloskerry to Tresmere / Through minty meadows, under bearded trees...' Today the 'ACE', and the Southern network, have been 'rationalised' out of the deep west, with even the tracks dismantled. But all this *is* South Western talk; and for many the Brittany of Britain has always belonged to the Great Western company.

For long, indeed, after not merely amalgamation but the nationalisation of 1948 the Great Western preserved its individuality, its unique air of aristocracy and of the aristocrat's mild eccentricity. This was the system on which, not so very long ago, one might travel next to a squire who kept a pair of gold-plated scissors especially for clipping the return halves off his first-class tickets (in another pocket he had a pistol for shooting wasps), or discover in the toilet a Dominican priest keeping rainbow trout alive in the hand-basin. This was where great trains stopped — or did not stop — at small stations such as Badminton to honour ancient agreements with landowners. This was where Professor Joad (a once-eminent philosopher, ticket-bilker and player of mixed hockey) delayed the 'Limited' itself at Reading whilst he engaged a porter in a semantic discussion on the meaning of the verb 'to stop' as applied to a railway train. And it was at Reading too — and in

The Great Eastern railway's *Norfolk Coast Express* leaving Liverpool Street in the first years of the present century. The locomotive, of the famous 'Claud Hamilton' class, is resplendent in the royal-blue livery of the company.

quite recent years — that the then manager of the line, Gerald Fiennes, asked an inspector why he did not use his whistle to hasten the transfer to a main-line express of travellers descending from a local train which had just arrived from the affluent country around Newbury.

'Sir', protested the shocked official, 'we do not blow whistles at people from *Newbury*.' But even this story can be capped by one from an ex-prime minister when he felt that he was being treated to quite remarkably attentive service. Were all former premiers, Mr Harold Macmillan enquired, looked after with such care?

'Oh no, sir', was the reply this time, 'Only former directors of the Great Western.'

A few ghosts of the old traditions still haunt such branch-lines of the west as the amazing run from Looe to Liskeard; and another heritage from a more leisured and luxurious age is to be found in that unique institution, the British railway tea. For the tea-cakes now universal on all regions were surely first cast at Swindon, just as they are still best enjoyed amid the blossom of the Vale of Evesham or by ' ... Brunel's wall / Between the red cliffs and the rise and fall / Of Channel tides...' on an express for Torbay some summer's afternoon when white sails dot the sea. But even sixty years ago the Great Western flyers did not live on holidaymakers, or even on children travelling to Britain's lusher schools. Indeed, this was one of the first companies to appreciate the importance of what is today a staple of railway economy — the occasional and long-distance, as opposed to the commuting, businessman.

For instance, in the later 1900s another of its short cuts enabled the GWR to become a seriously competitive line between London and the Midlands. Its rival here, the North Western, had the advantage of termini nearer to the heart of the capital's business. But the GWR services threatened to become so attractive that on its 2 ¼ hour *City to City Express* of 1910 the LNWR had to compete by introducing from the USA a facility not to be seen again on European rails until the 1930s in Germany — a lady secretary whose services, together with that of a far-from-portable typewriter, could be hired during the journey.

A dozen other trains from the Great Western alone cry out for mention here. There was, for instance, the *Cambrian Coast Express* which threaded its way through seaboard galleries and over the timber bridges built by 'Davies the Ocean', and that *Cheltenham Spa Express* which the public rechristened the 'Flyer' which made scheduled world records of 66 mph in 1929 and 71 ½ mph in 1932, on one journey in the latter year notching-up a classic 82 mph. But the GWR *was* only one system, and there are many for whom the greatest moments of Britain's railways are to be found along the two major ways from London to the Scottish Lowlands.

The east coast route — in amalgamation days that of the London & North Eastern railway — ran by way of York and Berwick, following the traditional Great North Road: the more westerly journey offered by the LMS, the 'premier line', was by way of Carlisle and the steep Border hills. Both routes served Edinburgh and Glasgow alike, and thereafter could vie for the traffic to the whole of Scotland. In addition, there were at the peak of the railway age at least two other ways to the far north; but these ran over rougher ground and the slogan 'St. George for England — St. Pancras for Scotland' appealed only to the most fervent supporters of the erstwhile Midland railway. A tribute should, however, be paid here to the journey still worked by the *Thames-Clyde Express* — a slow way from London to Glasgow, but a beautiful one.

It was between the two major routes, though, that there took place the most dramatic competitions in all railway history. Trains can often be seen apparently racing on parallel tracks, there are plenty of examples of contrived races between railways and other media, and ever since the Rainhill trials there had been competitions in performance. But the true railway race is a rare event; for it demands that genuinely competitive companies (such as could not exist in the planned networks of continental Europe) should own rival routes between A and B which can be covered in approximately the same time. Such conditions have arisen once or twice in the United States, but they presented themselves in their most classic form in Britain at the end of the last century.

Until 1888 the east- and west-coast consortia had been content to cover the 400-odd miles to Edinburgh in about 10 hours; but in that summer the two routes entered into a competition which within a few weeks produced runs up to 2 ½ hours faster. For the next 7 years the official timings were stabilised at 7 ¾ hours for the east coast route and 8 hours for the west: then, in 1895, the race entered a new and even more stimulating phase. For though the traffic being fought for was the same as in 1888 — huge house parties moving north for the grouse-shooting season — the race this time was run for another 140 miles onwards to Aberdeen, deep into the Highlands.

It began without publicity or pre-arrangement and was never publicly admitted even to exist; but from the first July night when the west coast companies announced a one-hour acceleration the consortia were at each other's throats. Timetables were torn up; carriages were stripped of every inessential accessory (and attendant) in the interest of weight-saving; tardy passengers were manhandled at intermediate stops whilst spectators cheered, or were thrown out of their sleepers at 0400 hours; and so 10 minutes were saved one night and a quarter of an hour the next until eventually the 525 mile journey was achieved in 8½ hours at an average of well over 60 mph, a peak of 77 mph had been recorded, and Britain could claim the world's fastest trains. Effectively the race ended at a junction south of Aberdeen where the rival routes converged to a single track; and on one classic night the announcement bells in the cabin there clanged with under a minute between them as the signalman saw two plumes of steam sweeping almost side-by-side up the valley in the northern dawn.

Yet for all their excitements — and their real value in accustoming the public to high speeds — such races had little effect on day-to-day (or night-to-night) running, for the second series like

8.0 P.M. EXPRESS, EUSTON TO ABERDEEN, AUGUST 22nd, 1895.

PARTICULARS OF RUNNING BETWEEN EUSTON AND CARLISLE.

Timing Stations.	Time of passing.	Time between Stations.	Distance between Stations.	Speed in miles per hour	Average Speed between stops.
	H. M. S.	MINS. SECS.	MILES.		
Euston ... dep.	8 0 0	17 0	17·3	61·0	
Watford ... pass	8 17 0	13 30	14·2	63·1	
Tring ... .. ,,	8 30 30	12 30	15·0	72·0	Driver, R. Walker.
Bletchley ... ,,	8 43 0	34 0	36·0	63·5	64·3 miles per hour.
Rugby ... ,,	9 17 0	13 30	14·6	64·9	
Nuneaton ... ,,	9 30 30	11 0	13·0	70·9	
Tamworth ... ,,	9 41 30	22 30	23·4	62·4	
Stafford ... ,,	10 4 0	23 30	24·6	62·8	
Crewe... ... arr.	10 27 30				Load, 3 = 4½
,, ... dep.	10 29 30	21 55	24·1	66·0	
Warrington pass	10 51 25	10 10	11·5	67·9	
Wigan ... ,	11 1 35	13 40	15·5	68·0	
Preston ... ,,	11 15 15	18 50	20·6	65·7	Driver, B. Robinson.
Lancaster ... ,,	11 34 5	5 37	6·5	69·6	67·2 miles per hour.
Carnforth ... ,,	11 39 42	11 28	12·8	67·0	
Oxenholme ,,	11 51 10	12 50	13·1	61·2	
Tebay... ... ,,	12 4 0	6 0	5·8	58·0	
Shap Summit ,,	12 10 0	11 0	13·3	72·5	
Penrith ... ,,	12 21 0	14 30	18·0	74·4	
Carlisle ... arr.	12 35 30		299·25		

Above: Although appearing in prosaic tabular form, the details here present one side of the stirring close-of-century race in which rival east and west coast routes fought a hard battle to provide the fastest services to Aberdeen.

The doyen of all trains to the north was — as it remains — the *Flying Scotsman*.

8.0 P.M. EXPRESS, EUSTON TO ABERDEEN, AUGUST 22nd, 1895.

PARTICULARS OF RUNNING BETWEEN

CARLISLE AND ABERDEEN.

Timing Stations.	Time of Passing.	Time between Stations.	Distance between Stations.	Speed in Miles per hour.	Average speed between stops.
	H. M. S.	MINS. SECS.	MILES.		
Carlisle ... dep.	12 38 0				
		39 30	39·75	60·3	
Beattock ... pass	1 17 30				
		13 30	10· 0	44·4	
„ Summit „	1 31 0				
		21 0	23·75	67·8	Driver, A. Crooks, Engine No. 90.
Carstairs ... „	1 52 0				
		10 30	10· 5	60·0	
Law Junction „	2 2 30				
		5 0	5·75	69·0	60·5 miles per hour.
Holytown ... „	2 7 30				
		19 30	20· 0	61·5	
Larbert ... „	2 27 0				
		7 30	8· 0	64·0	
Stirling ... „	2 34 30				
		33 0	33· 0	60·0	
Perth ... ... arr.	3 7 30				Load 3=4½
„ ... ... dep.	3 9 30				
		29 30	32· 5	66·1	
Forfar... ... pass	3 39 0				
		18 0	19·25	64·2	
Kinnaber Jun. „	3 57 0				
		12 30	15· 5	74·4	Driver, J. Souttar, Engine No. 17.
Drumlithie... „	4 9 30				
		7 0	6·75	57·8	
Stonehaven „	4 16 30				
Aberdeen—					65·4 miles per hour.
Ticket Statn. arr	4 30 0				
		15 30	16· 0	61·9	
„ „ dep.	4 31 0				
Aberdeen ... arr	4 32 0				
			240·75		

Another way to attract customers to the rival Scottish routes was by the provision of new stock, as exemplified by this beaver-tailed car on the *Coronation* introduced in 1937.

the first ended in a restrictive agreement and the leisurely timing of 8 ¾ hours from London to Scotland was so tightly enforced that for more than a quarter of a century the companies had deliberately to waste time in long 'refreshment' stops. They could only compete, as airlines do today, in their facilities; and the earliest evidence of *this* warfare had already appeared in 1893 when the western route's daytime service presented the first train in Europe which could be perambulated from end to end. For decades after this facility had become routine the noon-ish departure from Euston — the precursor of the *Midday Scot* — was indeed known to railwaymen as 'The Corridor'.

But the late 1920s brought the renewed competition in speed associated with what (as few of the 'Boy's Book of Inventions' of the period guessed) was to prove the penultimate age of steam; and this competition became even tenser in the 1930s. The first of the new breed of northbound flyers in fact never reached Scotland; for it was the record-making *Silver Jubilee* to Newcastle of 1935 which inaugurated that tradition of linking train-names to national events which was to continue down to *The Elizabethan* of 1955. (It is typical of our times, though, that 1973 did *not* see the debut of 'The European'.) Then, two years later, another celebration provided the excuse for the mounting of the west-coast *Coronation Scot* and the east-coast *Coronation*. The latter of these, which set up heroic records on trial runs before becoming the first train regularly to cover this route on a schedule better than that of the Victorian racers as it disposed of nearly 200 miles at 72 mph, was distinguished by a beaver-tailed observation coach for which a supplementary fare was charged by the hour — and also by the very necessary provision of rattle-proof cutlery.

If through the advent of war alone, these expresses ran for only a season or two before their special cars were banished to that limbo which awaits so much purpose-built stock, and eventually even the meretricious 'streamlined' casings (bullet-nosed on William Stanier's LMS, wedge-shaped on Nigel Gresley's LNER) were stripped from most of the locomotives of the age. But all the while the flagship of the fleet, the east-coast *Flying Scotsman* which had left Kings Cross at 1000 h. ever since 1862 (though it did not acquire its name until 1923) had been improving its own performance, until its time to Edinburgh was brought down to 5 ¾ hours.

Similar improvements were made to the train's stock, so that the 1930 set included not only a *Louis seize* restaurant but a ladies' retiring room and hairdressing salon. The latter seems to have been under-used, since in 1938 the *coiffeur* was replaced with a mere ladies-maid: but throughout the thirties male passengers could pass the time whilst their women-folk were being titivated by not merely reading bulletins assembled from news received on the train's wireless but studying radio-photographs of — for instance — the finish of the Derby. Other distinctions of the *Flying Scotsman* were that it became Britain's heaviest train, with up to two dozen cars grossing 800 tons, that (thanks to the device of providing a corridor tender which enabled the locomotive crews to relieve each other

— or themselves — *en route*) it made the journey to Scotland non-stop, that it was one of the only four British named trains to run during the Second World War (and was indeed twice machine-gunned, with the fireman on one occasion being wounded but continuing work), and that even after nationalisation it preserved a reminder of a decade when trains struggled for individuality in *couture* as well as performance. For it still wore the Stewart tartan on not only its name-boards but on its last corridor-connection.

Despite all their achievements in speed — later, of course, to be eclipsed by the better-than-five-hours promised and already in part achieved by the electrification of the west-coat route — none of these trains ever *quite* achieved the glamour of their designedly-slower sisters which remain the direct descendants of the racers of the 70s and the 90s, and which make the night journeys to Scotland. Threshing up over the Shap and Beattock gradients in the frosty small hours of a winter night, or rolling over Robert Stephenson's curving Border bridge across the Tweed on a summer dawn, the *Aberdonian* and its companions and predecessors have captured the imaginations of travellers for a century and remain very well patronised today. And the most privileged of such passengers have been those who, instead of being decanted at Waverley or St. Enoch stations in the grim early hours, have continued to Aberdeen, to Inverness, or over that incomparable line — the last of importance to be built for the railways of Britain — which still leads to Mallaig and the Western Isles.

On such a journey also one may be regaled with Scotland's own contribution to good eating, the northern breakfast; for the Scottish region of British Railways still pays suitable honour to the Aberdeen kipper and the 'finnan haddie'. This is not to suggest, though, that (even apart from those teas) other regions did not have such gastronomic eccentricities as the Great Western's radishes; and it is not so long since BR cheese was invariably served to the accompaniment of celery if not celerity. There has always been strength in the bottled-sauce quarter, too. One well-travelled Norwegian, for instance, recently ordered England's traditional roast beef for the first time on an up Newcastle boat-train, and when this was served at Durham fell in with what he took to be local custom by sloshing the accompanying condiments around. Darlington was in sight before he at last had an edible if chilly meal before him; for a little horse-radish goes a long way...

The catering departments of Britain's railways have also long been strong in sheer *matériel* — though wine-lovers can be distressed by the frequency with which the corkscrew gets mislaid. Operating over a thousand expresses a day which boast some kind of refresh-ment facility, BR boasts a fleet of eupeptic if unstable restaurant-cars three times the size of Germany's, and its cellarage and mobile resources indeed challenge those of the Wagons-Lits company itself. One reason for this disproportion is, at first sight, unexpected; the restricted loading-gauge of Britain's railways means that corridors are too narrow for the general adoption of the *vente ambulante* service of continental nations and so, however uneconomically, the cus-

The up east coast night mail approaches Doncaster about 1863. In the 1830's there was in Birmingham a man named Geach who took a very active part in the construction of the early railways and he then worked some of them by contract for their owners. To finance all this he founded the Midland Bank which later became the London City and Midland but which has now reverted to its original title. His elder son managed the bank and the second boy, Howard, accompanied his father as personal assistant on his travels. He was a very good artist.

This is the new Great Western royal train which was built for Queen Victoria's Diamond Jubilee celebrations and it is seen here conveying her from Windsor to Paddington for her state drive from there to St. Paul's Cathedral in June 1897.

tomers must go to the snacks rather than *vice versa*. But no such mechanical explanation can be given of the fact that, whereas a German dining car carries some 60 drinking glasses of various types (which seems generous enough), the British figure was in pre-plastic days nearer 200. This is enough to suggest that BR had visions of its buffet cars being patronised mainly by celebrating rugby-football clubs and by cossacks drinking toasts to their mistresses.

Yet all this discussion began with sleeping rather than dining cars. The splendours — or, for the insomniac, miseries — of night travel are, of course, not confined to the Anglo-Scottish routes; for until recently it was possible for the brave to be deposited at 0700 h. at a Cumberland station improbably known as Corkickle which was served by *couchettes* converted to their nocturnal guise by pulling down sepia photographs of Manchester town hall, and there is still a slow part-sleeper to Penzance which makes such stops as Bristol at 0300 h. But it is only on runs of 300, 400 or more miles that the traveller — alone or with a chosen companion, of course, *not* in the hideously-enforced intimacy of a shared second — can take real possession of his world of some 40 square feet.

For it *is* his, and his name is displayed on a manifest at every stop along the line, as well as on the train itself, in witness of that fact. This is his womb, if one can accept a womb lit by an almost invisibly-dim blue glimmer which hurtles around at 70 mph. Outside there are blizzards, blast furnaces, mercury-lit highways, night shifts, dying sheep, students with tired eyes, pain-racked invalids, men sorting mail and above all the peasants in the day-cars of passing trains. But inside there is only *luxe, calme et volupté*.

There, as T.S. Eliot wrote in his guise of 'Old Possum':

... the berth is very neat with a newly folded sheet
And there's not a speck of dust on the floor.
There is every sort of light — you can make it dark or bright;
There's a handle you can turn to make a breeze.
There's a funny little basin you're supposed to wash your face in
And a crank to shut the window if you sneeze.
Then the guard looks in politely and will ask you very brightly
'Do you like your morning tea weak or strong? ...:

whilst another good Christian (and a canon to boot) confessed to his 'childish and snobbish' pleasure at the deference which even the humblest sleeping-car passenger received. These tributes were written twenty or thirty years ago; but neither nationalisation nor the general decline of service have adversely affected the standards of that splendid corps of sleeping-car attendants of whom every member seems equipped to serve as at least a footman in a moderately stately home.

The £2 or so spent on a BR sleeper ticket, indeed, remains one of the best bargains available to the human ego and is certainly better value than anything the CIWL can offer. What is more, the ambience itself retains traces of the traditional magic. For though plastic surfaces may have replaced polished mahogany there are still mysterious cupboards holding water-decanters, tiny druggets, and even a device, surely restricted to such means of transport, (for it can be found in Wagon-lits) for hanging one's fob watch on . . .

Almost all sleeping-car trains, then, are great trains. But there are few other absolutes, and many contributors to this book have had to seek for their own answers to the question 'What is a great train?' — and have found the qualities as difficult to define (if, at times, as easy to recognise) as those of a great man. The selection in these pages must hence be largely a personal one, and every reader will have his own candidates for additions or deletions.

Thus, for some, greatness would be associated with the distant memory of a blue 'Claud Hamilton' hauling its teak coaches across the flats of Fenland or in under that sulphurous roof of Liverpool Street which was regarded by one American visitor as the most impressive of all entries to London: is it really half a century, these greybeards will wonder, since Britain lost such locomotive liveries as 'The Midland lake, the Caledonian blue / The Brighton "Stroudleys" in their umber hue', and with them coaches in 'The bronze green . . . of the Cambrian / GNS red and white; North Eastern plum . . .' Others will recall day-long journeys from Plymouth to Liverpool, with all the red sandstone splendour of the marcher country awaiting beyond the Severn tunnel (but rarely a refreshment car in which to toast it). The 1650 h. — or thereabouts: in any case it was *really* the 4.50 pm — to Oxford has featured in the autobiographies of numerous former undergraduates; but Cambridge had far more railway variety to offer, and on the erstwhile Great Northern line was served several times a day by the *Garden Cities and Cambridge Buffet Car Express*, known to four student decades by the more convenient name of 'The Beer Train'. Other travellers from Paddington might in any case prefer to wait for the 1710 h., Britain's last train to drop a slip-coach; and far to the north the Newcastle and Carlisle line still preserves qualities all its own. Above all, most would grant that 'great' is more than titularly apposite to the late and lamented Great Central railway.

Built in a megalomaniac but internationalist dream at the very end of the nineteenth century and of the railway era, this led from the infinite calm of Marylebone station (the best place in London for one's prayers, according to a Jesuit), through that tunnel under Mr Lord's cricket ground which caused so much acrimony, across green fox-hunting shires and by way of remote stations to end, after a last dive through the Pennines, almost incidentally at Manchester. Even at its busiest the *Master Cutler* usually provided its passengers with elbow-room as ample as the train itself enjoyed on its generously deployed tracks; but such custom as there was was 'carriage trade', and one felt that the GC expresses were patronised, as well as hauled, by 'Directors'.

With all this choice one thing is certain — that one does not make a train great simply by giving it a name. Today, for example, few remember the routes of such Victorian speedsters as *The Granville* (though, in 1877, this was probably Europe's first train to carry an *official* name), of the *Scarborough Flyer*, the *Peak Express* and *The Palatine*, all of which endured until after the Second World

Left: A restaurant car of the 1900s operated by the 'West Coast to Scotland' companies.

Right: A corner of a LNWR restaurant car of the 1900s. Although this vehicle was converted in part to form the dining car of a royal train, this part of the carriage was unaltered and is typical of the furnishings and layout of the time. Note the wine coasters on the carriage side.

Below: The kitchen of the London & North Western Railway's *American Special*, an express which ran in connection with the Atlantic liners which docked at Liverpool. Amongst the *batterie de cuisine*, a British note is struck by the enormous kettle on the stove.

War, or even of the quite-recently-vanished *Bon Accord* and *St. Mungo* expresses in Scotland. There were — and are — also trains such as the *Red Dragon* and the *Cathedrals Express* whose performances were unexciting even when they lived up to the promise of the timetable. In the days of steam these rarely received the supreme accolade of a crowd of business travellers — as well as of small boys — gathering round the cab to felicitate the driver on a noble run.

Certain names, too, should never have been inflicted on any train — names which were the British equivalent of that *Wiener Walzer* which one envisages as progressing across Austria in three-quarter time. The subject of the titling of trains (as opposed to locomotives) has never been definitively dealt with, but few would regret the death of the Victorian practice of christening expresses after racehorses. *The Flying Dutchman*, the *Afghan* and *The Zulu* — semi-official names for Plymouth flyers in the days when the broad-gauge Great Western was hard-pressed to exceed averages of 45 mph — sound dry in the mouth by comparison with that of today's *Golden Hind*, let alone of the *Limited*, and the South-Western's *Beeswing* was little more euphorious. But even now there can be sad solecisms: the idea of naming a Highlands express 'The Duke of Cumberland' was admittedly only a novelist's fancy, but nobody ever informed British Railways that *The Heart of Midlothian* was certainly the title of a Walter Scott novel (as were *The Talisman* and *Waverley*, also appropriated to railway use) but was, behind that, the soubriquet of a prison...

By contrast, there are trains which did not receive the compliment of even such a 'family' name as *Trans-Pennine Express* yet which capture the imagination. The railways of Britain (as of France) have never been at their best in inter-regional running, in operating expresses avoiding the national capitals; and apart from the Bristol-Birmingham link the best performances hence tend to have been those of holiday services linking the Midlands and the North to south and west coast resorts. There was once, for example, a train called the *Sunny South Express*, a rare name-bearer among those which (at least on summer Saturdays) crept over those tracks between Willesden and Clapham junctions which are London's answer to the *ceinture* of Paris and which gave northern readers of the timetable the idea that Rugby and Redhill were adjacent stations. Amid the true cross-country trains — the *Cornishman*, *Devonian* and the like — only the *Pines Express*, running from the Midlands to Bournemouth over the old Somerset & Dorset line, ever passed into railway mythology.

Yet during the Second World War, when the lines of the west were so disorganised that the arrival indicators at Paddington seemed permanently set at ninety-nine minutes late, there was a nameless North-Eastern train — itself the successor to a long-forgotten 'ports-to-ports' service — which carried the mail between York and Cardiff. This was, night after night, as punctual as it was clean and comfortable, and proved itself a great express indeed in its humble fashion. It was also of commendable velocity; but even

London & North Western royal saloons. These were built in 1903 to replace the charming but dated car used by Queen Victoria. There were two cars, one for King Edward VII and one for Queen Alexandra, and the interiors were designed to look as far as was possible like the cabins of the royal yacht.

Top left: King Edward's smoking saloon, lined with the same veneers as are used to make violins and furnished with solid but comfortable armchairs.

Right: Queen Alexandra's day saloon. The train saw much service, since it was used by King George V as a mobile headquarters during the First World War and by his son during the Second War.

Bottom: The royal dining car, showing the table set for a meal.

high speed is not essential to distinction in a train, for it must always be remembered that (contrary to popular superstition) express speeds were low by present-day standards before 1900 and, with a few exceptions, remained leisurely until the 1930s brought external challenges from the air and the road and internal competition between steam, diesel and electricity.

Perhaps what *is* indispensable — at least in Britain — for a train to claim to be 'great' is that it should make a reasonably long journey at a reasonably high speed for its period, and that it should run punctually to a regular schedule for the benefit of *bona fide* travellers. This latter stipulation, for instance, rules out what was undoubtedly the most luxurious thing ever to occupy British metals, the LNER's *Northern Belle* which made week-long 'land cruises' in the summers between 1933 and 1939. Since nearly half of its fourteen double-headed coaches comprised first-class sleepers, smoking and 'retiring' rooms, shower baths and the like, this could accomodate only sixty passengers, with each being supported by over ten tons of hardware. In fact, it (and its companion, the *Eastern Belle* of 'trips *de luxe*') could do almost anything except fulfil a train's first purpose, which is to carry something from A to B.

But given the above criteria, a great train can break almost any of the rules. For instance (and although this book is not concerned with even the fastest of ordinary freight trains), it need not even carry passengers: for from the very earliest days of Britain's railways up to and beyond the age when W. H. Auden wrote his film-script for *Night Mail*, the image of the Royal Mails racing through the night has borne a magic inherited from the stage-coach era. Today the grille-windowed parcels vans and travelling sorting offices have lost their distinctive livery, their royal cipher and — perhaps most sadly of all — their gear for picking up and discharging mail-bags at 70 mph. But (in the unlikely event of the traveller having a supplementary ½ p stamp on him) he can still post a letter directly into the up mail at Truro at midnight, or at Crewe in the small hours, and know that it will be in London before he is. Although BR regard the whole business as rather uneconomic, the mail must still get through — barring brigandage and villainy, that is, for even in our unglamorous late twentieth century there was a recollection of a tradition older than railways or even Dick Turpin when a £2m postal special was held to ransom in misty exurban fields in the greatest robbery in transport history.

Yet there are three categories of trains which have an *a priori* claim to be considered great. And the first of these comprises Britain's all-Pullman fleet.

Through those anomalies which began long before amalgamation, and which survived long after nationalisation, the distribution of the Pullman cars which were *themselves* an anomaly has always been uneven. Some companies would not look at them, but others so long relied on them for catering as well as comfort that in the south of England Pullmans largely took the place of ordinary restaurant cars. Even after electrification, those who lived near the main line to the south coast indeed learned to distinguish an

Top left: A 'club' train introduced by the South Eastern & Chatham railway in 1889 which consisted of two Wagons-Lits company Pullmans and accompanying vans. It was used on the Dover-London route, but did not prove a success and was withdrawn after four years.

One of Britain's modern 'Inter-City' trains. Though lacking all the glamour of their named counterparts, they provide comfort and high-speed running.

Eastbourne from a Worthing express a mile away by the position of its contrasting Pullman cars — and even to repeat the feat at night by noting the seductive pink glow from the tablelamps.

The aristocrat here was of course the all-Pullman *Brighton Belle*, electrified in 1933 but itself the descendant of a noble family of expresses which linked London to its most favoured resort and which combined luxury accomodation with reasonably high speeds. For as long ago as the 1840s there was a 90 minute non-stop service on this 51 mile line, and by the start of the century timings had been reduced, by way of 75 minutes in 1850, to the even hour schedule which endured throughout the Second World War and so turned the ordinary 'Brighton non-stops' into Britain's fastest trains. These predecessors, whose ultimate ancestor was a *Brighton Sunday Pullman Limited* of 1899 which so enshrined the decor of that age of lincrusta ceilings and padded doors that special clerestoried brake-vans were built for it, bore such names as the *Southern Belle* (consisting, in 1908, of the first British-built Pullmans), the *Pullman Limited* and the *City Limited*: the latter, terminating at London Bridge, is a reminder that even in stage-coach days there were those who commuted between the stock exchange and the sea.

Though certain branches of the Southern region experimented from time to time with all kinds of curious but cosy and comfortable little *coupés* for family and business groups, the electrified *Belle* itself lacked the intimacy of those 'club trains' which, between 1895 and the coming of the diesel multiple-unit, linked Manchester to its more delectable dormitories; for these latter were true clubs with their own membership rolls, rules and almost hall-porters. But the *Belle* possessed a personality so outstanding among the world's trains that it found many fans even in the heartland of the USA. Its journey was brief, its speed was unremarkable — though in a trick film the BBC managed to hustle it up to 825 mph — and towards the end its running became not very soothing. But it partook of the character of Brighton itself — rich in contrasts, bracing, and slightly naughty.

Back in 1910 the Metropolitan railway used to run a midnight train down from London (where the lavatories were locked until it was clear of the Underground tunnels) to the stockbroker country of the Chilterns. Since the 'Met' was so conscious of creature comforts that eight years earlier it had devised the world's first buffet cars, this boasted a Pullman — the earliest electrically-hauled one in Europe — with 'tiny portable electroliers of a very chaste design' somehow blending into a 'scheme of decoration ... of the latter part of the eighteenth century, with remarkably artistic effect'; and of it many legends are told. (It must certainly have appealed to the Oxford University Railway Club, which at this period flitted around the country digesting Lucullan meals in dining-cars.) Despite its more conventional timings, the *Brighton Belle* had something of the same quality. Most of the passengers who paid the few shillings supplement in first or third-and-later-second class were, of course, accountants and shoppers going up for the day and trippers going down; but there was often enough the faded but blue-rinsed dowager countess, or shamefaced would-be *divorcé*, to provide a certain piquancy. And above all there were two unmistakable communities. In season there were those racing men whose endless game of solo whist seems to continue in every Pullman car in the country — and who are never, of course, to be confused with the *owners* for whose convenience the GWR provided in the 1930s some magnificent private saloons whose *coupés* offered luxury within luxury, and who can travel to the Grand National in some style. And always there were the theatricals.

These thespians may no longer command whole trains for their own use, as they did in the days when Herbert Tree's special service set up a record by travelling from Balmoral to Dublin — 600 miles, including a long sea crossing — between 0200 h. one morning and curtain-rise on a sleepless cast the evening of the same day. But it was another and much later Actor-Manager, Lawrence Olivier, who led through the columns of *The Times* a splendidly-British battle defending the right of the kipper to remain on the *Brighton Belle*'s breakfast menu. For once the passenger prevailed against the authorities; but it was a short-lived victory. For in 1972 came the complete withdrawal of the service.

It was not that it was an uneconomic one, for only a few years earlier the frequency of *Belle* services had been stepped up from three to four return trips a day. But after forty years the unique electric multiple-unit cars had reached the end of their life, and the cost of replacing them was claimed to be prohibitive. British Railways were saying, in effect, that they could no longer afford any rolling stock of individuality; and so the *Brighton Belle* joined her sisters to Thanet, to Bournemouth and (at week-ends only, but equipped with one of Britain's rare observation-cars even if this *was* made deliberately uncomfortable) to Devon — all later born and sooner to die — in comparative immobility. But it was not in extinction, for the three sets of five cars were sold, mainly to brewery companies, for a total price of over £20,000.

Away from the Southern region, the Pullman company's operations were of latter years almost entirely confined to all-Pullman trains — particularly on the North Eastern routes, where the *Queen of Scots* made the long journey to Edinburgh and the *Yorkshire Pullman* behaved like a typical businessman by dividing its attention between the manufacturing cities of the West Riding and the handsome spa of Harrogate. But now the last Pullman services are disappearing from all over Britain, a land where they took root as never on the continent. Even before the end, too, British Railways had struck a blow against personality by abolishing the handsomest of all liveries, and at the same time there vanished from the outside of the cars the lovable and slightly-dated names. It was all sensible enough, for the company itself had for many years been absorbed into the nationalised railway structure. It was *very* sensible — and thoroughly deplorable.

Furthermore, British Railways had since 1960 experimented with a quite different type of train bearing the hallowed name — diesel multiple-units which went blue before the rest of the

Top: An 'Inter-City' express hauled by a diesel locomotive in the days when these still bore names.

Left: Electrification in Britain will soon extend all the way from London to Glasgow. Here a British Railways 100 mph electric locomotive runs near Watford hauling an 'Inter-City' express on the main line from London to the Midlands and the North-West.

Bottom: The Pullman name is not yet quite extinct on British Railways. This is the *Manchester Pullman*, which leaves London at 1800 h. and arrives at Manchester at 2030 h.

Much more character, if perhaps less comfort, was displayed by this saloon carriage built for the LB & SCR in 1873. It is not clear whether the sherry and biscuits formed part of the service.

country's stock and whose double-glazing and air-conditioning lent them the status of honorary trans-european Expresses. Though early seen on the Bristol run, these diesel Pullmans showed their paces most nobly on the beautiful, tough and now-abandoned Midland route to Manchester while the main line was being electrified. They introduced the British public to the rail travel of the future, with its lack of sense of speed and its feeling of slightly claustrophobic isolation from the outer world resembling air transport. But, as in the post-electrification *Manchester Pullman* with its schedule of 150 minutes for nearly 190 miles, their main link with a great name was that a supplement was charged for providing table service. For though the first-class-only train had itself been largely exiled from Britain's rails by the start of the century, the word 'Pullman' still serves to overcome a time-honoured and laudable prejudice against privilege fares. The second category of trains which are indisputably special are the 'special's themselves.

In the great days not merely private coaches but private trains were far from rarities — for the railway, being the only means of travel capable of beating 15 mph, was looked to in any emergency from the political to the medical. Newspapers, for example, would charter a carriage and locomotive with steam up to be kept ready at a Channel port whenever hot news was anticipated from the continent: there are stirring tales in fact and fiction of private chases where the slogan was 'Follow that train!' and every major company was ready to provide a special at a few minutes' notice for the man ready to pay £5 a mile. But when one thinks of chartered trains one thinks first of the royal progresses and state visits which run like a purple thread through railway history — and, in particular, through the history of Britain's railways.

Considering the detailed planning, the dislocation of ordinary running (no other train, for instance, is permitted to proceed alongside a 'royal', though royal coaches are surprisingly often coupled to normal services), the pages of standing instructions and special movement orders, the pilot engines and the security men and all the rest, it is remarkable how often such journeys have been marked by major or minor incidents. The keynote was set by the chain of disasters which characterised Louis-Philippe's visit to Queen Victoria in 1842, but nearly a century later the plans for the opening of new docks at Southampton were all but disorganised by a derailment at Winchester an hour before the King's special was due to pass. And in still more recent times there have been such embarrassing moments as the discovery that one oriental potentate's religion did not allow him to sit on cow-hide (so that a Pullman had to be hastily re-upholstered), or the even more urgent occasion when the official in charge of King Farouk of Egypt's train went to inform His Majesty that he would be at Victoria in five minutes, only to find the monarch mysteriously vanished and his aides sleeping off the effects of excessive champagne.

Fortunately, the Pullmans ran softly enough for a frenzied hammering to be heard from the end of the corridor. A wrecking-bar was hurriedly applied to the stout (and long-unoiled) latch of the smallest room on the train, and the sovereign — who had remembered royalty's first law, which is never to miss an opportunity to relieve oneself — scrambled past the shattered door just as the strains of his anthem boomed out from the platform band.

A few years later Queen Elizabeth and Prince Philip were unaware of a tiny incident which marred their return from a routine holiday journey to Sandringham. The royal coaches were nearing Liverpool Street when, as a signal outside the station was pulled off, its arm parted from its bracket and fell to the ground with a sickening clang. If the train was to arrive punctually there was no time to follow the rulebook procedure: and so a porter was sent to the top of the signal mast where he clung, holding the arm in the upper-quadrant position until the coaches were past.

Many such state trains have been boat-trains; and because Britain is an island it is boat-trains which form the third group of those expresses which are born great rather than have greatness thrust upon them. There are some for whom the prime magic is associated with those specials which still slip in to Waterloo bearing the names of the world's last long-distance passenger steamships; but the glories have departed from 'Lady Liner' whereas, for at least another decade, Britain's first link with a wider world will continue to be by way of the Channel ports.

It is true that even here recent years have seen a loss of romance if not of trade: perhaps things have never been the same since boat-trains ceased to be ruled by the tide-tables, as they were in the days when Charles Dickens was heroically involved in a derailment. Thus, the *Normandy Express* no longer clanks across the streets of Southampton — though the Channel Island trains *do* still make their even more eccentric progress through Weymouth. The special departures board which used to bring the 'Arlberg', the 'Nord' and half a dozen other of Europe's great expresses into the eastern station at Victoria has been replaced by a routine type of flip-flop indicator which reduces even Venice to the status of Surbiton — with, in the interim, continental departures being advertised in the kind of multicoloured-chalk handwriting used only by British railwaymen and British fishmongers. And, above all, the *Golden Arrow* is now no more than a golden ghost.

Introduced in 1929, fighting the depression years but later reinstated in splendour after the war, the English-side *Golden Arrow* was not only one of the most illustrious but also one of the handsomest of all the world's trains: it could even be argued that only a matched rake of Victorian clerestory cars headed by a Stirling 'single' ever challenged, in its very different way, the sight of those glittering coaches hauled by an immaculate 'Merchant Navy' locomotive (or, in the last years of steam, by the specially-deputed Britannia, 'William Shakespeare') across the weald of Kent. The English train *was*, of course, only part of a service which involved a special ship and, on the French side, a connecting train which had acquired some Pullmans three years earlier and which not only served Paris but had cars which were attached to Riviera expresses. But — if only because the British have on the whole believed in

Third-class passengers were early provided with dining facilities by the Great Northern railway.

operating trains as *trains* and not as temporary assemblages of carriages to be divided and reassembled in an endless game of put-and-take — the short run from London to the coast set the visual hallmark on the service. And it was sad to see it reduced, with ordinary cars steadily taking the place of the Pullmans, until at the end of 1972 it was finally withdrawn.

Another slightly-faded service is that of the various 'Continentals' from London to Harwich and thence to Holland and Denmark. The Esbjerg crossing, with Danish buffet catering on the boat, is still perhaps the pleasantest if slowest way of reaching the mainland from Britain; but the rolling stock of the morning and evening services today consists of second-hand, second-class Pullmans, hardly worthy successors to the sets built in 1904, 1924 (which only four crews were permitted to haul), and finally 1936. With the last of these the *Hook Continental* afforded in its first class a Pullman-plus standard of comfort, with splendid winged and swivelling chairs; and this was also the first British train to be wired for sound, even if the only use made of its announcements circuit was to warn the passengers in thick Dutch and thicker Danish of the rather obvious fact that Harwich was approaching.

Parkeston Quay, too, remains the terminal of Britain's oddest boat train, the cross-country service which makes what has been called the 'unimaginable journey' from Manchester and which (since a section also once served Liverpool) was termed a boat train at both ends: certainly it could take a tourist from Amsterdam to New Amsterdam with the minimum possible contact with British soil. This service — dating from 1821 — once had the extraordinary distinction of featuring as Table Number 1 of Cooks Continental Timetable; and it is the last survivor of a whole fleet of cross-country boat trains such as that which ran from the Midlands to Redhill and there divided for Newhaven and Dover, or that which served the port of Goole and in memory of which a Manchester station bears carved into its façade, amid the expected roll of such destinations as Bolton and Preston, the unexpected word 'Belgium'. It is sad to confess that the Manchester / Harwich journey is now at least an hour shorter *via* London...

Yet from the long roster of Britain's quasi-international services one name shines out in blue and gold, the name of the *Night Ferry*. It was in 1936 that the old Southern railway made its greatest advance ever in improving rail links to the continent by introducing a service of sleeping cars which were ferried across the Channel with their passengers (hopefully) slumbering undisturbed, encapsuled within one transport medium which was itself encapsuled in another. And these were no common sleeping cars either but rather the magnificent carriages of the Wagons-Lits company, differing from their mainland companions in little else than that they were accommodated to the loading gauge of the British system.

So the great bronze blazons of the *Compagnie* appeared at Victoria some forty years ago (and more than forty years after the CIWL had withdrawn the boat-train cars with which it invaded Britain in the 1890s). With the inevitable wartime interruption they have

Platform scene in Devonshire in the 1920s.

116

been seen there ever since, too, bringing to routine-entrapped Londoners a sense of horizons opening up towards the Mediterranean, the Baltic and even the Pacific, despite the fact that the coaches themselves rarely ran further afield than Paris (and, later, Brussels). Furthermore, the *Night Ferry* has not faded in its appeal as has the *Golden Arrow;* for if only because of its discretion it is a favourite means of transport of today's celebrities and Eurocrats just as it was of King Edward VIII — or in the days when Hitler dreamed of arriving in a conquered London aboard it. The stock itself is now the oldest running regularly in Britain — as well as the only material not painted in standard BR livery — and some of it is beginning to cause embarrassment in view of uncertainty as to the building of a Channel tunnel. But there are travellers for whom this very antiquity is an extra recommendation, travellers who, for the sake of bronze door fittings which close with a satisfying *clunk*, will excuse a little of that roughness in riding which comes with old age.

With the *Ferry* slipping out from Victoria on a spring evening there closes this selection from the great trains of Britain — long-past, just-past, and present. For the future there seems, at first sight, little enough to hope for. Speeds will of course continue to rise, especially with the introduction of the Advanced Passenger Train; but there is reason to think that even comfort will decline, whereas true luxury (quite a different thing) is a losing cause.

And yet, and yet... The history of British Railways since nationalisation has been one of constant reversals of policy (it is not so long, after all, since a chairman said that his public was 'not interested in high speeds'), and even by the petty and pusillanimous minds of accountants it may suddenly be realised that a fine train with a fine title and inheritance can offer something unknown in any other field of transport — and something which is therefore saleable. In any case, trains tend to be greater than the men who run them. For already the 'motorail' type of car-carrier-plus-sleeper services (since 1955 one of BR's outstanding successes) have introduced such strange trajectories as from Stirling to Newton Abbot and have produced what are, in their own lumbering but convenient way, great trains of the late twentieth century.

Meanwhile, for those who love the past and the sense of a century and more of tradition, a few last shining titles are still to be read from the timetables if not from those too-costly headboards — *Royal Scot, Aberdonian* and the like. At a time when the world's other great railway administrations are showing their appreciation of the prestige and revenue brought by illustrious names, BR has reduced its roll to a mere thirty or so, with even the *Cheltenham Spa Express* recently thrown on the scrap-heap; but the *Irish Mail* still leaves from Euston after dinner, the *Flying Scotsman* from Kings Cross after breakfast, and the *Cornish Riviera Express* from Paddington at coffee-time. And beyond the customs barrier at Platform 2, Victoria, the *Night Ferry* is there to lead out to those wider worlds where one poetaster (and president of Britain's Railway Club) would: '. . . Oft-times, as a mirage, see / The long sleek coaches of the Wagons-Lits / That wait the traveller on Calais quay.'

The *Night Ferry*, Britain's only truly international train. It is here seen headed by one of Oliver Bulleid's 'Merchant Navy' airsmoothed Pacifics.

Great Trains of Europe

The man with the cigar glances at his watch as the train gathers way: it is 1335 h. On the platform a tired-looking woman waves: the man smiles briefly and settles into his second-class corner seat. Outside, below the window, a chipped metal placard bears the legend:

SUD EXPRESS

PARIS

Bordeaux – Facture – Morcenx – Dax
Bayonne – Biarritz – La Négresse
Guéthary – Saint-Jean-de-Luz – Hendaye

IRUN

(MADRID – LISBOA)

British royalty — in the person of King Edward VII passing incognito as 'the Duke of Lancaster' — visits Biarritz in 1907. This symbolises an influence which was reflected in the running of many of Europe's luxury expresses.

The man draws the final puffs from his cigar and drops the butt into an ashtray. He picks *Le Figaro* off the seat beside him and lays it across his knees. He takes a handkerchief from his pocket, tucks a corner into his collar, extracts a bundle from the briefcase by his feet and, opening it, begins to chew crunchily at a long split loaf stuffed with ham. He wears a crumpled blue suit and his chin is grey with stubble. Spy? Smuggler? Seducer? So the novelists and film-makers would have us wonder. But in reality he is just a dull cog in the French bureaucratic wheel, a dutiful son bound for Bayonne and a routine visit to his mother, and really rather seedy — like the olive-drab train in which he travels.

Sud Express: even today, the Spanish, Portuguese and Moroccan timetables announce this train with a kind of faded flourish. Its connections with Africa are given — from Madrid by an overnight sleeping-car train to the port at Algeciras, thence by the waiting ferry to Tangier, and from the quay side there by air-conditioned express to Casablanca. But the process is not speedy, allowing a day in Madrid, and even on the French side it is far from *super de luxe*. Edward VII would no longer use it to Biarritz, nor Alphonso VIII to San Sebastian. Yet, until quite recently, the

The TEE *Lemano* crossing the Lausanne-Geneva motorway on its journey through the Alps to Milan.

1907 also witnessed the running of a through express from St. Petersburg to the Côte d'Azur — the *St. Petersburg — Vienna — Nice — Cannes Express*. It is here being hauled by one of the PLM's *coupe-vent* locomotives.

A direct connection between Berlin and the south was established by the *Nord-Süd Brenner Express*, which ran between Berlin and Milan from 1906 on.

The *Sud Express*, bound for Spain and Portugal by way of Bordeaux, seen leaving Paris in 1923.

French portion of this train carried only first-class passengers, some in Pullman splendour; these latter were served from a separate kitchen with meals superior even to those of the ordinary dining car. Today the 'Sud' no longer rates a supplement for speed or merit, the Pullman is no more, and the shared dining car lazily serves the same menu at lunch and dinner.

At Irun, as the passengers quit the arrival platform, the throng pushing through the narrow doors seems predominantly darker-skinned, more impatient, more gregarious, more Iberian. Their suitcases are larger, some bulging, some tied with string; among them are an assortment of bundles and wicker baskets. The queue files past the Spanish police to wait hopefully in the customs hall where officials probe and question and, all being well, wield their messy chalk.

It is already dark when the surviving passengers emerge on to the long and narrow departure platform, flanked by the towering broad-gauge Spanish and Portuguese carriages. The *Sud Express* on this side of the frontier, stretching endlessly into the distance, comprises eight or nine coaches for Madrid — mostly second class, some of them *couchettes* — while behind is a select cluster of more elegant carriages bound for Lisbon.

Among the latter, in its distinctive blue livery, is the train's only sleeping car, bearing ornately along its length the title *Compania Internacional de Coches-Camas*, and below this the words *Sud Express: Paris–Lisboa*. There are no shiny-suited Gallic clerks here; through the dimly-lit windows one glimpses in one sleeping-compartment a slender grey-haired man with a *hidalgo*'s aquiline nose and, in another and in the act of closing her door for the night, what legend would have one believe to be the adornment of all overnight expresses in Europe — a blonde, cool, full-bosomed and alluring.

The rest of the Lisbon portion comprises sumptuous first-class-only day coaches and, at the back, a smart blue *fourgon* for the baggage and mail; this section, detached during the night at Medina del Campo, will be joined at dawn by a restaurant car for the run through Portugal itself. And a beautiful run it is, down the lush wooded valleys towards the Atlantic, giving a leisurely arrival in Lisbon in the afternoon following departure from Paris after a journey of nearly 1,200 miles.

But this is a last reminder of old glories, for as these words were written it was announced that even the Lisbon 'Sud' would in future be burdened with second-class cars. If the *Sud Express* is not what it was, however, there are good reasons. Striving to keep up with changing markets, techniques and tastes, the railway administrations of Europe are continually experimenting with new services; and the *Sud Express*'s fall from grace was a deliberate act of policy consequent upon the introduction of the *Puerta del Sol* — an overnight express linking Paris with Madrid by means of sleeping and couchette cars which are adjusted at the frontier to suit the change of gauge. The high speeds now attainable on French tracks, combined with this new through-coach facility, make possible a service leaving one city centre early in the evening to arrive in the other shortly after breakfast the next morning, a run more than three hours faster than the *Sud*'s; and this service is offered at a price, including dinner and breakfast in the restaurant cars, less than the corresponding air fare. Similarly the historic *Rome Express* has now been overtaken by the *Palatino*.

But if the *Sud Express* has lost its old prestige, it meets a growing demand for second-class travel along this route on the part of both holiday-makers on a budget and workers in transit — not to mention Bayonne-bound clerks. The 'Sud' is dead, long live the 'Sud': and hail to its princely heir, the 'Sol'.

Going back in history, an example of the influence of fashion on railway development — and of the latter on regional development — is to be found in the story of the Côte d'Azur's rise to prominence as a winter resort for the wealthy. Since the late eighteenth century, the environs of Nice had been favoured by a handful of northerners in search of winter sunshine. Then in the 1860s — when, according to Prosper Mérimée, more English than French were to be found in Nice — there were two important developments: the city was ceded by the Italians to the French and the railway from Paris reached the coast, continuing along it to the new Franco-Italian frontier at Ventimiglia in 1872 and so serving a region hitherto difficult of access.

Before long, a feature of the winter timetable in those parts was to be the frequent service of first-class-only stopping trains by which even the richest visitors were happy to follow their daily (and nightly) social rounds. Naturally, there were also cruder trains for such peasants as Maupassant's lactating lady who, on a stifling hot journey along the line, offered her swollen breast to slake the thirst of a young man sharing her compartment — an offer which was promptly accepted. The affluent had whiter breasts and rosier *tétins* to toy with, and cushioned privacy in which to enjoy them; but even so, for those travelling from afar to enjoy the Riviera's amenities, the going could still be fairly hard. As recently as 1886, we have it from Baroness de Stoeckl:

'All went well till we arrived at Calais, where, as usual, there was a wild rush for the buffet as in those days there were no restaurant-cars on the trains. Everybody ordered the same: *Un potage, un demi-poulet, pommes purées, un demi de vin rouge*. We only had twenty-five minutes in which to eat this. A railway official would come to the door every five minutes and shout, "*encore quinze minutes avant le départ du train*", and so on.

'Waiters flew frantically in every direction, at last came the cry, "*dans cinq minutes le train part pour Paris*". Then a general rush, *garçons* making out *les additions*, the travellers trying to finish the *demi-poulet* and at the same time struggling into their coats, picking up bags, etc. Then running like maniacs along the platform, maids with anxious faces pointing to the various compartments, the porters shouting "*Prenez vos places, le train part*".

'There were no lavatories and no corridors; most people took with them a most useful domestic utensil, the emptying of which necessitated the frequent lowering of the window.'

The Lisbon section of today's *Sud Express*.

At one time the feature of the *Sud Express* was its rake of Wagons-Lits Pullman cars. (Note the elliptical window by the toilet, a characteristic of European Pullmans). But they were gradually reduced, and have now been entirely withdrawn. The last survivor ran as late as 1969 and is here seen next to a car whose exterior of unpainted and corrugated metal is characteristic of the latest generation of passenger stock in France and some other European countries.

The railway from Vienna to Trieste over the Semmering pass was opened in 1854 primarily for strategic reasons. Its steep gradients and heavy engineering made it one of the wonders of the railway world at the period, and it proved a model for later bores through the mountains of Europe. This painting says much concerning both the civil and mechanical feature of the line.

Although great expresses themselves have rarely appeared on the world's postage stamps, many of these have featured the locomotives which hauled them. This selection shows a Swedish stamp of 1936, with class F 4–6–2 of 1914; Monaco 1968, celebrating the centenary of the Paris-Nice railway; Denmark 1947, the centenary of Danish railways; France 1937, with a Nord Collin streamlined super-Pacific; Germany 1935, the centenary of German railways — first the 'Flying Hamburger', and second, streamlined 4–6–4; Spain 1958, International Railway Congress, Talgo II; Angola 1970, Benguela railway, wood-burning 4–8–2 + 2–8–4 Beyer Garratt; Switzerland 1962, multi-current electric TEE unit; India 1953, 2–2–2 'Express' built 1856, and Class WP 4–6–2 built by Baldwin in 1947; USSR 1948, 5-year transport plan, Class IS 2–8–4; Japan, 1972, centenary of Japanese railways, super-speed express on the San-Yo line; Australia 1970, completion of transcontinental standard-gauge railway.

Cie Intle des WAGONS-LITS
LES WAGONS-LITS DE
2e CLASSE
SERVICES VERS
PARIS ARCACHON
PARIS TOULOUSE
Cie DES CHEMINS DE FER DU MIDI

The Baroness fared a little better after a change in Paris, the train to Nice having compartments which: —

' ... consisted of three large seats with padded backs, these had a handle which one pulled and down came the bed. There were no sheets or blankets but one could hire pillows for a franc, from a porter who wheeled a small trolley on which rows of clean white pillows hung from a pole. The *chaufferettes* or footwarmers were changed at various stations during the night.

'The door would be flung open and men in blue blouses would haul out the cold *chaufferettes* and push in others steaming hot. The clash of their being hurled on to the platform was terrifying. One had a travelling rug, but one never undressed, it was not considered safe in case of an accident. For years later, even when sleepingcars existed, I would remember Mama's warning not to undress in case of accidents and I would lay [*sic*] on the bed fully clothed.

'In the early hours of the morning, the train stopped at Toulon and a chipped cup of coffee with a *croissant*, already moist from the overflow on the saucer, would be thrust through the window; that was all, yet one lived through it...'

But the British traffic was soon wooed with faster and more luxurious trains direct from the Channel to the Riviera. At the time of the Baroness's journey the Wagons-Lits company was ten years old, sleeping compartments with bed linen and toilet facilities (and restaurant cars too) had been in service on the *Orient Express* for three years, and even on her own route the *Calais–Nice–Rome Express* was already running with sleeping-car accommodation: this was succeeded in 1889 by the *Calais–Méditerranée Express*, the direct ancestor of today's *Train Bleu*. As for speed, the 18 hours from Paris to Nice of 1883 was reduced to about 14 by the turn of the century — quite a feat, even when compared with the *Mistral*'s 9 hours of some seventy years later.

There survives today, in the smart Cimiez quarter of Nice, a statue of Queen Victoria. This powerful woman, through her annual presence in that city in the late 1890s, bestowed upon the area the kind of accolade which made it a mecca of lesser royalties and their entourages in the *Belle Epoque*. Her son Edward helped too, for before becoming obsessed by Biarritz and the Côte Basque he favoured Cannes while regarding the Riviera in general as 'un pays de bonne compagnie où tout le monde se retrouve, comme dans une *garden-party*'.

In the wake of royalty there inevitably came the gentry and the *nouveaux riches*, the international smart sets and the social climbers with their trunks of fine clothes, servants, hat-boxes, jewel-cases and bulging money-bags. The Austrians were early on the scene, their presence facilitated by the *Vienna–Nice Express* introduced in 1898. Next year the Russians, whose Dowager Empress had reconnoitred the coast as far back as 1856, were brought in from the cold by an extension to the route of this train, which was then tactfully if ponderously renamed the *St. Petersburg–Vienna–Nice–Cannes Express*.

The interior of a dining car on the Semmering line in 1905 — one of a series of paintings, with the artist's signature inscribed on a tablecloth.

Elsewhere, this book relates one version of the remarkable collaboration between the Austrian and the Canadian Pacific railways. The service operated (and then in the teeth of opposition from Germany, which claimed that the ease of emigration to the New World from Trieste was robbing the German countries of potential military recruits) for only two years: but the CPR-style cars survived their confiscation and it is even rumoured that one of them ended its days as Mussolini's private coach. Right is shown the cover of an advertising brochure. Below, Wagons-Lits and CP join on the inaugural run.

The *Orient Express* in its earliest days — a bilingual poster of 1885 and the train itself in Turkey in 1905 when it had changed very little from its original form.

In 1900 the Germans, no longer content with a Cannes-bound section detached from the rather roundabout *Nord–Sud–Brenner Express*, gained the more direct *Riviera Express*: this originated in Berlin, but a few ambitious Dutch were admitted to it by courtesy of a section from Amsterdam. In 1908, the impatient Italians were at last rewarded with the *Rome–Cannes Express*. There were also royal, noble and merely rich personages from countries as distant as Sweden and as near as Belgium; and even the French contributed their own *Nice Express* in 1900 after having tended for a while, with Gallic caution and reserve, to leave the stage to foreigners while ministering to their needs and growing rich on the proceeds. As for Switzerland, Europe's tourist country *par excellence* found — with its Alpine tunnels now nearly complete — an additional source of wealth in the handling of much of the north-south as well as east-west railway traffic.

The Côte d'Azur, magnet of so many of Europe's historic expresses, is fortunate in having never lost its appeal. After the First World War, for example, the Americans adopted it: due largely to their influence (and notably, perhaps, to that of the railway millionaire Frank Jay Gould, the society hostess Elsa Maxwell and the international Gerald Murphy) it became a summer as well as a winter resort by the simple expedient of opening its ample facilities all the year round. But access was still chiefly by rail, of which at that time Scott Fitzgerald wrote:

'Unlike American trains that were absorbed in an intense destiny of their own and scornful of people on another world less swift and breathless, this train was part of the country through which it passed. Its breath stirred the dust from the palm leaves, the cinders mingled with the dry dung in the gardens'.

The trend towards a summer season suited well the new European 'whoopee'-makers of the twenties — most of whom, being obliged to work for their living, vacationed when the days were hot enough to frolic quietly by the sea and the nights warm enough for more zestful fun and games beneath the stars. The Côte d'Azur in its new guise was an ideal playground: and the British were once again conspicuous, their journey to Paris now being facilitated by the all-Pullman *Flèche d'Or* of 1926. Several cars from this were attached to the latest in *de luxe* sleeping cars and so became the kernel of a revitalised *Calais–Méditerranée Express*.

This train was itself challenged, three years later, by the equally golden *Côte d'Azur Rapide*, for this was the era in Europe of the glamorous Pullman expresses with their individual armchairs at softly-lit tables for two, of 'grand-hotel' decor and of impeccable service by hand-picked stewards. While these trains were well suited to the few millionaires-playground circuits, such lavish accommodation was not destined to spread widely or to survive long; indeed, after the Second World War the Pullman services on the continent gradually petered out, the last such cars running in 1971. And today even the *Train Bleu*, its through cars from Calais withdrawn, serves mainly Frenchmen — as so does the famous *Mistral*, the last word in European opulence, all first class with restaurant

The *Barcelona Express* seen in 1905 between Narbonne and the Spanish border. This train maintains a sleeping-car service, leaving Paris in the evening and arriving in Barcelona in time for lunch the next day.

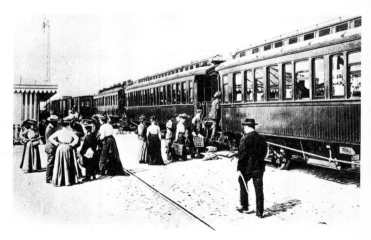

The *Transatlantic Express* at Cherbourg in 1908 — a service run from Paris to connect with the liners for America. The rolling stock, provided by the Wagons-Lits company, came from the short-lived SECR 'club train' from the Channel ports to Victoria.

Beyond the Mediterranean (and encouraged by the Thomas Cook agency) British tourists were soon in evidence. Left, top: the *Star of Egypt*, with its white-painted CIWL stock is seen still running in 1954. But the heyday of the Egyptian services was before the First World War, when a magazine (below) could caption this contrast of the fashionable train and the swarming platform: 'The Flight into Egypt, 1908 — the tourist-laden evening express from Port Said to Cairo'.

One of the earliest needs to be filled by luxury trains was the transportation of mails and passengers to the Far East. To avoid the frequently rough crossing of the Bay of Biscay, British travellers patronised expresses which used the Mt Cenis route to Brindisi, there to embark on a liner for Suez, India and the further east. The poster below notifies passengers that from 1890 the *Indian Mail* will carry only postal traffic, and that the *Peninsular Express* will replace it with a passenger service. At bottom right the *Indian Mail*, which left London once a week is seen in its mail train guise.

CHEMINS DE FER DU NORD & DE PARIS-LYON-MÉDITERRANÉE
Compagnie Internationale des Wagons-Lits et des Grands Express Européens

PENINSULAR-EXPRESS

Train de Luxe de la Malle des Indes
ARRIVÉE & DÉPART:
GARE DE PARIS-NORD
18 JUILLET 1890

A partir du Vendredi 18 Juillet 1890, le train de la Malle des Indes, partant tous les Vendredis soir de LONDRES pour BRINDISI, par CALAIS, le CHEMIN DE FER DE GRANDE-CEINTURE et le MONT-CENIS, sera exclusivement affecté au Service Postal et ne prendra plus de Voyageurs.

A partir de la même date, les Voyageurs devant s'embarquer à BRINDISI sur le paquebot de la Malle des Indes effectueront leur voyage par un train de luxe : LE PENINSULAR-EXPRESS, composé de wagons-salons, restaurant et voitures-lits entrant à la gare de PARIS-NORD pour y relever les provenances du Nord de la France, de la Belgique, de la Hollande et de l'Allemagne et y prendre des Voyageurs pour MACON, CULOZ, AIX-les-BAINS, CHAMBÉRY, TURIN, ALEXANDRIE, BOLOGNE, ANCONE et BRINDISI.

DÉPART DE LONDRES	TOUS LES VENDREDIS	à 3 H. 15 DU SOIR
PARIS-NORD ARRIVÉE	ID.	à 11 H. DU SOIR
DÉPART	NUIT DU VENDREDI AU SAMEDI	à MINUIT 15
ARRIVÉE A BRINDISI	LE DIMANCHE	vers 4 H. DU SOIR
DÉPART DU PAQUEBOT	ID.	vers 10 H. DU SOIR

Au retour, le train de la Malle des Indes, qui part de BRINDISI aussitôt après l'arrivée du paquebot, continuera à prendre des Voyageurs.

A partir du 18 Juillet, ce train contiendra une voiture mixte avec lits et restaurant pour les Voyageurs à destination de PARIS, qui sera détachée à PIERREFITTE-STAINS et conduite à la gare de PARIS-NORD.

LE NOMBRE DES PLACES ETANT LIMITÉ, MM. LES VOYAGEURS DOIVENT
PRENDRE LEURS BILLETS D'AVANCE
AUX AGENCES DE LA COMPAGNIE DES WAGONS-LITS
ET A LA GARE DE PARIS-NORD

cars, bar, hairdressing salon, boutique, bookshop and secretarial services, but with three seats across the carriage instead of the former Pullman's two.

For today's British, however, there is the newer *Flandre–Riviera Express*, with through sleeping and couchette cars from Calais; the Germans and Dutch are still served by a *Riviera Express*, though it no longer gets closer to France than Vintimille: and from Milan along the whole length of the Riviera runs the daytime *Ligure*. The other international trains serving the Côte d'Azur are still numerous and varied, but anonymous. Sleeping or couchette cars penetrate the area daily from Brussels, Hagen, Irun, Geneva, Port Bou and Rome as well as Calais, and there even survives a direct link with Vienna — though only in the form of day cars, and the train to which these are attached creeps so bleakly across the northern plains of Italy that it appears in mourning for a lost empire — or, perhaps, just the sound of carefree laughter.

And yet, over nine decades ago, it was Vienna and the east rather than Marseilles and the south which saw the first of all *Grands Express Européens* when, in 1883, Georges Nagelmackers launched the legendary *Orient Express*. Initially this ran from Paris, by way of Munich, Vienna, Budapest and Bucharest, with the entire journey (which had to be completed by boat) taking just over 80 hours. A connection from London and Ostend, the *Ostend–Vienna Express*, was added in 1894, by which date the train had extended its run right through to Constantinople and brought the time from Paris below 70 hours.

But the sponsors had seen to it that Britain was well represented even on the 'Orient's inaugural run in the person of Henri Stefan Opper de Blowitz, the Paris correspondent of *The Times*. In the conscientious manner of that period, the journalist earned his keep by keeping a detailed diary on which to base his despatches. From this blow-by-Blowitz account we learn that the train was 'a marvellous sight. It consists of two sleeping cars, two vans for baggage and provisions, a restaurant car and' (leaving nothing to the imagination) 'a locomotive and its tender'. Blowitz noted with approval the smooth running of the train, enabling him to shave efficiently even at the breakneck speed of 50 mph.

Another and even more profuse chronicler of the event was Edmond About from France. From his reports one discovers that there were twenty beds in each sleeping car, a *salon* for the ladies and a smoking room for the gentlemen. The refrigeration system enabled passengers to enjoy butter from Normandy throughout the journey, while the skill of the chefs made it possible to vary the menu to include national dishes of the countries across which the express travelled. And a little later, in 1896, that most prolific of all railway writers, J. P. Pearson, records that the woodwork in the *Orient Express* sleeping cars was 'dark brown, with a dark yellow leather, which had a gilt figuring in the corner as relief. Berths and carpet matched one another in a dark blue material with a greenish-white pattern, and the ceiling was painted with a blue, flowered cornice and a large "star" design on a whitish-blue

Yugoslavia's railways have always been used by the great international expresses; but today there are some rapid internal services too, such as this diesel express between Zagreb and Belgrade.

For passengers from Copenhagen to Berlin the *Neptun Express* takes just under six hours, including a ferry crossing to Warnemünde.

The interior of a Wagons-Lits restaurant car for luxury trains.

'ground', while in the smoking room there were 'arm-chairs in red plush, a red-figured carpet and diamond-shaped panels in brown and green on the side walls and ceiling'.

Since that inaugural run there have been so many variants and off-shoots of the 'Orient' that one may be pardoned for falling into a state of confusion and false nostalgia. (Perhaps in reality too, few pale young dancers have found themselves in the situation of Graham Greene's Coral, who on a snowy night between Vienna and Belgrade surrendered her virginity to a Jewish currant-trader). But among the great names on the west-to-east route are those of the *Simplon* (formerly *Simplon-Orient*) *Express*, the *Arlberg* (formerly *Arlberg-Orient*) *Express*, and the *Direct-Orient Express*. And these in their turn have bred new relations such as the *Tauern-Orient Express*.

For through all vicissitudes there has remained before the Wagons-Lits company and the railway administrations of the west (if not always of the Balkans) the challenge of providing a service which should span Europe. And so it is still possible to travel from Paris to Istanbul by a through *Direct-Orient* car, this now being a 60 hour run through the Simplon tunnel. At Belgrade the *Tauern–Orient* from Munich arrives within a few minutes of the *Direct-Orient*, innumerable connections having been made en route by both with places as distant as Calais and Copenhagen; and, the two trains linking up, the whole is then divided again into the *Marmara Express* (for Istanbul) and the *Athens Express*.

The Calais connection is simple, consisting of one sleeping car and one couchette car which join the *Direct-Orient Express* in Paris to be detached the next morning in Milan. That from Copenhagen is more complex and illustrates the interknit quality of these trains whose personality resides in their name-plates rather than in a continuity of assembled stock; for the Scandinavian link begins as part of the ubiquitous *Alps Express*. This leaves the Danish capital at tea time and, after a short hop by train ferry, enters Germany to reach Hamburg in the late evening. Here a sleeping car is connected as far as Munich, with a breakfast-time arrival the next morning. The passenger may now disembark, spend a day in that romantic city and continue in the evening by the *Tauern-Orient Express*, so avoiding Italy; or he can remain with the 'Alps' on its southward run across Austria into Italy, arriving in Venice at tea time.

Either way, however, the traveller from Copenhagen on the *Alps Express* has to remember that this itself continues south from Verona through Bologna to Rome and so transfer to one of the Venice-bound cars attached in Germany; and then again between Verona and Venice, with his car now forming part of the *Direct-Orient Express*, he has to move along into one of those proceeding beyond Venice. Usually this section includes sleeping and day cars destined to go right through, according to the day of the week, to Istanbul or Athens, arrival in either city being in the morning of the fourth day after leaving Copenhagen. As to catering, our Danish friend will have experienced a variety of facilities, ranging from buffet services between Puttgarden and Hamburg and (if he went that way) between Verona and Trieste to a full-scale restaurant car from the Turkish frontier to Istanbul.

If he is still active after his part in this railwayman's jigsaw-puzzle the Istanbul passenger can, by crossing the Bosphorus to Haydarpasa, join a through sleeping car of the 'Orient' family's Asiatic cousin. Born in 1930, Agatha Christie's *Taurus Express* traverses the mountains and deserts of Turkey and Syria, dividing on the way, to reach Beirut some forty-five (or Baghdad some fifty) hours out of Haydarpasa. It was the Germans who, for military reasons, pioneered this route towards the true orient. But it is thanks to Georges Nagelmackers of Belgium that today, and mainly in sleeping cars of the company he created and with restaurant cars of the same company attached where needed, one can still in a few days (and with only one change) travel the 4,000 miles or more from Paris, Calais or Copenhagen to Baghdad, passing through eight countries en route.

And further still: for, since 1971, the *Vangölü Express* has run from Haydarpasa to Teheran, with sleeping cars in Turkey and coaches with a superior type of couchette compartment in Iran. This is a three day journey, involving a lift by train ferry across Lake Van and thence a run over tracks newly-laid to by-pass the former loop through the USSR.

The full history of the 'Orient' fleet demonstrates the ability of Europe's railways to adapt to political change, but they have always had to adapt too to changing challenges from other forms of transport. And just as today the train, whilst competing directly with both aircraft and car, is happy to act as a feeder to airports and a carrier to motorists, so in the heyday of the ocean liner it was quick, by means of boat express and quay-side stations, to service sea-borne, inter-continental travel.

The British, with their world-wide commitments, were again the first market; and so as long ago as 1855 the French railways provided a train known as the *Malle des Indes* which carried mails (only) from London to Marseilles. There they were loaded into orient-bound P & O ships, so saving several days in transit whilst preserving the secrecy of diplomatic and financial information. The *petite ceinture* line skirting the suburbs of Paris — for which unromantic by-pass British travellers using the through services from the Channel ports to southern climes have long been grateful — soon enabled the 'Malle' to circumnavigate that city and so save another hour or more. Then, in 1869, the train was extended to Brindisi via the new Mont-Cenis tunnel and the liners called at the Adriatic port, so saving more time yet.

This service continued until 1914 with few changes — though passengers were admitted from 1880, the train at that time taking 48 hours from the Channel to Brindisi. In 1890 it was indeed split into two, with the passenger portion being known as the *Peninsular Express* and the former service to Marseilles being reinstated as an additional amenity for passengers. This train, called the *Bombay Express*, was destined to survive until 1939, when the Second War came. Until engulfed by war, the 'Bombay' offered a splendid facility

The dining car of the Italian *Rialto* express from Milan to Trieste.

Another example of 'art deco' —
and a reminder of a recently
vanished glory of European travel.

for Britons and their ladies privileged to go about imperial business in 'posh' style: with an afternoon departure from London after a leisurely lunch in club or hotel the passengers reached Calais in time to join a sleeping-and-restaurant-car express which conveyed them swiftly through the night to provide an after-breakfast arrival at Marseilles. Here their ship awaited, ready to bear them towards Suez, India and worlds beyond.

Before the opening of the trans-Siberian route, in fact, the lucrative British mail contracts did a surprising amount to shape express running on the mainland. Thus, with Belgian connivance, the Germans offered a route direct to Salonika and thence by sea to connect with the P & O liners at Port Said. Later, passengers and mail were intended to be conveyed without change of carriage from Calais to Cairo, bridging the Bosphorus by train ferry and the Suez Canal by a swing bridge: the track and the bridge were built but, though through trains ran on the Levantine section in the 1940s, war, politics and the air age ended that dream. And today, when such luxury trains of the Nile as the *Star of Egypt* are themselves fading memories, the only *wagons-lits* operating in North Africa — small-windowed and white-painted against the heat, in contrast to the company's normal livery — are on a solitary survivor in Morocco.

But though in the battle for the mails the French were usually the victors, the service they sponsored was not always faultless. From Foxwell and Farrer's census of 1889, for instance, one learns that the Brindisi mails, though heavily subsidised by the 'English post office', were being run at speeds well below those of internal trains, the average over the route as a whole being only 26 mph. This was still good by contemporary Italian standards, however, and two years later the sleeping cars of the new passenger portion of the Brindisi service were still fitted with special handbrakes for use on the Italian part of the journey. These were worked by men who, exposed to wind and weather, were obliged to tie themselves in place to avoid being thrown on the line by the train's violent movement.

In 1900 France led continental Europe in speed, having twenty trains whose average exceeded 56 mph. As the new century dawned, too, the French railways were playing host to a growing variety of boat trains, both regular and irregular. There was the *Sud Express* itself, which provided connections at Lisbon with ocean liner services to South Africa and South America and at Algeciras with Suez-bound vessels calling at Gibraltar. There were the *Trans-atlantique Express* from Paris to Le Havre and the *New York Express* from Paris to Cherbourg. Soon there would be the *Barcelona Express*, offering connection at Port Vendres with sailings to North Africa, and the *Lloyd-Riviera Express* for German and Dutch passengers joining ship at Genoa; and later still the *Rotterdam-Lloyd* and *Netherland-Lloyd Expresses* fed, at Marseilles and Genoa respectively, a succession of eastbound liners.

The daily *Barcelona Express* also helped to open up the Costa Brava to tourists. It did not, however, always run over its present

THE GRAPHIC POCKET FOREIGN HOTEL GUIDE.

BESET BY TOUTS.

N.B.—The Traveller will escape all the annoyance here depicted provided he has previously consulted the pages of his "Pocket Foreign Hotel Guide."

THE GRAPHIC POCKET FOREIGN HOTEL GUIDE,
(WHICH CAN BE CARRIED IN THE WAISTCOAT POCKET)
CONTAINING A
Complete Alphabetical List of the Principal Hotels on the chief Tourist Routes in Europe.

PUBLISHED AT THE OFFICE OF "THE GRAPHIC," 190, STRAND, LONDON, W.C.; 15, RUE BLEUE, PARIS; and at WILLMER AND ROGERS' NEWS COMPANY, NEW YORK, UNITED STATES.

PRICE SIXPENCE.

A vivid reminder of the dangers that lay in wait for the *fin de siècle* traveller in Europe.

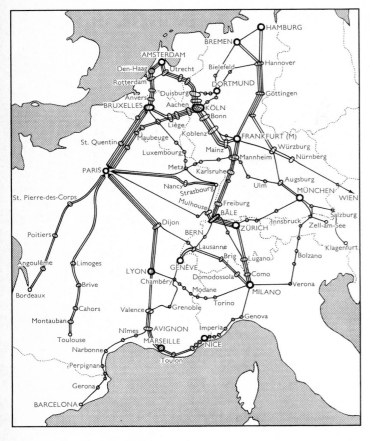

This map shows the spread of the high-speed Trans-Europe-Express network. Designed to take the businessman from one centre to another with the least possible delay, these trains have outclassed aircraft for comfort, reliability — and speed on journeys of up to 400 miles.

trajectory down the splendid *route mauve* of the western flank of the Massif Central, for at one period it was routed through the heart of those formidable hills. More recently this line (or, at least, the easy part of it) was used by the *Thermal Express* to the Auvergnat spas — a reminder of the importance of another factor in developing the great trains of Europe, the appeal to over-nourished Edwardians of all the watering-places ranged between Marienbad and Montecatini.

Of the boat trains, though, the cream was formed by those serving the vast, fast and opulent leviathans on the New York run. Even in the years after the Second World War there were several liner sailings each week across the North Atlantic, each with an attendant express. Today, these are few except those which serve as a seasonal means of conveying package tourists; and the connecting boat trains have inevitably dwindled into dull, every-day versions of their illustrious forebears.

Similarly the humble yet historic Channel packet no longer serves the luxury trade; but the railway maps of Europe still show clear traces of a former British domination there. For spokes of the train-operator's wheel radiated in every landward direction from the Channel and North Sea ports: Cherbourg, Le Havre, Dieppe, Boulogne, Calais, Dunkirk, Ostend, the Hook, Esbjerg... At the quay sides the sleek sleeping cars, Pullmans, saloons, compartment coaches and diners awaited the arrival of the steamers from England and the pleasure of their passengers. Without the islanders' patronage the development of international express trains on the continent would have been a good deal less spectacular: there would, most probably, have been no *Sud Express* (established 1890), no *Rome Express* (also 1890), no *Nord Express* (1896) and no *Train Bleu*. And even the family of 'Orients' might have been much truncated.

Furthermore it is still possible today to take ship from England and entrain at one or other of these ports, without change of carriage, for the south of France, Switzerland and northern Italy by way of the *ceinture* loop round Paris; for Germany (and again, but avoiding Paris, for Switzerland and Italy); for Copenhagen or Vienna and even for Berlin, Warsaw and Moscow.

Perhaps the greatest change has been that the typical passenger now uses a couchette rather than a first-class sleeper berth. All this, and much more, is illustrated with painstaking accuracy in that fascinating and expertly-edited monthly named *Cooks Continental Timetable*. The only guide of its kind, this is consulted in *agences de voyages* and *Reisebüros* across the continent and the world: it is now over a century old but in this respect, at least, Britannia still rules Europe's rails.

Another, and more recent, British gift to the mainland has been the concept of the car-sleeper service — though the motorist has so grown in importance everywhere that today, for every car-sleeper train originating at a port served by Channel ferry, there are at least five from other centres in France, the Benelux countries and West Germany. For the greater part, however, these cater for the seasonal flows of tourism. And in influence and spending power today's most important patron of the international express in Europe is the travelling businessman.

It is his kind who form the new elite; but though they are the successors to those grand and wealthy people who looked for (and usually got) the space, elegance and attentive if not obsequious service *en voyage* which they found in their own ornate mansions, today's executives are of a different breed. They carry briefcases: they live in gadget-operated homes; and they work in an ambiance of air-conditioned or centrally-heated office suites, four-star hotels, credit-card restaurants and hire-cars or chauffeur-driven limousines. With the spread of standardised amenities, they expect a predictable and consistent environment, a kind of upholstered retreat insulating them not merely from the cares of travel but even from awareness of which frontier they last crossed.

Ever since 1922 the railways of Europe (and, to an increasing extent, of the world) had operated a body known as the *Union internationale des Chemins de Fer*: beginning quietly with work on the standardisation of braking and coupling systems, this had become a leader in fields ranging from timetable-planning to technical research. In the mid-fifties the European national administrations and the UIC resolved that the businessman should not be ceded to the aeroplane — which for distances of up to 400 miles between city centres was no faster than the train, and which could never compete in comfort and facilities — and so conceived a new type of international express. These trains would belong to a rejuvenated Europe, and they would not only be fast in transit but would eliminate those long frontier waits — demanded for both technical and bureaucratic reasons — which made the progress of the traditional international 'express' a fairly dismal performance interrupted by customs checks on baggage and railwayman's checks on equipment extending down to the last light bulb.

The first of these custom-built trains — christened *Trans-Europe Expresses* — ran in 1957, and since then the story has been one of almost unbroken success. While there are, technically, numerous varieties of TEE — some electric on different or multiple systems, some diesel-hauled, some with only open-plan cars, some with compartment stock — neither their external liveries nor their internal appointments differ greatly at first glance. These trains are all first class only, with a heavy supplement for the businessman to pass on to his company; they all offer food and drink to international-hotel standards; they are all close-carpeted, sound-proofed and air-conditioned; they call (briefly) only at principal cities; they run, for the most part, at the start and finish of the office day: and they are all named, some having inherited titles made famous by conventional expresses in earlier years. Another link with the older network is in their restaurant facilities, the catering in many of these trains being provided by the Wagons-lits company. In other respects, however, the TEEs — which now account for nearly half of the continent's eighty-odd named trains — are separately administered.

The *Rheingold* TEE, which links Holland (and London) with Switzerland and Italy.

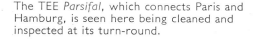

The TEE *Parsifal*, which connects Paris and Hamburg, is seen here being cleaned and inspected at its turn-round.

One of the foci of the TEE system is Frankfurt, which like many continental stations has the advantage of being located centrally in its city. With twelve converging routes, twenty-six platforms and one of the most complex signalling systems of Europe, Frankfurt may be taken as the starting-point for a journey to be contrasted with that offered by today's *Sud Express* at the start of this chapter.

It is a grim winter's morning, and snow is falling from a leaden sky as the *Saphir* glides in from Nuremberg a few minutes behind schedule. A cluster of passengers wait in the gloom, their faces pinched with cold, as the train comes to a halt. Its three coaches — two compartmented, one an open saloon — and restaurant car are joined swiftly by two additional carriages: an electric locomotive takes its place at the former rear end of the train: and within nine minutes the *Saphir* is on its way down the Rhine, via Bonn and Cologne, to Brussels.

The lost time is soon made up on the curving stretches of line bordering the great river; but the train's suspension is so good and the track so smooth that there is hardly any sensation of movement and only an awareness that the steep mountains, with their snow-flecked vineyards, are steadily falling away. From the hushed luxury of the train the passenger contemplates the patient barges — and even the cars and lorries — which are so quickly left behind. At Koblenz, as the *Saphir* waits poised for departure, a woman runs on to the platform with her child. She pleads with the guard as he swings in through the only open door, but the express streaks mercilessly away leaving her hunched figure breathless on the platform. The system is relentless: at Bonn the train is scheduled for a one-minute stop and, as the second hand on the station clock creeps up to the sixty-second mark, the doors close and the *Saphir* is in motion once again.

Into Cologne station it runs, dead on time; and there, sharing the same platform, stands the gleaming *Rheingold*, pausing briefly on its own southward run for passenger transfers. While there are some connoisseurs who will advance the 80 mph *Mistral*'s claims to be the most luxurious of the TEEs, the *Rheingold* is of special interest both historically and in the ramifications of its contemporary performance. Its long but rapid journey begins in Holland in the early morning, one section of the train starting at Amsterdam and another, connecting with the overnight ship from Harwich, at the Hook of Holland. In mid-morning a third section, which initially formed part of a sister train known as the *Rheinpfeil* with coaches originating at Hanover and Dortmund, joins the Dutch sections; and the complete train, with restaurant car and one of Europe's very few vista dome observation cars, then continues down the Rhine to Basle, which is reached in the mid-afternoon.

Had one chosen the *Rheingold* rather than the *Saphir*, one would hence have reached another station famous in European railway history — and one familiar to the many overnight travellers whose sleeping cars, converging in the early morning, are here shunted around to be shared among adjoining trains. For Rhine-ringed Basle is a meeting point of three countries. Indeed, an earlier

A German TEE in Westphalia.

A poster of 1929 for the *Côte d'Azur Pullman Express*, which epitomises both 'jazz-age' publicity and the dawn of the last great age of steam.

station there was so surrounded by water that, at night, a drawbridge was raised to prevent illegal entry or exit — or, perhaps, the capture of a cherished train.

When Basle station was moved into its present and more central position, it was designed specially for its multi-national and rapid-shunting role; but at first all was not well organised. In 1900, apparently, with 'six through lines from one end of the station to the other there was only one platform face, and all trains from either Germany or Switzerland were dealt with at this... Any stragglers on the platform were rounded up by pompous German officials in semi-military uniforms and driven down to the Swiss end of the station.' But things go better today, and the *Rheingold* suffers no indignities. It divides at Basle into three sections — one for Geneva, one for Chur and one for Milan — but the manoeuvre is conducted swiftly with all the sections being on their way within 30 minutes of arrival. And late in the evening, only 14 hours after the start from the Hook of Holland, the last section of the *Rheingold* comes to rest well over 700 miles and 4 nations away.

Today's *Rheingold* is a descendant of an earlier train established in 1928 with an eye, particularly, on the Swiss-bound traffic from England. In those days it carried both first- and second-class passengers, but all the coaches were distinguished by their special cream and violet livery. The train was suspended during the Second World War, but returned to service in 1946 between the Hook and Basle with some fine new stock in royal blue with silver lettering. Various improvements followed until, in 1965, the *Rheingold* joined the TEE elite.

But it is — inevitably — the French who hold the speed record for the TEEs (and, probably, a world record) with their internal run from Paris to Bordeaux by the *Aquitaine*, most of it achieved at an average of over 90 mph. Many other TEE services radiate from Paris. There are trains four times a day to Brussels and twice a day to Amsterdam, for instance, sometimes by expresses with long-established names such as the *Ile-de-France*, *Brabant*, *Etoile du Nord* and *Oiseau Bleu*. Then, among those penetrating Germany, there is the *Goethe* by which Frankfurt can be reached in a morning's run from Paris. *L'Arbalète* does the same for Zurich-bound passengers, and the *Cisalpin* for passengers on their way to French Switzerland — or, via the Simplon tunnel, to Milan. Of the other great Alpine tunnels, only the St. Gotthard plays host to TEEs, taking the *Gottardo* and the *Ticino*. This route, linking Zurich with Milan, is among the most dramatic in Europe.

Milan, as well as being the terminus of such internals as the *Settebello* to Rome, is itself an important TEE centre, being the starting point for trains to Munich (the *Mediolanum*) and Bremen (the *Roland*), for the *Lemano* to Geneva, and for the *Ligure* to Avignon. This latter connects with the *Catalan Talgo* from Geneva to Barcelona — an odd-man-out among the TEEs, for it consists of the low-slung, articulated coaches which are Spain's own contribution to railway technology. The *Catalan Talgo* shares with the *Puerta del Sol* the distinction of having bogies which are adjustable at the frontier to match the change of gauge.

So it is possible by leaving Milan at breakfast-time to enjoy a run — for the most part of exceptional scenic beauty along the Mediterranean coast — which ends at Barcelona in good time for a Spanish dinner the same evening. And while these long-distance trains, whether TEEs or of conventional type, may not carry many passengers all the way, their timings are usually such as to attract a succession of short-run traffic. A good example of this kind of coming-and-going service is provided by the *Edelweiss* TEE which, in the course of linking Amsterdam and Brussels with Strasbourg and Zurich — a 9½ hour daytime journey — manages without fuss and with minimum formality to traverse five countries, an international feat so far unmatched by any other TEE. Similarly there are trains such as the *Direct-Orient*, the composition of which may include cars from several lands travelling continuously for many hundreds of miles over periods of up to four days: in these the passenger who survives from start to finish is certainly rather exceptional.

Yet there are always a few for whom it is better to travel hopefully than to arrive. Imagine oneself, then, in Rome on a day in early summer, relaxing after an alfresco lunch and with a copy of the 'CCT' open, just as wanderlust attracts one to the land of the midnight sun. That challenge is easy enough to meet — at least with a generous budget supporting one — for there is a train within the hour running as far as Stockholm, the *Italia Express*. And so we board the sleeping car that will deliver us into Stockholm two mornings later. At Florence a restaurant car attaches itself, bringing our dinner: it is taken off before the Italian border but at Frankfurt another arrives, providing breakfast and lunch. The train waits nearly two hours in Copenhagen, providing time for at least a *smörgasbrod* dinner. That night, for the second time, we cross water by train ferry; and now we are in Sweden.

A change of train in Stockholm follows, with a day to enjoy the city, and in the evening we leave for Narvik. We can choose between two trains here, *Nordpilen* and the *Lappland Arrow*. Both have sleeping and restaurant cars for parts of their journeys, and the former offers couchettes all the way. The next afternoon, the third out of Rome, we are inside the Arctic circle, heading up out of the silvery Swedish lowlands into the mountains and towards the steep Norwegian fjords.

Narvik is the ultimate limit of Europe's network of international expresses: to continue our trip it must be by ship back to Bergen. But from there we can travel by the *Bergen Express* for more than 300 spectacular miles across the mountains to Oslo, where other of Scandinavia's comfortable internal trains await — or where, hungry for more sea air, we can re-embark for Copenhagen.

From the Danish capital a train with a time-honoured name will take one south to Paris — the *Nord Express*. Originally, though, the 'Nord' ran between Paris and St. Petersburg, and the recollection of that fact may turn thoughts eastward. For though in the years

Mitropa, the German catering and sleeping car company, fought the Wagons-Lits company for the privilege of serving meals on the extensive private railways of Switzerland. Thus, the Rhaetian narrow-gauge system was served by Mitropa...

after the Second World War links to Russia became tenuous, a quite sizeable fleet of through cars now cross the plains of eastern Europe once again. Indeed, as we study the timetable bills under the timber roof of Copenhagen station (and perhaps note the running of the *Englander* boat-train which was dieselised as far back as 1935) our eyes may be caught by the announcement that alternate evenings see the departure of the *Ostsee Express*, Copenhagen/Berlin/Warsaw/Moscow.

All one needs is the patience to collect the necessary visas and then make a journey of just under two days, resisting the temptation to leave one's sleeper for the sake of side-trips to such legendary cities as Prague, Cracow and Czestochowa. And then, having seen the sights of Moscow, what could be more convenient than to return west, not by another of the off-shoots of the 'Nord' family, but by the *Chopin*? For this train travels via Minsk and Czechoslovakia to Vienna: and there it connects with another sleeping-car express which will land the traveller from Rome back at his starting point after a round-Europe trip of perhaps a fortnight and 5,000 miles.

If, amid all this choice, there is still not a train for our needs we can of course lay out a little more on a train of our own, a *private* train; for it is still quite possible. Europe has a long tradition of specials — royal trains, presidential trains, millionaires' personal carriages and the like — and France, for example, keeps in good order its presidential train for ceremonial tours. But anyone who borrows a VIP coach should take care to avoid the fate of Paul Deschanel who, after falling out of *his* presidential train, felt obliged to give up rail travel.

At midnight, not far out of Paris, the president needed air and leant out of the window. Suddenly he 'felt faint, lost his balance and fell head first on to the track'. Later, a level-crossing keeper 'discovered him pyjama-clad walking barefoot beside the line'. Having put the stranger to bed in his own house, the keeper reported his find by telephone to the nearest station, saying that 'a man calling himself Deschanel claimed to have fallen out of the presidential train'. The message was relayed down the line, reaching one of the train attendants at about 0500 h. But 'the story seemed so improbable that nobody took any notice, and it was not until the valet took the president his breakfast at seven o'clock in the morning that his disappearance was discovered'.

Fortunately, though, most journeys have happier endings; even if they fall short in the kind of adventure that befell Graham Greene's dancer and salesman, and travelling on one's own one may be pleased to have the company of that cigar-smoking clerk on the *Sud Express* — who on further acquaintance may well prove less uninteresting than he looks. In any case the romance of rail travel lies not only in one's fellow travellers; it lies too in the cities and countries traversed, in the distances which separate peoples and the lines and trains uniting them. And these trains await us still as they have done for over a hundred years: the *wagons-lits*, day cars, inter-city trains, boat trains and now TEEs: the great expresses of Europe.

... Whilst the Montreux-Oberland Bernois was the province of the Wagons-Lits company. Here the *Golden Mountain Pullman* is about to set off on its inaugural run in 1931 from its Montreux 'terminus' — the forecourt of the main-line station. Note (again) the elliptical Pullman window.

The *Balkan Express* stops at small station in Greece where it connects with the metre-gauge *Thessalonian*.

A 2-10-0 hauls an express near Sofia

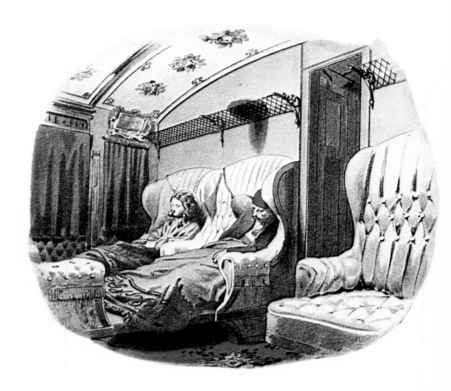

Scenes on the Kiev-Odessa line in 1864.

Left top: second-class coupé.   Right top: second-class washroom.
Left below: first-class coupé in its day position.   Right below: first-class coupé made up for night travel.

Great Trains of Russia

It is hardly surprising that, in a half-Asiatic land of enigmas wrapped in mysteries, even the railways should show paradoxical faces. The contrasts of war and peace are striking enough, for the only nation ever to mount on rails a church complete with bell-cote was also that of which a commentator wrote 'Almost as soon as the lines were laid in Russia they bore fatal electric rumours of unrest, soldiers, refugees who never knew whether the next town would be friendly'. But there are subtler contrasts which seem to reach into the very soul of the land.

On the one hand Russia's railways have been — and remain — of such immense practical importance as the nation's nerves and sinews that (as in the days when the 1907 Pekin–Paris motor race was won by driving along the tracks of the trans-Siberian line) there are still snowy wastes where the best 'road' is a plate-layers' track straggling for a hundred miles beside a forest branch: on the other hand they remain the material of myth and legend. These aspects are indeed so fused that the reality often seems stranger than the fiction. *The Idiot*, *The Kreutzer Sonata*, *Dr Zhivago*, above all *Anna Karenina*... the railway images in these novels are as powerful as any in world literature. But are they more unforgettable than that of Tolstoy himself dying in the stationmaster's house at Astapovo as the news cameras turned on his wife battering at the door, of the Grand Duchess Anastasia (if it was indeed she) arrested amid the marshalling yards of Perm, or of Lenin arriving, safely late, at the Finland station?

And yet, railways came to the holy Russian empire later than to most countries of western Europe. The first line of all was laid from St. Petersburg — later to become Petrograd, and later still Leningrad — to the tsar's winter palace in 1842; but this was a humble affair, as was the railway which ran to some imperial pleasure-gardens which had been christened, after a London model, Vauxhall. (The latter has, however, left its mark in the dictionaries, for *vokzal* is still Russian for a terminus.) And it was not until nearly a decade later that the era of main lines began with the linking of the port of Peter the Great to the nation's second city, Moscow.

But after that event a crow could hardly have flown more directly than a train travelling between those cities 403 miles apart, for the route taken was outstandingly straight and level. The latter quality was partly due to nature, for the worst gradient (at first 1 in 125, but later eased to 1 in 165) was encountered crossing the Valdai hills; but the directness was thanks to Tsar Nicholas I who, having decided on a railway, called in a surveyor and drew a

Sonya Tolstoy (centre) arrives by special train with her medical advisors at the country station of Astapo in 1911. Her husband lies dying there but is unwilling to see her.

The *St. Petersburg-Moscow Express* crossing the frozen steppes in the winter of 1904.

A station of the Trans-Siberian railway in 1901 with moujiks waiting to sell fresh milk, food and fruit to the passengers. Even in the days of state marketing the practice continues.

straight line with a ruler from his capital to Moscow. He then turned to the astounded man with the famous words — '*Voilà votre chemin de fer*'.

Since it rarely pays to argue with Russian heads of state the railway was built accordingly, using masses of unpaid serf labour plus a leavening of wage-earning semi-skilled men. But it was exceptional so far as early Russian lines were concerned in being so solidly and expensively constructed.

By late November, 1851, the first trains were able to run on what was then called the Nicolai, and today the October, railway. The line has always enjoyed the best and fastest service in Russia, but speeds remained extremely low until very recently. Thus, in its early years the concern could show no timings better than 30 hours; and even by 1866 Russia's finest internal express was leaving St. Petersburg at 1430 h. with a requirement (not always met) to reach Moscow at 1000 h. the next day. This called for an average speed of 21 mph with nine intermediate stops. There was, though, a train running in the mid-sixties which put up a rather better performance between St. Petersburg and Warsaw, then a city of the Russian empire. This averaged 23 mph over the entire distance, and put on a spurt of 37 mph over the 40 level miles between Pskov and Ostrov.

Nicholas' successor, Tsar Alexander II, took an almost exaggerated interest in railways, and he and his advisers began to see them as a means of keeping control over the outposts of his empire. He also obtained a luxurious and exotic train for his own use, buying it from Napoleon III of France after the latter's disastrous capitulation at Sedan. The coaches were modified so that they could run on the broad gauge which Russia had arbitrarily adopted as well as on European metals, and the train's fifteen saloons, already luxurious, became mansions on wheels as elaborate as the private cars of American millionaires at that period. The Tsarina's boudoir, with its marble bath, was probably the most lavish rail vehicle ever to run in Europe, and another coach was fitted out as a children's nursery.

Even this train, though, was subject to derailments — as were others used by the Tsar or his family, since unlike Queen Victoria the Emperor had stated that he regarded it as a personal affront if his train was not driven at the highest possible speed. Not much of an expanding network of tracks, however, could sustain running at above 30 mph, and the history of Russia is hence peppered with accidents to royal trains. One serious disaster killed no fewer than sixteen members of the imperial retinue.

As the era of Anna Karenina approached and the steamy slackness, lavish first class and cattle-truck thirds, bad couplings and fur-hatted aristocrats in the snow (which in some quarters still form the popular image of Russian railways) became established, reasonably fast schedules appeared on lines used by the court and important visitors. Thus, St. Petersburg was linked to Moscow by five trains a day in 1880, the best taking 15 hours with eight intermediate stops to give an average of 26 mph. In the years

The *Trans-Manchurian Express* waiting in
Harbin station in 1923. The train is drawn by
a well-maintained Russian locomotive, and the
rolling stock is of Wagons-Lits material. This
train ran until 1931, when Japanese pressure in
Manchuria caused it to be withdrawn.

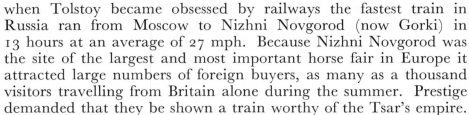

As an advertisement for its Russian services, the CIWL staged an exhibit at the Paris Exhibition of 1900 showing some of the wonders of the Trans-Siberian Railway.

when Tolstoy became obsessed by railways the fastest train in Russia ran from Moscow to Nizhni Novgorod (now Gorki) in 13 hours at an average of 27 mph. Because Nizhni Novgorod was the site of the largest and most important horse fair in Europe it attracted large numbers of foreign buyers, as many as a thousand visitors travelling from Britain alone during the summer. Prestige demanded that they be shown a train worthy of the Tsar's empire.

Yet even by 1889 — the date-line for Foxwell and Farrer's classic survey — Russia could boast only one train which (if by the skin of its teeth) got in above their 29 mph qualification for an express. This was the 2630 h. (first class only) departure from St. Petersburg to Moscow. The longest of its eight stops was 12 minutes, and the fastest intermediate timing was 1 hour 16 minutes for the 44 miles between Okulowka and the Nicolai's one important town of Bologoye. No train in Russia as yet had a name, and no fast trains carried third-class traffic; but a run on the South Western railway in the Ukraine was noted in 1889 which showed an average speed of 29 mph over the 97 miles from Kazatin to Kiev. Somebody in the imperial court, seeing what was possible, then put pressure on the South-Western administration (which was rather less creaking than that of most Russian railways at the period) to speed up the Kiev-Odessa trunk line. For Odessa, then as now, was an important ice-free port and naval base, and there were many comings and goings by senior officers and administrators between the Black Sea and St. Petersburg.

This led to the running of Russia's first named train in 1894, when the Kiev to Odessa night express became the *Courier*. It travelled the 405 miles (almost an identical distance to St. Petersburg-Moscow) in 12 hours 9 minutes at an average speed of just over 33 mph. One section, between Fastov and Kazatin, was run at 40 mph, outstandingly the fastest performance in Russia in 1894. Naturally the *Courier* was first class only, and persons without priority tickets had little chance of boarding it.

Eleven years passed before a faster train appeared in the time-tables of Holy Russia. This too had a name, being curiously known as the *Courier Number One*; and it ran on the prime route from St. Petersburg to Moscow, leaving the capital of the tsars at 2230 h. and reaching Moscow at 1000 h. the next morning. It made eight stops and carried first-class-priority ticket holders only, some of these enjoying the luxury of sleeping in the varnished teak cars of the Wagons-Lits company. There was also in 1905 a day express which performed fairly well, leaving St. Petersburg at 0945 h. to arrive at the Kursk station — one of Moscow's eight termini — at 2120 h. Indicative of the growth of a middle class in Russia and of the liberalism enforced upon the tsars by the explosive events of 1905 was that this train carried first- and second-class passengers, both of whom could use the restaurant car.

But Russia was looking eastwards well before the turn of the century; and having built most of its railway network to serve European Russia it was time to make some impact upon the vast and inhospitable wastes of Siberia. A few cities already existed there, including Omsk on the Irtisk River (the seat of the Governor-General of the Steppes) and Irkutsk on Lake Baikal, a fur-trading base and wealthy merchants' town hopefully known as the Paris of Siberia. To reach these was a formidable journey by river or carriage, and it was indeed quicker for someone in St. Petersburg to get to almost any capital city in the world than to central Siberia. The overland journey to the 'Siberian far east', for instance, could take *two years*, though in mid-winter and by using troika sledges the journey to Irkutsk over the snow and ice could be done in a month.

The next Tsar, Alexander III, hence declared a trans-Siberian railway essential to the empire and laid its foundation stone in the May of 1891. The days of the serfs and their free labour had ended in 1868, but exiles and convicts took their place. The construction was of low grade, with a single light track and few earthworks, and so such rapid progress was made that inside ten years the Baltic was linked by a more-or-less-continuous railway route with the Pacific at Vladivostok, nearly 6,000 miles away. The bridge over the Ob at Novosibirsk, built in 1897 and named after the Tsar, was the biggest engineering feat on the line. Crossing Lake Baikal, passengers and goods had initially to use ferries prefabricated in Britain (or, in winter, temporary tracks laid on the ice), since work on the line around the mountainous southern shore of the great lake was extremely difficult. Through Manchuria the route ran over the metals of the Chinese Eastern railway, perhaps never a stable proposition in any sense but one that caught the imagination of the world at the turn of the century since it provided a link to Pekin.

By the end of 1900 passenger trains began to make what remains by far the world's longest rail journey. Not all completed it intact, and many are the stories told of trains rolling off the embankments as the lines gave way and coming to rest in the forests of silver birch. Fortunately, with speeds so low, casualties were not serious; but the delays were enormous. During the first years of what Russia termed the Great Siberian railway, people set out from Moscow in high hopes of reaching Vladivostok in two weeks, but they always allowed an extra week for mishaps.

It was the railway-minded British who had christened the train the *Trans-Siberian Express* after the Russians had announced the start of a public service: for the completion of the line was a matter of great importance for British travellers to the Far East and indeed to the Foreign Office in London. French and German diplomats, too, realised that they were going to use it. All at once, the journey to an embassy in Peking or Tokyo was cut from six or seven weeks to barely a fortnight — if all went well. The service had an impact on long-distance travellers akin to that of flying boats thirty years later, and the powerful British P&O shipping line became seriously worried by it.

For in the quality of its services and appointments, at least, the trans-Siberian route set standards which would have been regarded as high in France, let alone Russia. The huge train crews, for instance, were instructed in a staff booklet as to the most meticulous details of

Part of the appeal of the Trans-Siberian route was the fact that diplomats and businessmen could travel to China and Japan faster by train across Russia than they could by ship. This poster of 1909 explained the journey, gave prices, and also stated the tariff for 'nourishment' en route.

L'EXTRÊME ORIENT
par le
TRANSSIBÉRIEN

Paris
Moscou, Vladivostock dans les trains de la
Cⁱᵉ des Wagons-Lits
(la voie la plus courte et la meilleure marché)

de PARIS en CHINE (Mandchouria)
en 13 jours

de PARIS au JAPON (Tsuruga)
en 17 jours

Le port de Tsuruga est le plus rapproché de toutes les villes du centre du Japon, 15 heures de chemin de fer le sépare de Yokohama.

PRIX TOTAUX des billets de 1ʳᵉ CLASSE et de
SUPPLÉMENTS WAGONS-LITS
pour le JAPON au départ de PARIS :

PARIS à TSURUGA : 1262 fr. 65

PRIX de la NOURRITURE de MOSCOU à VLADIVOSTOCK
à raison de 3 repas par jour pendant 12 jours
92 fr. 50

Pour tous renseignements complémentaires s'adresser :
PARTOUT aux AGENCES de la Cⁱᵉ INTERNⁱᵉ des
WAGONS-LITS
et lire le Guide Officiel : Sleeping-Car.

— A dater du 14 janvier 1909, —
nouveau train de luxe direct "PARIS-MOSCOU" en correspondance avec le Transsibérien

This wood-burning locomotive with its
'hard' class rolling stock epitomizes rail travel
across the vast plains of central Russia at
the end of the nineteenth century.

Wagons-Lits tickets or 'bulletins' issued in 1903 for a journey from Paris to St. Petersburg, and from there to Moscow and Lake Baikal. Mme de Souza was a journalist, and the bulletins were signed by Georges Nagelmackers.

Le Transsibérien

Première grande Excursion de luxe en Russie

ORGANISÉE EN

TRAIN DE LUXE SPÉCIAL

PAR LA

Cie INTERNATIONALE DES WAGONS-LITS

ET DES GRANDS EXPRESS EUROPÉENS

Itinéraire

MOSCOU — NIJNI-NOVGOROD (VISITE DE LA FOIRE) — DESCENTE DU VOLGA EN BATEAU JUSQU'A SAMARA (VISITE DE KAZAN, CAPITALE ANCIENNE DU ROYAUME TARTARE) — TRAVERSÉE DE L'OURAL A PARTIR DE SAMARA EN TRAIN DE LUXE, LE TRANSSIBÉRIEN, VIA TCHELIABINEK ET TOMSK JUSQU'A KRASNOIARSK ET RETOUR A MOSCOU.

5 Août   24 Août 1898

their craft: the ashtrays and spitoons must be scrupulously cleaned after every use, the attendants must dust everything (and in the right sequence) many times a day so that the passengers should have 'no cause for complaint during the long journey', the temperature must be held at a steady 14° C, and above all attention must be paid to the train's condition on arrival at Irkutsk, the half-way house where the manager charged with cleanliness and minor repairs kept his keen eyes on these unique expresses.

The first such trains, running twice weekly, were known internally as *International Expresses* when they comprised *wagons-lits* (plus a bath car with porcelain tubs, a gymnasium and a lounge with a piano), and *State Expresses* when they were the alternate departures made up of Russian stock. But both these were short-lived, since outbreak of war between Russia and Japan implied troop trains passing all the time and heavy work needed to improve the track. Even at their best the 'Internationals' and 'States' had not managed to average more than 15 mph, and derailments averaged two per trip.

The year 1905 was a bad one for Russia, with war in the Far East, the total loss of the imperial fleet, uprisings and massacres and financial troubles. The railways were soon in poor shape apart from those which radiated in a great cross from Moscow — north to St. Petersburg, south to Odessa, east to Nizhni Novgorod and west to Warsaw — and a standard history of them points out that in 1905 'the pride of many a main line was a train making 25 kilometres [15 miles] an hour between stations, and requiring from its passengers a supplement for the privilege of travelling at so great a velocity'. The locomotives were mainly underpowered and the tracks weakened by the extremes of Russian weather, particularly the spring thaws. Long station stops were needed whilst the engines took on water through small-diameter pipes, and on the railways of the Ukraine alone no less than 6,357 derailments were reported in 1905. Corruption among ticket inspectors had become rife, and it was said that (at least on secondary lines) more persons travelled without paying than purchased tickets. But imperial Russia somehow pulled herself together after defeat, and by 1907 the railway scene, as well as the financial and political one, was looking better than it had ever looked — or would look again for many a year.

The seven years from 1907 to the outbreak of war in 1914 saw major improvements to transport throughout the vast land, and an influx of foreign travellers such as J. P. Pearson as well as of foreign investment. The first through service from Berlin to Moscow was achieved by a bogie-changing device on the Polish border in 1912, when two sleeping cars were lifted up and converted to the 5 ft gauge. (This device was not seen again until the 1950s, when it appeared with improvements at Brest-Litovsk). As for the trans-Siberian 'Internationals', they kept to the tracks most of the time and by 1912 were offering a weekly service from Moscow — now rapidly overtaking St. Petersburg as the commercial capital of Russia — to Tokyo in eleven days, with only nine being spent on the train to Vladivostok. Often half the first-class passengers — who

The *Krasnaja Strela* or 'Red Arrow' overnight train to Leningrad in Moscow in 1966.

still had access to shower baths and a travelling gymnasium — were western European diplomats and their families, with a leavening of British and French businessmen. Some Americans too came to Europe this way, crossing the Pacific from San Francisco.

Meanwhile, in the last peace-time year of the Nicolai railway, Russia's fastest train left St. Petersburg as the *Courier Number One* at 2200 h. and entered Moscow 10 hours later, averaging just over 40 mph including four stops. Such running was not to be experienced again anywhere in the country for over forty years. The 'International' had its best-ever summer and its equipment now included not only more porcelain baths but a quiet library and reading-room car: it was never again to aspire to such standards of comfort. Completion of the 'Chinese avoiding line' from Chita enabled the 1914 services to stay in Russia all the way to Vladivostok, so that there was now no need for Cossack guards to protect the trains against Manchurian bandits.

Total chaos followed the end of the war with Germany, the October revolution and the civil war. There were no great trains and few trains of any kind running, though Czech divisions somehow took control of the trans-Siberian railway and used it to reach their homeland *via* Vladivostok and America, their power on arrival clinching independence. Yet one train of this era is officially regarded by every good revolutionary as the finest ever to run in Russia or perhaps the world — that which the Germans allowed to pass, sealed, through Europe and on to the Finland station in Petrograd, carrying Lenin and his entourage back from exile in Switzerland. The engine which hauled this, and the carriage which the future leader used, are preserved as part of Soviet history. But the armoured, book-lined saloon wherein Trotsky read the poems of Mallarmé has long been destroyed in fact and memory.

Various five-year-plans during the 1920s and 1930s put the Russian railways back into fair physical shape — and, oddly enough, the passenger operations made all the profit. Even more unexpectedly, private railway companies were not entirely eliminated by the soviets until about 1923, since some had an essential nucleus of trained foreign staff. But in 1917, in his last year of rule, Tsar Nicolas III had nationalised just over two-thirds of all the railways in Russia, and by 1924 the system was fully under state control. A passenger train which averaged more than 20 mph was at that time a rarity, as was any where all the passengers travelled inside the carriages.

After the first flush of Marxist fervour had passed together with dreams of universal revolution, Soviet Russia realised that she could not isolate herself from the world — and especially from the world of commerce and finance. It became essential to attract visiting businessmen and even tourists, and so great strides were made to restore the main-line trains to some semblance of comfort and efficiency. Two classes were again introduced (so once more upsetting the die-hard Marxists who had objected when fares were re-instated on trams and trains in 1923), and these were called 'soft' and 'hard' as they are to this day. Modern overnight 'hards' can be better than the old 'softs', though, the main difference being in service (there are two *provodnik* sleeping-car attendants in 'soft', charged with such duties as distributing chess sets and samovars as well as stoking the heating stoves and rounding-up straying passengers), and in the provision or otherwise of an upholstered mattress and cushions.

In 1929 Intourist was formed in the new capital of Moscow and charged with the tasks of (to put it politely) looking after foreigners and arranging internal travel for Russians. By 1930 it was again possible for west-Europeans to enter Russia and even Siberia by train. One who accepted the challenge was the explorer, railway enthusiast (and brother of the creator of James Bond), Peter Fleming, who in addition to suffering a journey to Samarkand in conditions less comfortable than those of today's *Uzbekistan*, crossed Russia twice — in 1931 and 1933. On the whole he enjoyed it, though the train's performance was rather akin to that of an 'International' back in 1904 and left him sitting on the side of his carriage surveying 'the "Trans-Siberian Express" sprawled foolishly down the embankment... The mail van and the dining car, which had been in front, lay on their sides at the bottom. Behind them the five sleeping cars, headed by my own, were disposed in attitudes which became less and less grotesque until you got to the last which had remained, primly, on the rails.'

It was, said Peter Fleming, 'an ideal railway accident... We suffered only four hours delay. They found another engine. In a sadly truncated train the Germans, a few important officials and myself proceeded on our way. Our fellow passengers were left behind ... and did not seem to care.'

By 1939 the trans-Siberian line had been double-tracked all the way from Moscow to the Pacific, a fact which stood the Soviet Union in good stead during the Second World War. In fact, by the late 1930s the railways were in reliable condition at least so far as the main lines were concerned, with trains available to foreigners listed in the international timetables. The erstwhile Nicolai railway remained the premier line, with the 'Krasnaja Strela' or *Red Arrow* — its crack express, and the fastest in Russia — leaving Moscow at 0030 h. to arrive in Leningrad at 1025 h., giving an average of over 40 mph. There were three other trains daily on the October railway classified as 'fast' and averaging 30 mph or better. Moving into a field where transit times must always be measured in days rather than hours, the 1937 timetable showed trans-Siberian trains leaving Moscow on Tuesdays, Thursdays, Fridays and Sundays at 1700 h. and reaching Vladivostok at 1345 h. on the ninth day. More important for foreigners were the connections — arrival at Peking at 1840 h. on the tenth day, Tokyo at 0710 h. on the eleventh day, and Shanghai at about the same time. All this was highly competitive in an age which, although it already used long-distance air travel, accepted ten days to Australia in flying boats.

Another shattering war wrecked most of the railway system in European Russia but left the trans-Siberian line not only intact but

Another modern, custom-built Russian express, the *Druzhba* or 'Friendship' on its long journey from Moscow to Tiflis.

strengthened behind the Urals. A tremendous amount of rebuilding had to take place, and there were factions which argued for investment in roads and aircraft rather than railways. But for once sanity prevailed: the tracks of the world's largest railway administration were reconstructed and modernised, and in particular electrification swept through the system so that the last steam locomotives were built in 1956. Today the trans-Siberian line runs 'under the wires' from Moscow to Petrovsky Zarod, nearly 4,000 miles away, and is scheduled to be electrified throughout by 1975.

Russia is, like all 'socialist' countries, blind to the tourist appeal of the more recent past; and when the time comes for its last main-line journey behind steam the occasion will (if regarded as an occasion at all) presumably be treated as one for a rejoicing unmixed by any nostalgia or thanks to a medium which — more than any *ukases* — enabled a ragbag of ethnically-contrasted 'autonomous republics' to function as one of the world's greatest powers. But meanwhile, if only for a few years, the trans-Siberian line can provide a splendid journey behind steam, including a length which requires double-heading and banking to climb over the summits of the Yablonovy mountains. The whole journey is made daily from end to end in summer and four times weekly in winter; but tourists (and a surprising number *do* make the trip for its own sake) must change trains in Khabarovsk and spend an enforced day sightseeing with Intourist.

This is because the secret naval port of Vladivostok has for many decades been closed to non-Russians. However, a new harbour has been developed at Nakhodka, where the steamer to Japan and Hong Kong berths alongside a modern and luxurious boat train which has covered the 564 mile journey from Khabarovsk in 16 hours. This train, with its two-berth sleepers equipped with showers, is in marked contrast to the current 'Trans-Siberian Express' (known internally as the *Rossia* or 'Train Number One'), whose sixteen sets use mainly older rolling-stock with four-berth compartments and which no longer boasts any special facilities beyond a six-language menu to tell one what dishes are not available. However, some summer working are beginning to get one or two new two-berth sleepers — though Russian rolling-stock in general preserves a rather pleasant period atmosphere with even the most modern cars displaying red velours, oriental carpets and massive bronze castings.

But the finest trains in modern Russia remain the high-speed expresses on the line where it all began, between Leningrad and Moscow. There are now eleven departures a day under the wires installed by 1962, the fastest — called *Aurora* after the cruiser preserved in Leningrad which sounded-off the 1917 revolution — taking one symbolic minute under 5 hours to give a fine average speed of over 80 mph. The *Auroras*, whose catering is restricted to snacks served at seats, leave both ends of the line after lunch to arrive in the early evening. The *Red Arrow* continues as a sleeping-car train with the usual — and correct — accent on overnight

A locomotive of the IS (Iosef Stalin) class, photographed in Georgia.

comfort rather than speed, taking a well-scheduled 8½ hours.

Recent years have seen the introduction of such internal named trains as the *Azerbaijan*, the *Ritsa*, the *Kavkaz* and the *Druzhba*, running at relatively high speeds to the south and south-east from Moscow, whilst on the trans-Siberian line the *Baikal* — an express made up of semi-'streamlined' coaches — runs as far as Irkutsk. But more significant, perhaps, are the results of that thaw in a long and useless 'cold war' which led to the realisation of a seventy-year-old dream when through cars first ran from Paris to Moscow in 1960. For today there is a whole fleet whose passage is simplified by the use of gauge-change machinery at seven frontier points. Thus, as this book has already mentioned, the *Chopin* with its surprisingly light-hearted, TEE-type name now runs from Moscow to Vienna, as well as the *Praga* to Prague and the *Danubius* to Bucharest on a voyage almost as long as that of the *Orient Express*.

It is only a minor annoyance that on some of these journeys the carpets have to be rolled up to allow the mechanics to get at the bogie-bolts — and that a supplement is charged for this 'service'. For few could have hoped, at the height of the 'iron curtain' years, that from 1963 onwards one would be able to board in Moscow's Byolorussian station a coach of the *Ost-West Express* and so find one's way directly through to the Hook and the packet-boat to England, 2½ days and 1,600 miles away.

The Trans-Siberian railway.

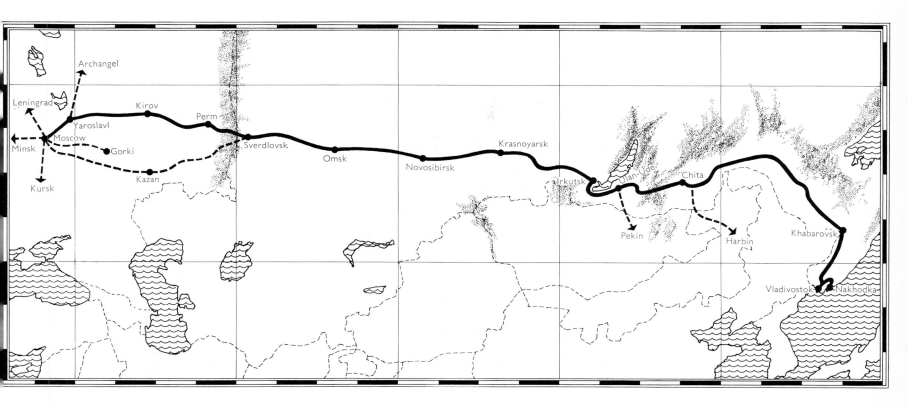

Great Trains
of North America

The importance of George Mortimer Pullman in initiating North American — and, indeed, world — luxury travel can hardly be over-stressed. An earlier chapter has said something of the splendid cars which he and his contemporaries put at the public disposal, but his influence had many secondary aspects: for example, even today the American system of calculating fares from a basic cost with supplementary tariffs for luxury facilities, which contrasts with the European 'class' structure, is linked back to the Pullman tradition. And certainly the increase of US train speeds from the depressing levels normal around 1870 to the more impressive runs which were being made at the turn of the century can be seen as deriving from Pullman's vision of travel becoming something more than a crude necessity. For those who were prepared to pay for the luxuries of sleeping and diningcars to say nothing of baths, travelling secretaries and all the rest, expected speeds to match.

These improved timings, however, did not come immediately; and though there were trains running in the 'seventies and 'eighties which could be regarded as 'great' in their appointments, they were rarely so in their schedules. Certainly the various expresses which were in this period known as 'Cannonballs' did not live up to their titles, and they looked to the future mainly in that they *were* named. For the christening of American trains is a tradition dating back as far as 1847 (when a service from Boston to a nearby harbour was officially referred to as the *Steamboat Express*), and in due course some 700 trains — the *majority* of US long-distance services, though including some of rather leisurely performance — were to bear titles. Even today, around 200 named expresses remain.

So it is that a survey of the great trains of North America need pay comparatively little attention to events before the closing years of the nineteenth century. (By this period, ironically, the magnificent handcrafted Pullman car was giving way to plainer mass-produced vehicles and even the characteristic open vestibule was becoming less universal, though it was to be a few more years before the first steel-bodied stock made its appearance.) The new high speeds owed much, of course, to rivalry between America's multiplicity of competing companies. But almost equally influential were a handful of long-distance runs made for advertising purposes or in privately-chartered trains which showed that scheduled times could be cut by over 50 per cent even on systems characterised by their light single tracks.

One such journey had indeed been made as early as 1876, when a theatrical company accepted a booking schedule which implied

George Mortimer Pullman: (1831-1897).

A fierce member of the Ute tribe stood guard on the cover of the 1901 edition of the Colorado Midland railway's timetable.

THE COLORADO MIDLAND RAILWAY

THE COLORADO MIDLAND RAILWAY

JANUARY 1901

THE DENVER LITH. CO.

MONON ROUTE
Louisville, New Albany & Chicago Ry.

Pullman Palace Car Route

TO FLORIDA

THE SHORT & DIRECT LINE to all Points South.

CHICAGO
MICHIGAN CITY
MONON
LAFAYETTE
INDIANAPOLIS
CINCINNATI
LOUISVILLE
MEMPHIS
ATLANTA
MONTGOMERY
THOMASVILLE
MOBILE
PENSACOLA
NEW ORLEANS
TALLAHASSEE
JACKSONVILLE

Pullman Sleepers to LAFAYETTE Indianapolis Cincinnati and Louisville.

1869. May 10th. 1869.
GREAT EVENT
Rail Road from the Atlantic to the Pacific
GRAND OPENING
OF THE
Union Pacific
RAIL ROAD,
Platte Valley Route.
PASSENGER TRAINS LEAVE
OMAHA
ON THE ARRIVAL OF TRAINS FROM THE EAST.
THROUGH TO SAN FRANCISCO
In less than Four Days, avoiding the Dangers of the Sea!
Travelers for Pleasure, Health or Business
Will find a Trip over The Rocky Mountains Healthy and Pleasant
LUXURIOUS CARS & EATING HOUSES
ON THE UNION PACIFIC RAIL ROAD.
PULLMAN'S PALACE SLEEPING CARS
RUN WITH ALL THROUGH PASSENGER TRAINS
GOLD, SILVER AND OTHER MINERS!
Now is the time to seek your Fortunes in Nevada, Wyoming, Arizona, Washington, Dakotah Colorado, Utah, Oregon, Montana, New Mexico, Idaho, Nevada or California.
CONNECTIONS MADE AT
CHEYENNE for DENVER, CENTRAL CITY & SANTA FE
AT OGDEN AND CORINNE FOR HELENA, BOISE CITY, VIRGINIA CITY, SALT LAKE CITY and ARIZONA
THROUGH TICKETS FOR SALE AT ALL PRINCIPAL RAILROAD OFFICES!
Be Sure they Read via Platte Valley or Omaha
Company's Office 72 La Salle St., opposite City Hall and Court House Square, Chicago.
CHARLES E. NICHOLS, Ticket Agent.
G. P. GILMAN, JOHN P. HART, J. BUDD, W. SNYDER,

THE Short Line LIMITED
VIA
625
N-W. **CHICAGO AND NORTH WESTERN Railway.**
CHICAGO TO ST. PAUL AND MINNEAPOLIS
THE FINEST TRAIN IN THE WORLD. **IN 12 HOURS AND 30 MINUTES**
Leaves Chicago at 7.30 p.m. daily except Saturday,
ON AND AFTER MAY 2d. 1886.

Intercolonial RAILWAY CANADA
NOW OPEN BETWEEN
QUEBEC, RESTIGOUCHE MIRAMICHI, PICTOU ST. JOHN AND HALIFAX
THROUGH EXPRESS TRAINS
Between QUEBEC and HALIFAX in 24 HOURS.
STEEL RAILS AND IRON BRIDGES.
No Custom House Obstructions. Excellent Refreshment Rooms.
NO CHANGE OF CARS.
PULLMAN PALACE SLEEPING CARS
ON ALL EXPRESS TRAINS
CLOSE CONNECTIONS made at Quebec with the Gr... ...s between Montreal and Quebec
THE SCENERY ALONG THE LINE IS T... ...THE ENGINES AND CARS

closing one night in New York and opening in San Francisco five days later. In the event, the three-car 'Lightning Express' completed its run of just over 3,300 miles in 84 hours, so clipping a whole three days from the regular transcontinental timing. As reported by that great chronicler of the American railway past, Lucius Beebe, highlights of the episode were the re-greasing of a 'hot box' by a hardy roadmaster who held on by one hand as the train roared ahead, a display of live-fire and Roman candles as it raced through Cheyenne at night, and a final descent from the high Sierras with the air-brakes not functioning. Speeds peaking to over 72 mph, however, led to such uneven riding that beds could not be made nor hot meals cooked, and the male actors preferred to arrive on the west coast with four days' growth of beard rather than dare the use of a cut-throat razor.

In the new century such spectacles became more common, a typical example being the publicity run in 1905 of the 'Scott Special' from Chicago to Los Angeles in under 45 hours: here, though, the claim that a climax of 106 mph was reached must be regarded with some reserve, and perhaps the running owed most to that very fast work at the change of engines which was speeded by the distribution of silver dollars to anybody around at the time. But one must turn from such isolated early achievements to a more orderly consideration of the expresses which began to network the United States, Canada and Mexico from 1890 onwards. And on a geographical basis first place must be given, for both historical and commercial reasons, to the trains of that eastern seaboard which runs from Boston southwards to New York, Philadelphia, Baltimore and Washington to form what is now known as the north-east corridor, and which continues by way of Richmond and Charleston to the holiday lands of Florida.

As the railways between Boston and New York developed in the nineteenth century, trains took over from the once popular and palatial Long Island Sound steamboats. Among the first of the great expresses of the east was the *New England Limited* of 1891 — 'a complete new train of cars resplendent in white and gold', whose presentation as well as whose name was already typically American. For this the Pullman company provided seven parlour cars, four passenger coaches and two 'royal buffet' smokers. These cars were divided into two rakes owned respectively by the New York & New England and the New York, New Haven & Hartford railroads, the dining car which operated between Boston and Willimantic, Conn., provided by the former company.

The parlour cars and smokers were furnished with velvet carpets, silk draperies and white silk curtains; revolving chairs were upholstered in old-gold plush. The outstanding elegance of these trains, however, was in their white livery delicately ornamented and lettered in gold. Although the locomotives were in traditional black, it was reported that the coal in the tenders was whitewashed. The scheduled time for the run between the 'hub of the universe' and the nation's largest city — just under 230 miles by this route — was 6 hours.

A timetable cover of 1881 illustrates what was for many years America's most substantial tunnel and certainly the world's longest in building-time.

A collection of posters advertising various railroads in Canada and the United States

It was not long before the 'Limited' became known locally as the 'ghost train'. The service was well advertised, and the following verse was widely circulated:

> *Without a jar, or roll or antic,*
> *Without a stop to Willimantic,*
> *The* New England Limited *takes its way*
> *At three o'clock on every day,*
> *Maids and matrons, daintily dimited,*
> *Ride every day on the* New England Limited;
> *Rain nor snow ne'er stops its flight,*
> *It makes New York at nine each night.*
> *One half of the glories have not been told*
> *Of that wonderful train of white and gold*
> *Which leaves every day for New York at three*
> *Over the N.Y. & N.E.*

After only four years the 'ghost train' became even ghostlier when in 1895, the president of the New England line decided that it was too much trouble to keep the livery clean. Already there was a successor to hand, however; for in 1903 Charles S. Mellon became president of the New Haven line and, as a protégé of banker J. P. Morgan, proceeded vigorously to reshape the New Haven (and, indeed, much of the public transport of New England). Almost immediately he inaugurated a five-hour Boston/New York flyer which soon became a favourite of the bankers and brokers of the 'city of the bean and the cod'. This 45 mph train, which departed each terminal at 1700 h. and boasted 'limited and superior accommodation' including private state-rooms, was christened the *Merchants' Limited*.

A brochure published by the New Haven in 1913 advertised the service between New York and Boston as follows, and shows how the fleet had been expanded if not accelerated in ten years: 'Three of the most magnificent trains in the United States, if not, indeed, in the entire world, are operated over the scenic Shore Line route by the New York, New Haven & Hartford Railroad... The *Bay State Limited*, the *Knickerbocker Limited*, and the *Merchants' Limited*, as they are known, are trains with marvellous equipment, and for trips occupying but little over five hours they are really palatial — truly Trains de Luxe!'

The *Merchants' Limited* was unusual in that it carried two dining cars. In one the service was *à la carte;* in the other, *table d'hôte* meals were offered. The latter, in particular, were veritable feasts. For one dollar, the New Haven offered a seven-course meal which included grapefruit, soup and relishes, followed by baked Savannah shad, roast prime ribs of beef, South Shore duckling with currant jelly, and roast short ribs with brown potatoes. Vegetables, salad, dessert, chocolate confections, cheese and a *demi-tasse* completed the repast. The menu noted that the table water was purified by a 'Boston filter'. A complete selection of champagnes, wines, hocks, ales, beers, liquors and cordials was offered, except during the

The interior of a typical early American railroad car in 1852. Note the view through to the open platform.

A frank and detailed view of the interior of a 'colonists' car on the Canadian
Pacific railway in 1888. Though following the general Pullman layout, these were decidedly plebeian versions
where the immigrant was expected to provide his own refreshment and bedding

THE NORTH-WESTERN LIMITED
CHICAGO—ST. PAUL—MINNEAPOLIS

DINNER

BLUE POINTS
CELERY

MULLIGATAWNEY   CONSOMME, PETIT POIS

RADISHES   MELON MANGOES   SALTED ALMONDS   OLIVES

BAKED HALIBUT, AU GRATIN
CUCUMBERS

SWEET BREADS, SAUTE, FRESH MUSHROOMS

BANANA FRITTERS

PRIME ROAST BEEF, NATURAL

NEW POTATOES IN CREAM   CAULIFLOWER, HOLLANDAISE

ROAST MILK-FED CHICKEN, WHITE CHERRIES

MASHED POTATOES   SUGAR CORN

ST. JULIEN PUNCH

SALAD ST. REGIS

RHUBARB PIE

CHERRY ICE CREAM   ASSORTED CAKE

ROQUEFORT, EDAM AND CAMEMBERT CHEESE

WATER CRACKERS   SALTINE CRACKERS
STRAWBERRIES   NABISCO WAFERS

COFFEE

EN ROUTE
THURSDAY, FEBRUARY 1, 1906   PRICE ONE DOLLAR

"COPIES OF THIS MENU," IN ENVELOPES READY FOR MAILING, CAN BE SECURED
ON APPLICATION TO THE CONDUCTOR

WINE LIST

			QUARTS	PINTS
Champagnes	MOET & CHANDON (WHITE SEAL)			$2.00
	POMMERY SEC			2.00
	G. H. MUMM'S (EXTRA DRY)			2.00
	VEUVE CLICQUOT (YELLOW LABEL)			2.00
	RUINART, VIN BRUT			2.00
	IMPERIAL (COOK'S)			1.25
Red Wines	ST. JULIEN (CALIFORNIA) (CRESTA BLANCA)		.75	.40
	ST. JULIEN (CALIFORNIA) (GOLD MEDAL, CORDOVA)	.25	.75	.40
	ST. JULIEN (CRUSE & FILS FRERES)			.75
	TIPO CHIANTI (ITALIAN SWISS COLONY)			.50
	PONTET CANET (CRUSE & FILS FRERES)			1.00
	CHATEAU LAROSE " "			1.75
	MEDOC TYPE (ALTA VISTA)			.50
	CHATEAU MARGAUX TYPE " "			.75
	CHATEAU LAFITE TYPE " "			.75
White Wines	SAUTERNE (CALIFORNIA) (CRESTA BLANCA)		.75	.40
	SAUTERNE (CALIFORNIA) (GOLD MEDAL, CORDOVA)	.25	.75	.40
	SAUTERNE (CRUSE & FILS FRERES)			.75
	CHATEAU LATOUR BLANCHE " "			1.50
	TIPO CHIANTI (ITALIAN SWISS COLONY)			.50
	RUEDESHEIMER (CARL ACKER)			1.00
	SAUTERNE TYPE (ALTA VISTA)			.50
	CHIANTI TYPE " "			.60
	MOSELLE TYPE " "			.50
Sparkling Wines	BURGUNDY TYPE (ALTA VISTA)			1.00
	SAUTERNE TYPE " "			1.00
	MOSELLE TYPE " "			1.00
Waters	SALVATOR	SPLITS, .15		
	CLUB SODA			.25
	CONGRESS OR HATHORN			.25
	WHITE ROCK LITHIA	SPLITS, .15		.25
	APOLLINARIS	" .15		.25
	HUNYADI	PER GLASS, .15		.35
	LONDONDERRY LITHIA	SPLITS, .15		.25
	RED RAVEN	" .15		
Beers	PABST "BLUE RIBBON"			.15
	SCHLITZ' "PALE"			.15
	BLATZ' "WIENER"			.15
	MILLER'S "HIGH LIFE"			.15
Whiskies	OLD FITZGERALD RYE OR BOURBON	INDIVIDUALS, .20		
	NATIONAL CLUB BOURBON	" .20		
	SCOTCH OR CANADIAN CLUB	" .20		
	WESTMORELAND RYE	" .20		
	FLASKS, 50c AND 75c			
Miscellaneous	COCKTAILS—WHISKY, MARTINI OR MANHATTAN	" .20		
	HENNESSY BRANDY	" .35		
	AMONTILLADO SHERRY	" .20		
	BASS' ALE, WHITE LABEL OR DOG'S HEAD			.30
	GUINNESS' DUBLIN PORTER			.30
	BELFAST GINGER ALE			.25
	WHITE ROCK GINGER ALE			.15
	OLD TOM GIN	INDIVIDUALS, .20		
	CREME DE MENTHE	" .20		
	BENEDICTINE	" .20		
	EFFERVESCENT BROMO SELTZER	" .10		
	HORLICK'S MALTED MILK	" .15		

IMPORTED AND DOMESTIC CIGARS, 10c, TWO FOR 25c, 15c AND 25c

Above: The 'dollar dinner' on America's *North Western Limited* in 1906 provided good value for the money and was probably subsidised so as to attract passengers to the line.

Left: A drawing-room car built for the opening of the Union Pacific railroad in 1869...

...and a sleeping car (right) of the same period.

brief passage through dry New York state. Seven brands of cigars, including the favourite of J. P. Morgan himself, were also on hand.

Observation cars on the Shore Line trains, fitted with leather club seats, served as gentlemen's smokers, and news bulletins and stock market quotations were posted in these. The parlour cars were attended by porters and also maids — a feature which appealed to ladies travelling alone or with children.

By the 1940s the schedule of the *Merchants' Limited* had been reduced to 4 ¼ hours, at 54 mph. But before moving southward, it should be noted that the tradition of luxury travel on the Atlantic coast was older even than the earliest of this series of flyers, for two of the first long-distance expresses in the United States had been the day and night trains inaugurated in 1876 to carry passengers without change from Boston to the Centennial Exposition in Philadelphia. The original routing of these was *via* the New York & New England and the New Haven roads from Boston to the Harlem River north of New York, where a ferry conveyed the trains on a two-hour boat trip down the East River to Jersey City. There they were transferred to the Pennsylvania railroad for carriage to Philadelphia and Washington. The night train became known as the *Federal Express*, and the day operation was later named the *Colonial*.

This transhipment system naturally proved unsatisfactory, and in 1910 the opening of the Pennsylvania station and its tunnel network brought the Pennsylvania railroad into New York city from the west under the Hudson River and from the east under the East River. Seven years later, the great Hell Gate bridge connected the New Haven road with the Pennsylvania line and so eliminated the ferrying of Boston/New York trains. When the *Federal Express* first passed over the new bridge the long-cherished dream of an all-rail route from Boston to the south *via* New York was at last realised.

South of New York down to Philadelphia, Baltimore and Washington, the Pennsylvania competed with the 'Royal Blue' line — an amalgam of the Central of New Jersey, the Philadelphia & Reading and the Baltimore & Ohio companies. Here the 'Pennsy's' crack train was the *Congressional Limited Express* inaugurated in 1885; the B&O's 'Royal Blue' service, whose overall speed even then exceeded 45 mph, dated from 1890. The rivalry between these routes developed its greatest intensity in 1898, when each introduced luxurious new equipment built by the Pullman company.

The first of the 1898 trains to be completed was the Pennsylvania's restyled *Congressional*, which began service during the month of April. The cars of this were painted Brewster green, cream and red — a livery reported to have derived from a visit to the Pullman works by Pennsylvania executives when the private cars for Don Porfirio Diaz, president of Mexico from 1877 to 1911, were standing ready for shipment. This elegant stock, freshly painted in the Mexican national colours, so impressed the vice-president of the Pennsylvania line that he ordered the same livery to be applied to his New York/Chicago and New York/Washington 'limiteds'.

America's transcontinental line traversed the 'Bible belt' and although Sunday travel was unavoidable, suitable provision was made for divine services as in this Pullman car of 1875.

166

The 'Ghost Train', a fabled express made up of white and gold cars, shown leaving Boston for New York in 1891.

In November of the same year the sets for the Royal Blue line were out-shopped by Pullman for use on the *Royal Limited*. The cars of this were similar in design to those of the *Congressional* but were painted a rich deep blue, lined and lettered in gold. The dining cars were named 'Waldorf' and 'Astoria' after the then-new hotel. For decades the two expresses competed, until in 1958 the Royal Blue service was discontinued and the *Congressional* remained the premier train on the route until a new era began in 1969 with the advent of the frequent, high speed electric 'Metroliners'.

Still further south (and in vacation, rather than businessman's, country), the flagship of the 'Atlantic Coast' line was the *Florida Special* — a seasonal train which carried northern tourists to that land of sunshine. The builder of the Florida East Coast railway had been Henry Morrison Flagler, a founder of the Standard Oil company who was convinced that wealthy Americans could be induced to visit Florida instead of the French Riviera during the winter season. Accordingly in 1888 he built the Ponce de Leon hotel at St. Augustine and furnished it to rival the Alhambra palace of Granada. To transport the hotel's guests, Flagler arranged with George Pullman to build the electrically-lit and fully-'vestibuled' *Florida Special*.

The first run left Jersey City in the January of 1888 with seventy passengers, including George Pullman, aboard. A reporter noted that the conductor and his crew 'resembled Prussian officers, so gaudy and gorgeous were their uniforms'. During the night, as the train sped south between Richmond and Charleston, bonfires were lighted by the hundreds of onlookers who cheered its passing, and the Jacksonville *Times-Union* reported that the 'pioneer trip was made exactly on time. A large assemblage had gathered at the [Florida] station to welcome "The Aristocrat of Winter Trains" from the winterbound north'.

Just three years after the first run of the *Florida Special*, the Richmond & Danville railway system commenced operation of the *Washington and Southwestern Vestibuled Limited* between the federal capital and Atlanta, Georgia: passengers naturally soon shortened this jaw-breaking title to the 'R & D Limited' or the 'Vestibule', and also spent considerable time simply walking from car to car admiring the safe new bellows-connections of the all-Pullman train. More than thirty years later this express was to have a distinguished successor, when in 1925 the Southern railway, in conjunction with the West Point route, the Louisville & Nashville and the Pennsylvania, established the *Crescent Limited* which extended the route of the former 'Vestibule' southward to New Orleans and northward to New York City.

The new train was named in honour of the 'crescent city' of New Orleans. Five sets of *de luxe* cars and locomotives were required to 'fill the line', and a five-dollar supplement was charged for the facilities and the services of the crew of twenty-six who were assigned to each ten-car section. Furthermore, the Southern railway's class Ps-4 Pacific locomotives constructed by the American Locomotive company to haul this train were, with their 73 in driving

An express on the New York, New Haven and Hartford railroad being hauled by a Grant locomotive. The picture was taken about 1890 by a pioneer of railroad photography, A.F. Bishop of New Haven.

wheels and their stunning Virginia-green and gold livery, among the most beautiful engines ever built in the United States. All-in-all, the *Crescent Limited* was one of the handsomest assemblages of steam and steel ever to run on American metals.

Returning to the 'Vestibule', however, this was not for long without competition; for soon after its introduction the association of railroads which formed the 'Seaboard Air-line' responded with its *Atlanta and Washington Special*, known locally as the 'Cyclone'. This operated over the Richmond, Fredericksburg & Potomac railroad, and connected at Washington with the Pennsylvania's *Congressional Limited* for New York.

The operating relationship formed by the association of the Seaboard, the RF & P and the 'Pennsy' developed into one of the best-known passenger routes in America. Over this, for example, travelled the *Seaboard Florida Limited* — 'a train of quality for people of quality' — established during the winter season of 1903 as a competitor of the *Florida Special*. But south of Palm Beach the through Pullmans from the rival trains were hauled jointly by the Florida East Coast railway to central and south Florida.

Nor was that the end of the line; for in January 1912 an island-hopping extension of the Flagler system was completed to Key West, where travellers bound for Cuba could transfer to steamers for the ninety mile journey to Havana. But — alas — the 'overseas railway' was so damaged by a hurricane in 1935 that it had to be abandoned. It was rebuilt as a highway in 1938.

During the prosperous years of the Florida boom of the 1920s the Seaboard Air-line also created the luxurious all-Pullman *Orange Blossom Special* — and launched it to the accompaniment of such stunts as bathing beauties spraying the stock with orange-blossom perfume. Rather more permanently, the train's crew was outfitted in special uniforms with the name of the express embroidered in orange silk. But the 'Special' was discontinued in 1953; and fourteen years later those once-great rivals, the Seaboard and Atlantic Coast lines, were merged to form the 'Seaboard Coast Line' railroad. After that date the *Florida Special* survived as the premier train to the south.

Yet for many the true romance of the railroads of the US is embodied in their drive westward — a movement whose springboard was Chicago, soon to become the greatest railway centre in the world. From there to New York there were by the turn of the century no fewer than eighteen competing routes; but few would challenge the statement that the most famous train on them was to be the *20th Century Limited* — a name so magnificent, the *New York Evening Post* suggested, that it should never appear other than in capital letters. From 1902 onwards this worked a 980 (later reduced to 961) mile route mainly over the tracks of its owning company, the New York Central.

Further description of this great train must be delayed for a few pages, however, for the 'Century' was only the latest in a series of flyers whose history had begun some years earlier. It was conceived by the bewhiskered George H. Daniels, a former patent-

A warning from the prohibition era which speaks for itself.

Giant Alco-GE 6,000 hp 100 mph diesels haul a highly-coloured express for Santa Fe and Los Angeles out of Chicago in 1949.

medicine salesman who acted as general passenger agent for the NYC from 1889 to 1907 and who had a flair for drama. Daniels, for instance, was the inaugurator of the 'red cap' porter system, and he also persuaded the Government to feature another of his trains, the record-breaking *Empire State Express*, on its two-cent postage stamp of 1901. In 1898 this latter flyer was covering the 440 miles between New York and Buffalo in 8¼ hours — an average of over 53 mph, or rather better than the best that contemporary Britain had to offer on the London–Edinburgh lines, though the NYC had itself run a mile-a-minute special on the same route seven years earlier.

In this territory too there was naturally rivalry, with the NYC being fiercely fought by the Pennsylvania railroad whose own flagship, entering service in 1887, was the *Pennsylvania Limited*. With the benefit of a shorter (909 miles) if steeper route between New York and the 'windy city', this was in the earliest years of the present century running to a twenty-hour schedule. The competition between the two systems was even such that, whilst the 'Pennsy' used George Pullman's cars, the NYC favoured those of his rival Webster Wagner.

In due course the *Pennsylvania Limited* was to be succeeded by a still more famous train, the *Broadway Limited* with its 'K4' Pacifics, its Tuscan-red stock and — in the age of the streamliners — its 'master rooms' which were virtually mobile apartments with their armchairs and private bathrooms: perhaps it is worth noting here that the allusion to the 'great white way' in the title of the latter express was a secondary one and that the main reference of 'broadway' was to the fact that the Pennsy's tracks were quadrupled and even sextupled for close on a thousand miles. But the *Pennsylvania Limited* retained the historic distinction of being, before the *Florida Special* or Britain's west-coast 'Corridor', the first train in the world to be equipped throughout with Pullman's newly-patented improved 'vestibules' — the flexible bellows or concertina connections which allowed passengers safe if swaying access to the whole train.

In the nineteenth century the NYC group had some other fine expresses working various routes between New York and Chicago. For instance, during 1893 — the year of the World Columbian exposition — George Daniels inaugurated the Wagner-car *Exposition Flyer* which ran on a twenty-hour schedule *via* the 'Lake Shore' route. A companion train operated by way of the Michigan Central route through Canada between Buffalo and Detroit, and was described poetically (if with some historical liberties) in a contemporary brochure as follows:

'Victoria, Empress and Queen, was the first European sovereign to have a private royal train, and the old one, in use for many years, has recently been replaced by one of modern construction. Her imperial grandson of Germany has also recently had completed for him a train of sumptuous equipment. These are the modern equivalents of the famous post-chaise of Napoleon, in which he read and wrote, dictated to his secretaries, ate and slept, while posting to his capital or to his distant armies. They represent the

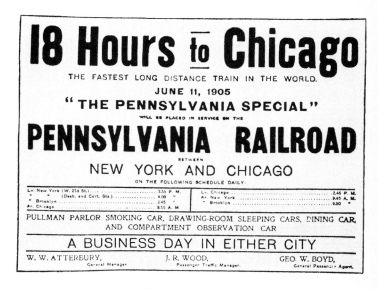

An advertisement of 1905 reflecting the rivalry between the Pennsylvania and New York Central lines for the passenger traffic between New York and Chicago; below, an earlier rivalry of 1870.

A Pennsylvania railroad limited of the 'Fleet of Modernism' in 1941.

Mixed traction heads a 'Royal Blue' line express — for as early as 1895 electrification was introduced to improve ventilation in the 3½ mile Baltimore tunnel.

The all-Pullman *Florida Special* hauled by a massive 4–8–2 of the Florida East Coast railroad, seen in typical Florida scenery in 1925.

marvellous progress made in mechanical science and decorative art in but little more than three-quarters of a century.

'America, however, is in this respect, as in many others, no whit behind the older nations of Europe, and the uncrowned kings of the exchange, the princes of trade and the stately empress-queens and dainty princesses of American society are satisfied with nothing less fine or perfect for their accommodation. All the resources of the skill for which our American mechanics are noted, guided by highly trained artistic sense, and supported by unlimited expenditure are fully drawn upon to produce the magnificent result of THE NORTH SHORE LIMITED.'

In 1897 Daniels established his twenty-hour service on a daily basis with another all-Wagner train, the *Lake Shore Limited*, each of whose three rakes comprised seven of the most sumptuous cars ever built for public service. The entire train sparkled in its light olive lined with gold; and this inevitably provoked a rejoinder, so that two months later the Pennsylvania company inaugurated one of the most colourful trains ever operated in the United States — the *New Pennsylvania Limited*, resplendent in a Brewster-green and cream livery and trimmed with so much gold leaf that the irreverent referred to it as the 'Yellow Kid'.

The NYC's reply, made four years later, was at last the afore-mentioned *20th Century Limited*. But on the same day in 1902 as this entered service the rival countered with its *Pennsylvania Special*. Like the railway races from London to Scotland, the NYC *versus* Pennsy war was reported throughout the newspaper world — though it should be noted that there was at first no attempt at clipping speeds and the battle was rather to keep to 45 or 50 mph schedules over indifferent tracks. (Similarly, the Scottish flyers were stripped down to the point of discomfort; but their transatlantic equivalents, where each sleeping car weighed almost as much as a whole British express, were so luxuriously appointed that a typical train carried fewer than fifty passengers.) Crowds gathered at the terminals at both ends of the line to witness the departures of the rival limiteds, and an English journal loftily commented:

'Surely it is only an experiment. There are over 900 miles between the two American cities. Can so high a rate of speed as will be necessary to accomplish the feat be maintained daily without injury to the engine, the rails, and the coaches? The operators will soon find that they are wasting fortunes in keeping their property in condition and then, loving money better than notoriety, the 20-hour project will be abandoned.'

The first 'Century' of 1902 was composed of both Pullman- and railroad-owned cars. The diners were 'attractively finished in Santiago mahogany ... all linen, silverware, and crockery were manufactured to order'. The buffet was equipped with club facil-ities which included a barber's shop, a bath and a smoking room. Similar equipment was to be found on the Pennsylvania trains.

When the 'Pennsy' reduced its running time to 18 hours in 1905 a speed war at last flared up and the English journalist was proved very wrong. The *Pennsylvania Special* was then soon advertised as 'the fastest long-distance train in the world' — and this was despite an early set-back, for on its maiden trip westbound the 'Special' had developed a hot box and lost valuable time. After entering the system's western division 26 minutes behind schedule the engineer, piloting a borrowed freight locomotive, is reported to have covered more than 131 miles in 115 minutes and to have speeded over a three-mile stretch at above 127 mph. Needless to say these figures (like that of Britain's contemporary 'City of Truro' with its mere 102 mph) have been challenged by many experts, and certainly the second claim seems wholly incredible. But undoubtedly some very fine performances were put up.

For many years the rivalry of these two great lines continued, with every improvement on one being matched by the other. In 1912, for instance, the 'Century' too was advertised as 'the fastest long-distance train in the world: 960 miles in 18 hours', and its new amenities included fresh and salt water baths, manicure service and a stenographer. As has been noted, trains on both lines now entered New York City by way of tunnels running into the newly-completed Pennsylvania and Grand Central stations.

The 'Century' became an important source of revenue for the NYC, for in 1926 its gross earnings were around ten million dollars. A fleet of 122 cars and 24 American Locomotive company 'Hudsons' was assigned exclusively to a service which almost daily operated in two or three sections, all hurtling across the countryside only minutes apart; and on 7 January, 1929, (ironically, in connection with the annual automobile show), 7 almost-identical 'Centuries' carried 322 revenue-paying passengers eastward from Chicago. It was reported that each morning the president of the NYC was handed a statement showing the arrival times of the 'Centuries' and the numbers of passengers each carried.

By 1940, after the NYC had added the *Commodore Vanderbilt* to its fleet and the Pennsy the *General*, the number of competing routes between New York and Chicago had been reduced to seven. But the two major companies still offered the fastest timings — now a mere 16 hours, equivalent to exactly a mile a minute over the NYC route.

Chicago and other cities of the mid-West were also well linked directly to Washington, with services operated by the Baltimore & Ohio and the Chesapeake & Ohio companies — both long-established and prestigious concerns (though, after 1962, amalgamated), and each in fairly recent years the operator of a crack express. The pride of the B&O was the *Capitol Limited*, inaugurated in 1923 in response to appeals from Chicago businessmen for a first-rate train to the national capital. The *George Washington* of the C&O (inevitably referred to as the 'George') was nine years younger and was largely created to serve Cincinnati. Its title celebrated the 200th anniversary of one who was not only the first American president but also a father of transportation in America — for Washington, when a practising surveyor, was responsible for an extensive network of roads, canals and trails in the eastern states. 'Capitol' and 'George' alike featured cars decorated in the

The *George Washington* carried an illuminated portrait of the train's namesake as its 'drumhead'. The express is here seen standing at White Sulphur Springs, West Virginia.

motifs of colonial America: both were hauled by Pacific locomotives which earned reputations for their beauty; and both included some of the first mechanically air-cooled cars ever produced. Their diners, which served colonial dishes in the atmosphere of early American taverns, were equally appreciated.

Renowned as they were, all such trains were outstripped in glamour by those which apparently spanned the continent. Strangely enough, though, there were never any regular coast-to-coast workings in the USA and the term 'transcontinental train' usually describes an express operating between the west coast and an inland city such as Chicago where a connection to the east will be waiting — though it can also be applied to a special or to a few through-*cars* transferred from one system to another on the model of the modern 'Orient' rather than of the 'Trans-Siberian Express'.

As earlier pages of this book mention, the first line to be built across the western wilderness and the mountains was the classic 'overland route' to California completed in 1869. The news of the joining of the Union Pacific and Central Pacific railroads was then flashed across the United States by telegraph (with, in some cases, special wires being laid to church belfries so that the celebratory ringers should lose no time), and soon brightly-painted steam engines and passenger cars had replaced the legendary pony expresses and stage-coaches of the early West. Only a little later trains including George Pullman's elegant cars brought civilisation to the wild country between the Missouri and the Golden Gate.

The first of the so-called transcontinental trains operated between Omaha and Oakland, opposite San Francisco: it took more than five days for the 1,775 mile trip, equivalent to an average of less than 14 miles an hour and little improvement on the best performances of horseback days. Seventy years later (and leaping over almost as many developments), the *City of San Francisco* ran all the way from Chicago over generally the same route, covering 2,261 miles in 39¾ hours at some 57 mph. The *City of San Francisco* and its companion 'City' trains to Los Angeles, Denver and Portland were luxurious yellow streamliners which contained every possible amenity including registered nurses. Operated by the Chicago & North Western, the Union Pacific and the Southern Pacific companies, they were completed in the decade prior to the Second World War and were among the last custom-designed trains produced in America before the imposition of controls. The precursor of this fleet had been the Union Pacific's first lightweight streamliner, which commenced service in 1935: originally known simply as M10,000 but later as the *City of Salina*, this was a then-revolutionary high-speed train composed of three aluminium cars powered by a 600 hp diesel engine. The first of all America's streamliners, it may be noted here, was the stainless steel *Pioneer Zephyr* which had entered service a few months earlier.

Far south of the overland route ran America's second-oldest transcontinental railway, the 'sunset route' operated by the Southern Pacific for just under 2,500 miles from New Orleans through the arid deserts of the South-west to San Francisco. The crack train

The *20th Century Limited* in 1909, seen in Indiana with a 'Pacific' locomotive heading seven wooden-bodied Pullman cars.

175

The *Broadway Limited* in 1938, drawn by a 'K–4' which has been subjected to streamlined treatment, hauling a consist of early, lightweight, metal-bodied Pullman cars.

This photograph, taken around 1935, records a brief but memorable period in American railroad history when the *Broadway Limited* (left) and the *20th Century Limited* (right) left Chicago simultaneously and, for a few miles, could race side by side towards New York.

on this was for many years the *Sunset Limited*, put in service in 1894 on a once-a-week schedule: the original running time, advertised as 'the shortest possible limit consistent with safety', was 75 hours, equivalent to 33 mph. The original *Sunset* was like an ocean steamship on wheels with sumptuous Pullman cars finished in costly woods and fabrics and equipped with a library and a bathroom. The dining car, named 'Epicure', featured 'viands peculiar to the lands and climate traversed' such as oysters, shrimps and corn cakes prepared by southern cooks. The *Sunset* proved so popular that it was soon running twice and then three times a week, until it became a daily service in 1913.

Yet another great line was the Northern Pacific, running 2,000 miles from St. Paul to Seattle along a northern tier of territories which were not even states in the age of its construction. After the northern territories achieved statehood, however, the company decided to inaugurate its own luxury express, and so in 1900 the *North Coast Limited* was created. Each of the eight sets of this, headed by a ten-wheeled locomotive, included a dynamo-baggage car equipped with an electric lighting plant which was accompanied by an electrician who tended the 300 lamp bulbs. Another innovation to be enjoyed during the 62 ½-hour trip was the observation-lounge car, one of the first of its type to be devoted exclusively to scenic purposes. On the rear of this was a platform surrounded by a brass railing to which was attached the electrically-illuminated crest of the Northern Pacific. Such ornamental signs, known as 'drumheads', later became so common in the United States and Canada that for many years no self-respecting train appeared without one.

Few railroad names, though, have such romantic overtones as that of the Atchison, Topeka & Santa Fe, which was built through the rugged and lawless country along the old Santa Fe trail. Its line stretched from Dodge City in Kansas, over the Raton Pass, and across the deserts of Arizona and New Mexico to reach Los Angeles in 1887.

The Sante Fe was later best known for its *Chief* and *Super Chief*, but for a brief moment in history the railroad scheduled one of the most elegant trains in the world — the *Santa Fe de Luxe*, a winter-season train for California with a capacity limited to sixty passengers. This ran from 1911 until 1918, and was one of the first supplementary-fare trains in America. The finest sleeping and club cars produced by Pullman were assigned to it, and the dining car operated by restaurateur Fred Harvey was provided with an 'air-cooling and air-washing device' which was of special interest during the desert crossing. Despite the enviable reputation earned by the *Chief* and *Super Chief* of later days, the AT & SF was never again to boast a train of the calibre of the 'de Luxe'.

Perhaps less renowned was the Great Northern railway, running high through the Cascade mountains of the Pacific North-west. The year 1905 was especially significant in the history of this line, for it was then that the dream of its 'empire builder' founder Jim Hill — the dream of travelling to the orient aboard a Great

A Union Pacific employee's timetable issued in 1867, two years before the driving of a spike at Promontary Point made possible a public transcontinental service.

Delightful both in itself and in its decorations is this 4–4–0 which drew the inaugural cars of the Northern Pacific line to the ceremony at Gold Creek, Montana, in 1883.

UNION PACIFIC RAILROAD--PLATTE DIVISION!

Time Schedule No. 1, for Construction Works.

Trains leave North Platte and Ogallalla daily, Sundays excepted
To take effect *Thursday June 6th* 1867.

BOUND WEST.			NAMES OF STATIONS.	BOUND EAST.		
NO. 1.	NO. 8.	DIST.		DIST.	NO. 2.	NO. 4.
8.00 *A. M.*	7.00 *P. M.*		*North Platte,* - -	50.30	4.00 *P. M.*	3.30 *A. M.*
9.24 do	8.24 do	16.90	*O'Fallons,* - - -	33.40	3.00 do	2.09 do
10.31 do	9.31 do	31.20	*Alkali,* - - - - -	19.10	2.08 do	1.00 do
12.00 *M.*	11.00 do	50.30	*Ogallalla,* - - - -		1.00 do	11.30 *P. M.*

A double-headed Union Pacific express with open-vestibule cars poses on the Dale Creek Bridge west of Cheyenne, Wyoming, in 1876. Note the two men perched in the truss near the centre.

The *Oriental Limited* follows the north shore of Puget Sound near Seattle, Washington.

Four lounge cars were built in 1929 for the
Rock Island line's *Rocky Mountain Limited* which ran between
Chicago and Denver.

The Union Pacific's 'Little Nugget' saloon was built for
the 1937 *City of San Francisco*. The decor represented the interior of
an old-time Western music hall.

Top, left: Part of the car 'Cassius' which served as an all-male club on the 1898 *Pennsylvania Limited*. In addition to the lounge, there was a barber's shop and a bathroom.

Above: The 1920s were the age of the dancing-car.

Above, right: The first-class Pullman sleeping car 'Reinz', built in 1885, was furnished with intricate marquetry on the upper berth fronts, polished brass oil lamps, and specially-imported fabrics.

Below, right: The amenities of this observation/lounge car built in 1926 for the *North Coast Limited* included a radio, a telephone (right) for use in terminals, and a lady's maid.

Marshall Foch observed the Pacific North-west from the rear platform of the *Olympian* shortly after the First World War.

An advertisement of 1911 for the *Santa Fe de luxe* express which made no secret of the fact that this was a service for the rich.

Northern train-and-steamship combination — was realised as the 20,000-ton ss 'Minnesota' embarked on her maiden voyage. Later that year the Great Northern placed its transcontinental train, the *Oriental Limited*, in service from St. Paul to Seattle; and four years later still, in honour of the Seattle World's Fair, the 'Oriental' became a Chicago–Seattle train. Unlike most other railroads in the United States at the time, the Great Northern operated its own sleeping cars.

It is interesting to contemplate the extent and scope of the *Oriental Limited*'s transcontinental service. At the same moment as one 'Oriental' departed the Union station in Chicago a second was speeding westward across North Dakota, a third was winding through the Rockies of Montana at Glacier national park, and a fourth completing its westward run at Tacoma. Meanwhile a fifth, eastward bound, was climbing into the Cascade mountains in the state of Washington, a sixth in the foothills of the Rockies, a seventh entering the Dakota side of the Red River valley, and the eighth lately arrived at Chicago. Each of these trains was identical in equipment and provision; and each would make a 5,000-mile round trip to form part of a daily service.

The last-built of all the transcontinental lines in the northern USA was the Chicago Milwaukee & St. Paul of 1909, which in the brief period between that year and the opening of the Panama Canal was one of the most prosperous railroads in America. Here the first expresses offering a *de luxe* service over the 2,200 miles between Chicago and Seattle and Tacoma began in 1911. The premier train was *The Olympian*, covering the journey in three days and advertised as 'Fit for the gods'.

Together with its sister, the *Columbian*, this was one of the few expresses to operate from Chicago to the west coast over one company's tracks, the only other such running over the Santa Fe route. It included the by-now-commonplace barber's shop, bathroom and library, and tea was served free of charge to ladies every afternoon. The St. Paul company (which also operated the *Pioneer Limited*, whose 83 ft long diner amazed a visiting British journalist) proudly announced that the train was entirely owned and worked by the railroad, and for years a feature was made of its 'longer-higher-wider' sleeping berths. In an era when most companies painted their passenger cars a standard Pullman green, this road used a bright yellow-orange trimmed with maroon and gold. An abundant supply of water power in the Rocky mountains and the Cascade ranges persuaded the company to electrify 656 miles of its main line between 1915 and 1927.

As the number of transcontinental lines had increased, so had competition, and hence the railroads sought every way of proving theirs to be the premier route. The long-established Union Pacific, for example, found an unusual claim on the grounds of public health: insurance companies, it pointed out, did not ask for an extra premium for travellers over its metals (as they appeared to do for those daring the deserts of the Santa Fe or the sub-Arctic wastes of the Northern Pacific), since the UP tracks lay 'within

'As the Centuries Pass in the Night' — a painting made for the New York Central line's calendar of 1924 showing the east- and west-bound *20th Century Limiteds* passing each other.

Overleaf: The *Overland Limited* which was in its time the fastest and perhaps the most luxurious train between Chicago and San Francisco, hauled by an 'Atlantic' locomotive.

the health limits between Omaha and Kansas City and San Francisco'. But since in later years it was speed which counted, this may be an appropriate place to recall a famous railway race of the 1930s.

During 1934 and 1935 three rivals for the important traffic between Chicago and the twin cities of Minneapolis and St. Paul all provided new trains which reduced the 400 mile journey to around 400 minutes. These three beauties were the *400*, the *Zephyr* and the *Hiawatha*, and for a time the situation again recalled that of Britain's east *versus* west coast rivalry. The Chicago & North Western's *400* was a steam-hauled train of conventional steel cars operated at speeds approaching 100 mph over some stretches. For the Chicago, Burlington & Quincy company — the 'Burlington route' — the Budd company built 'Twin Zephyrs', diesel-electric units resembling the *Pioneer Zephyr* previously mentioned. Finally, the *Hiawatha* of the Chicago, Milwaukee, St. Paul & Pacific — the last of the trio to enter service — was a steam-hauled, streamlined train liveried in orange, maroon and silver.

To take one comparison from performances put up in 1940–41, the eastbound *Hiawatha*, hauled by a 4–6–4 locomotive, had its time over the 78 miles from Sparta to Portage cut to 58 minutes, an average of 81 mph entailing sustained speeds of 100 mph since the route included a short single-track section near Tunnel City and some fairly difficult gradients. And at the same time the *Zephyr*'s schedule was reduced to 43 minutes over one 58 mile section, an average of over 80 mph supplementing an existing average over another 55 mile section of 84 mph.

To return to the sunset of the great age of American railroad construction, the last of all the transcontinental links was the Western Pacific, which was completed between Oakland and Salt Lake City in 1910 as the part-fulfilment of an ambition of financier Jay Gould and his son to control their own line from coast to coast. In 1915 this carried the *Scenic Limited* (a name revived from earlier years and later changed to *Royal George*) which was provided for those visiting the Panama-Pacific Exposition at San Francisco. The Western Pacific passed through some of the finest scenery in North America — a feature which keeps the Denver and Rio Grande western section alive today — and used a route pioneered on the narrow gauge. Tourist trains were manifold, and included the *Exposition Flyer* (inaugurated for the San Francisco Golden Gate Exposition of 1939) and its streamlined successor, the 1949 diesel-hauled *California Zephyr* whose stock cost over ten million dollars and included (to provide a facility no airline could rival) the first transcontinental 'vista-dome' cars in the United States. The scenery of the Rio Grande country was indeed so magnificent as to justify christening another such train as simply the *Panoramic*.

But north of the 49th parallel there are to be found lines which equal (and, some would say, surpass) in splendour the finest that the United States can offer. The first of these — which was also the continent's third true coast-to-coast route — was the Canadian Pacific, whose inaugural public service ran on 28 June, 1886. At

The *Columbian*, working over one of America's first trunk routes to be electrified, in the Bitter Root mountains of Idaho in the 1920s.

An observation car was attached to the *Olympian* for its spectacular run through the Rockies. This shows the train in 1939. Electrification had been extended to such stretches as that through the Montana canyon.

'On Time' was the title of the Pennsylvania railroad's portrait of the *Broadway Limited* as painted for the 1932 calendar.

The heroic age, as epitomized by an express of the Denver & Rio Grande system beating up the grade towards Soldier Summit, Utah, in 1911, with four heading locomotives and a banker.

2000 h. that day, amid the usual deafening cheers and booming cannon, a twelve-car train which included the dining car 'Holyrood', with its 3,000 dollars' worth of silverware slowly departed from the old Dalhousie Square station in Montreal. Two sleeping cars (named 'Yokohama' and 'Honolulu' for the cities on the Pacific 3,000 miles away), each containing a real bathroom with tub, were also included in the rake. Six days later, the CPR transcontinental arrived at Port Moody, British Columbia. The event was described by the Montreal *Gazette* as being 'second in importance only to Confederation'.

From its inception in 1880 by a dedicated group of Canadian and British railwaymen and bankers, the Canadian Pacific soon grew to become one of the world's great transport undertakings, complete with hotels, steamships, telegraph and express agencies and an airline as well as railways: a traveller could indeed almost span the world without leaving the aegis of comfort and security provided by this unique system. One of its first luxury expresses was the *Imperial Limited*. Inaugurated in 1899 as (then) 'the only transcontinental train run under one management', this departed daily from Montreal for Vancouver and covered 2,900 miles in 100 hours. The equipment for the 'Imperial' (whose engines were changed 21 times during the run) consisted of luxurious cars with interiors of a Louix XV style finished in ivory and gold. The exteriors were constructed of Honduras mahogany, varnished to the well-known CPR standard to form a red train of great beauty.

The special observation cars added to enable passengers to view the magnificence of the Canadian Rockies were, however, rather more primitive, being essentially open and low-sided freight wagons fitted with benches: early models lacked even a roof. A later CPR version which was equipped with a cupola, though, has been reported as the first example of dome-car design in North America; and yet another unusual passenger carriage developed on the CPR and used on its *Imperial Limited* was the colonist car, a sparsely-furnished sleeper similar to what was known in the United States as an immigrant car. Minimal sleeping and cooking accommodation — but no bedding — was furnished to settlers from Europe *en route* to their new homes.

The CPR participated in several joint operations with American railroads in providing well-equipped international services running southward from Montreal and Halifax to Boston and New York and westward from Montreal to Minneapolis and St. Paul, whilst another CPR international line was operated from Montreal and Toronto to Detroit and Chicago. On its own metals the company inaugurated in 1919 the all-sleeping-car *Trans-Canada Limited*, a Montreal/Vancouver train receiving connecting cars from Toronto. New Canadian-built locomotives were assigned to the 1929 edition of this express and its twelve complete sets — ten of which were in motion at any one time — were proudly described by the Vancouver *Star* as 'entirely of Canadian construction, having been built to Canadian designs, by Canadian artificers and of Canadian materials'. Today the *Canadian*, which at its inaugura-

tion twenty years ago could claim to be the world's finest train, follows the same route.

The second Canadian transcontinental line — the Canadian National, which also operated such border-crossing expresses as the *International Limited* — was neither conceived nor built as one system. It was the result of a union (brought about in 1919, when the railways were suffering from economic set-backs) of six major networks, some privately-sponsored and some government-owned. There are analogies here to Britain's 1923 'amalgamations', though the Canadian outcome was a fully-nationalised system running in competition with a private one.

The premier train of the CNR was the *Continental Limited*, trains Nos. 1 and 2 of which commenced operation in 1920. The run of about 2,900 miles from Montreal to Vancouver (achieved, eastbound, in just over 108 hours as against the 75 hours of today's *Super-Continental* which also offers nightly sessions of 'bingo') was by way of the metals of five former companies, and culminated in a journey through some of the most breath-taking mountain scenery in the world. One experiment made by the *Continental Limited* was to have an unexpected outcome after 1924, when the CNR introduced radio *en route*; for to provide this entertainment eleven broadcasting stations had to be operated across Canada by the company. This network soon afterwards provided the basis for the government-operated Canadian Broadcasting Corporation.

Canada had other notable trains — for instance, those running between Montreal and Nova Scotia or southward from the latter such as the *Gull*. But now it is time to return from Vancouver to the United States, where the west coast can show such distinguished expresses of its own as the Seattle/San Francisco *Shasta*. The most famous trains here followed the eighteenth century *camino real* of the Franciscan fathers between Los Angeles and San Francisco, and ran over the 470 mile main line of the Southern Pacific railroad — which was known to itself as the 'friendly line' and to everyone else as the 'Espee'. This company early operated the *Lark*, an all-Pullman overnight favourite of businessmen and cinema stars, and its companion *Daylight Limited*. The latter allowed passengers between 'SF' and 'LA' to enjoy the dramatic coastal scenery, especially over the 113 miles along the very edge of the Pacific near Santa Barbara.

Both trains endured into the age of streamlining, when they were powered by magnificent 'Golden Gate' 4–8–4 locomotives in orange, red, black and silver. The *Lark* of 1941 was the West's first train with private-room accommodation and also included an articulated, triple-unit club-lounge set more than 200 feet long, whilst for its daytime counterpart the carriage stock as well as the lcomotives was painted in that striking livery. The Southern Pacific at first advertised the 'Daylights' as 'The most beautiful trains in the West', but later expanded this modest claim to read, 'The world's most beautiful trains'.

Two other great (and early) axes of American railroading remain to be mentioned — that between Chicago, St. Louis and

The *Empire Builder* of the Burlington Northern line shown threading through the Rocky Mountains at Marias Pass, Montana, in 1967.

191

Overleaf: A special train for HRH Prince Henry of Prussia, which ran as a section of the *Pioneer Limited*, seen by night in Milwaukee station in 1902, illuminated by the locomotive headlights.

The Canadian Pacific's glistening *Trans-Canada Limited* leaving Montreal for Vancouver in 1925.

In 1910, open observation cars were a feature of runs through the Rockies.

The long consist of the Canadian National railway's *Super Continental* at Windy Point, near Jasper, Alberta, in 1964.

New Orleans, and that which linked St. Louis to the oil towns of Texas and Oklahoma before crossing the Rio Grande into Mexico. St. Louis was the main departure point for luxury train travel to Mexico City by Laredo and El Paso, and over the 'main line of mid-America' between Chicago and New Orleans ran the *Panama Limited* of the Illinois Central system, with connecting Pullmans from St. Louis onwards. This train had received its name in 1911 to commemorate the canal then being built, and was re-equipped in 1916 as an all-Pullman express scheduled to cover the 921 miles from the Great Lakes to New Orleans in 23 hours at over 40 mph. Throughout its territory it became almost a legend: for instance, at Vaiden the chancellor of the Sixth Mississippi district would recess his court for five minutes every day so that everyone could watch the train pass through the town, a ritual which he maintained for twelve years. The dining car of the 'Panama' was justly famous for its cuisine: a typical menu offered twenty-three entrees.

South-west from St. Louis too rolled the crack *Texas Special*, operated jointly by the St. Louis–San Francisco railway ('the Frisco') and the Missouri–Kansas–Texas railroad ('the Katy'). In the early years of railroading on America's last frontier these two systems had been serious rivals; but from 1915 they began an era of co-operation which included the joint working of their premier train over 'Frisco' tracks to Vinita, Oklahoma, where it transferred to 'Katy' metals for Dallas, Forth Worth and San Antonio. On this train too the menus of the air-conditioned dining cars offered the tempting cuisine of the South-west. So popular was the route that during the depression of the early 1930s the only new passenger equipment built anywhere in the United States was that constructed to serve the premier trains of the 'Frisco' and the 'Katy'.

Finally, sharing the business from St. Louis to the South-west with this combine was the great Missouri Pacific system whose flagship, the *Sunshine Special*, entered service in 1915. This international train carried through sleeping cars from St. Louis and Memphis, Tennessee, southward and westward to the principal cities of Texas and onward to Mexico City over the National Railways of Mexico, or to California over the Southern Pacific. Special lounges and dining cars in Spanish design — complete with soda fountains — operated through to dry Mexico City.

In addition, from June 1937 until December 1940, the Missouri Pacific and the National Railway of Mexico offered weekly a luxury tourist train named the *City of Mexico*. Only first-class Pullman accommodation was available in the cars which departed from St. Louis every Sunday evening and arrived in Mexico City the following Tuesday evening, some of the most elegant stock in the Pullman fleet being assigned to this service. It also had a flavour of the boat train, for until international air travel became fully established the expresses between the USA and Mexico helped provide the fastest route between Mexico City and Europe *via* New York and the transatlantic liners.

In Mexico itself railroading dates from the 1880s, when developers were invited in from the United States and Great Britain by

The *City of Mexico* was a *de luxe* express, aimed at the tourist market, which ran in the inter-war years on a once-a-week schedule.

A Mexico City — Vera Cruz daylight express of the Mexicano railway pauses in Maltrata station in 1925.

Bilingual menu from the 1931 *Sunshine Special*.

that railway enthusiast, President Porfirio Diaz. Three major rail routes from the border to Mexico City were built with Mexican and American funds, whilst a fourth line, constructed with English backing, connected the capital with the port of Vera Cruz. Sleeping and dining cars were at varying times operated over all these routes by the Pullman company or the railroads themselves. Several of the lines, being built to the 3 ft 6 in gauge, operated scaled-down Pullmans like those of the Colorado narrow-gauge.

In the early years of the present century the railways operating near the US/Mexico border began to experience economic set-backs; and though a large degree of nationalisation was resorted to, it was not until the 1950s that a major improvement of the Mexican railway system took place. But then trains were re-equipped with new passenger cars purchased in Switzerland or the United States and with modern diesel locomotives. Furthermore, as railways in the United States discontinued many of their passenger services during the 1950s and 1960s, the National Railways of Mexico were able to make bargain purchases of luxurious, nearly-new rolling stock for assignment to a growing number of excellent passenger trains such as *El Regiomontano* from Mexico City to Monterrey, *El Fronterizo* from Mexico City to Ciudad Juarez, the *Aguila Azteca* from Mexico City to Nuevo Laredo, *El Tapatio* (named after the dáncing girls of Guadalajara) from Mexico City to Guadalajara, and *El Jarocho* (a native of Vera Cruz) from Mexico City to Vera Cruz.

Meanwhile, though, direct passenger rail links between the USA and her southern neighbour were being reduced almost to vanishing point; for already hints have appeared in this chapter of the blight which increasingly affected the railroads of the United States in the 1950s, 60s and 70s. It was not merely that — as in Europe — branch-lines were condemned as uneconomic: in North America great trunk routes were reduced to a skeletal service and year after year familiar and glamorous names disappeared from the *Official Guide*. To cite just one statistic, more than 75 per cent of all public-carrier passenger traffic was by rail in 1930; but before 1970 the figure had declined to little over 7 per cent, and most of this represented suburban journeys.

There were three main reasons behind this catastrophic collapse — the over-commitment of American society to the automobile and the aircraft, a belief in private enterprise so rugged that, for decades after the United States had become the only major country in the world whose railroad system was still basically competitive, any form of state aid (and hence control) was rejected even by once-great companies now on the edge of bankruptcy, which would not have existed but for subsidies in the era of their construction, and finally soaring operating costs. To examine these problems further would be to exceed the confines of this book: it is perhaps enough to say that in the late 1960s the future of American railroading, outside of freight and perhaps commuter traffic, appeared dark indeed.

But — if only for environmental reasons — the US Government resolved that the passenger express should not die. After the First

The *Daylight*, pre-war pride of the Southern Pacific system, photographed near Santa Barbara, California, in 1937.

The *Empire Builder* of the Great Northern railroad, hauled by a 4–8–2 Baldwin, crosses the Stone Arch bridge over the Mississippi.

World War the great trains had certainly lost some of their glamour and individuality, and the depression too had proved a severe blow; yet from these set-backs the US railroads had emerged by their own efforts into a second golden age, following half a century after the first, of the air-conditioned, private-room streamliner.

But now more radical measures were called for; and so in 1970 Congress passed an Act which set up a National Railroad Passenger Corporation with the code-name 'Amtrak'. This was charged with providing efficient inter-city rail services within a national structure which abolished the old competitive routes, and was funded by federal grants supplementing the finance provided by the participating companies themselves. From 1 May 1971, the new body took over the management of a service which operated over 1,000 trains a week, covered 22,000 miles of track, and fed 350 cities — or virtually all those with more than 500,000 inhabitants.

Nor did 'Amtrak' neglect the glamour of the great names, for on its first birthday a refurbished *Broadway Limited* of sixteen cars in red, white and blue set off on its maiden trip to a considerable fanfare. This was followed by five other renovated trains, including the *Super Chief* for the service from Chicago to Los Angeles which worked the spectacular Santa Fe route through Kansas City and Albuquerque at an equally spectacular average of nearly 55 mph. The morale of both passengers and crews on these was boosted by attempts to return to the standards of the great days (for example, the silver finger-bowls were retained in the diners, and one journalist remarked that the corridor of the *Super Chief* was the one place in the USA where one could leave one's shoes in the expectation that they would be polished rather than stolen), with the addition of all the appurtenances of modern publicity. Thus, long-thighed girls in hot-pants, and male crew members in striped trousers, arranged flowers in the dining cars and dispensed linen table-napkins.

On a more northerly transcontinental route, 'Amtrak' introduced its own *Empire Builder* from Chicago to Seattle. A new *Florida Special*, aimed at an expanding leisure market, wooed passengers from the airlines with complimentary champagne, colour television and two cinemas; and in the West the *Coast Daylight* and *Coast Starlight* linked Los Angeles to San Francisco. Rebirth was in the air.

It may as yet be too early to assess the efficacy of this eleventh-hour acceptance of a measure of state involvement into US railroading. But it is clear that, even in the land where the road and what Lucius Beebe referred to as the 'barbarous and cheerless' medium of the air seemed on the verge of a total take-over, it has been appreciated that railways have a vital part to play in long-distance passenger work. And since the most committed of free-enterprise railway supporters would rather see subsidised expresses than no expresses at all, few will dissent from the hope that the 'Amtrak' trains — so often bearing names reaching back to the great years around the turn of the century — will roll on to a future as distinguished as their past.

An Amtrak 'Metroliner' of the US railway renaissance.

The spectacular Royal Gorge of the Arkansas river showing the *Pacific Coast Limited* of the Denver & Rio Grande railroad about 1910.

Right: Even in the 1970s, steam-power remained conspicuous and often glorious on the Indian sub-continent, as witness the *Madras-Trivandrum Express* here seen at Vilapurum.

Left: The observation car of the *Udharata Menike* or 'Highland Maid' train in Nanu-Oya, Ceylon in 1970.

Below: Perhaps the world's smallest 'serious' train to lay claim to the title of 'Express' runs on the 2 ft gauge line from Siliguri to Darjeeling. Here the *Himalaya Express* waters at Thindaria. The handrails in front of the cylinders are for the use of the men who sand the rails on the steep gradients of this famous line.

Great Trains of India

When the first railway in India opened between Bombay and Thana on 16 April, 1853, it did so amidst 'the loud applause of a vast multitude and the salute of 21 guns' in the presence of 400 distinguished guests. Admittedly the Governor of Bombay was not among these, having taken off for the cool of his summer residence in the hills; but his superior — the Governor-General, Lord Dalhousie — had considered the development of railways in the sub-continent of major importance. A commission set up by him in 1850 had recommended that a network of lines be constructed based on Bombay, Calcutta, Madras and Lahore — and, perhaps less wisely, that a gauge of 5 ft 6 in be used for this. Certainly the latter decision (which perhaps appears less unreasonable when it is remembered that the barrier of the Himalayas cut off the sub-continent from any likely connection with other lines) was amended when in the 1860s it was realised that for feeder lines a metric — or even narrower — gauge would be appropriate.

For few countries in the world presented such hazardous conditions for railway construction as did India. Great mountain ranges, almost waterless deserts, seemingly-impenetrable jungles, rivers that could quadruple their width in a few hours and change their courses as suddenly, mosquito-ridden marshes, temperatures that ranged from oppressive heat to killing cold — all were there in India. Couple this with an almost total lack of skilled workmen and one can appreciate the difficulties that confronted the builders. But the enterprising spirits of nineteenth-century engineers were not easily deterred by such challenges.

What the builders did have in plenty was a tough, resilient labour force. The building of the railways gave employment to many thousands, and without the stoicism of these workers the lines could never have been laid. Of later importance was the fact that many Indians soon became not only skilled and adept railway builders but also railway operators; but the primary task was to get the metals down.

And so, though that first line was of a mere 21 miles, by 1880 the total mileage was in excess of 9,000 and by the turn of the century a staggering 40,000 miles. A major incentive to this rate of building was the demand of the military. In the mid-1850s progress in construction was comparatively slow, but the great mutiny of 1857 made the authorities realise just how strategically important a railway system could be. It is no exaggeration to say that, had there been a better network in 1857, the mutiny might never have taken place.

A typical progress was that of the East Indian railway, which had set out from Calcutta in 1854 and in 1866 entered Delhi,

The *Royal Mail* leaving Bombay in 1907.

1,020 miles away. Then in March, 1870, one of the most important links was opened — the Bombay/Calcutta line of 1,300 miles across much difficult and diverse terrain. The significance of this event can be judged by the fact that it was graced by the imposing presence of the (then) Duke of Edinburgh, the son of the Queen-Empress herself.

The opening also marked the beginning of an extension of the Indian system which was to continue as late as the 1920s; and the year 1870 also saw the commencement of a planned network of metre-gauge lines. The system has been criticised as it inevitably meant a trans-shipment of goods, sometimes twice and even three times in the course of one journey. But there is no doubt that many parts of India (as of Switzerland) would never have had a railway at all had the broad gauge been made mandatory throughout the country.

More relevant to this book is that the same period saw the start of the tradition of those luxurious if sometimes leisurely expresses, mainly named from their terminal cities, which with their private saloons for nabobs and maharajas typify the years of the *raj*. Right from the beginning, though, upper-class travel in India had been equal to (and in some respects in advance of) that in most parts of the world. In the 1860s, for instance, first-class double-deck coaches were introduced. The upper deck, made suitably comfortable if not luxurious, was for the well-to-do passenger, while his servants occupied the lower section — for provision for servants has always been another characteristic of Indian long-distance trains, and to some extent still exists. Thus, in 1863 the Governor of Bombay had a four-wheel double-deck luxury saloon built. On the upper floor His Excellency had his sitting-room-cum-bedroom, and next to it a dining room. Below were the servants' quarters and stores, so that the whole comprised a small but commodious house on wheels.

Even for the slightly less privileged, the high standards can be judged by quoting from two travellers of the period. First hear what Louis Rousselet, a French author, had to say in a book published in 1865. He had travelled from Calcutta to Agra and back on the East Indian, a journey that had taken about 5 ½ days. 'I travelled over this immense distance with comparatively little fatigue', he wrote, 'sleeping at night on a comfortable little bed and walking up and down in my carriage during the day. At stations provided with buffets I found a servant who, when he had taken the orders for my meal, telegraphed it to the next station where my breakfast or dinner awaited my arrival.'

Rousselet was particularly full of praise for the design of his sleeping car. 'These carriages', he wrote, 'contained only two compartments in each of which there is but a single seat, the movable back of which takes off, and being fastened by leather straps forms a sort of couch of the same description as the beds in ships' cabins. On the opposite side of the carriage are two closets — one for the toilet and the other the convenience. By paying a slight addition to the price of the ordinary fare, you might travel thus surrounded by all the comforts so essential in this country.'

This was travel of a quality not to be known in Europe for at least another decade; and a few years after this another voyager whose name is synonymous with nineteenth century travel, Thomas Cook, was writing equally enthusiastically about rail travel in India. In February, 1873, he reported: 'For my party a saloon carriage with sleeping berths, baths and closets was allotted and this we kept for three weeks, attaching and detaching it where we liked for the whole 2,300 miles... The Indian sleeping carriages are a modification of the American system and although they do not in India furnish bedding and attendance, there is no extra charge for the carriage and it was cheaper to buy stuffed bed-quilts and pillows than to pay three dollars a night for the American accommodation.'

The *Bombay–Poona Mail* of the Great Indian Peninsula railway at the height of its glory in 1908 when it was described as 'One of the finest trains in the British Empire.'

One point is of particular interest in this quotation. It is the mention of baths — which had been introduced in the 1860s, putting India far in advance of any other country including the USA. Indeed, the royal coaches of Britain had no such refinement during the opulent reign of Edward VII, and it was not until the First World War that a royal train was equipped with them. But in 1870 the Duke of Edinburgh could have had a bath.

Keeping carriages cool was always a problem, and even with modern air-conditioning (which is regarded as a supplementary luxury rather than a necessity) it is one by no means completely solved. But in the 1860s the East Indian railway had installed an ingenious device in some of its cars. Again it is the observant Louis Rousselet who reports 'The Bombay to Calcutta expresses are now accommodated with carriages with *khas* [or absorbent bolsters] in matting which are kept moist by reservoirs specially provided for the purpose. This moisture enveloping the carriage preserves the temperature at a degree of coolness sufficient almost to extinguish the risk of incurring sunstroke or apoplexy.'

Considering the advances made in so many respects it is surprising that four-wheeled coaches persisted so long on Indian railways, for it was not until the early years of the present century that bogie stock was introduced. After that, though, it became almost universal on both broad and metre-gauge lines. The first dining car on bogies made its appearance in 1903 on the Bombay to Calcutta run which connected with the luxurious P & O shipping service; and perhaps it should be mentioned here that restaurant cars in India have always had to provide two basic menus, vegetarian and non-vegetarian, to cater for religious convictions.

Though in some respects the railways of India moved ahead of those of Britain, the British were the original designers and constructors of the system of the sub-continent; and that influence was (and to a certain extent still is) a pronounced one. But the Indian railways were not just slavish copies of their counterparts and had their own characteristics. From the beginning, for example, they were operated by a mixture of private and state enterprise, with at times the distinction between the two becoming more than complicated. Certainly the Government of India always had military considerations in mind, particularly in areas like the North-west

Another of the great mail trains which crossed the Indian countryside was the *Calcutta–Bombay Mail*, here seen hauled by a 4–6–0 of the Bengal Nagpur railway in 1906 when Calcutta was still the capital of India.

frontier where the threat of Russian influence — and possible invasion — was a major factor in development. Thus by 1892 the North Western railway had pushed to the frontier with over 2,000 miles of branch lines to its credit in addition to the long trunk routes. But another of the four horsemen of the apocalypse was never far off, and in 1880 a famine commission stressed the importance of the railway and its ability to move foodstuffs rapidly from one side of the nation to the other. Alas, this usefulness was to be proven on all too many occasions in subsequent years.

Yet although the central government of India was firmly in the hands of the British administration, a large part of the sub-continent was ruled by the princes whose various (and very varied) states were almost totally autonomous. Several of these built and operated their own railway systems, of which perhaps the most outstanding — and certainly that with the grandest name — was in Hyderabad. This rejoiced in the title of 'His Exalted Highness the Nizam's Guaranteed State Railway', though it was known more simply to most as 'the Nizam's' or by its initials. Not only had it the longest name but also the longest private track, with just over 320 miles. And as Hyderabad was in the centre of India, 'the Nizam's' connected with several major networks.

From 1907 onwards all the major lines, including much metre-gauge track, were purchased by the Central Government and then leased back to the companies to operate. By 1920 about 75 per cent of India's track was thus wholly government-owned, though only 21 per cent of the services were run under Government supervision. But in 1922 the Railway Board of India was re-organised and two of the main concerns were fully nationalised. Many miles of main routes were doubled, and this period also saw the start of a serious attack on the standardisation of locomotives (of which some 500 types were operating) and of much rolling stock. Possibly some plans were over-ambitious, for in 1937 a committee considered that 'In the past 15 years, stations, workshops and marshalling yards have often been built to be the last word in railway technique rather than on careful calculation of probable requirements, and prestige has perhaps counted far more than prudence.' However, one noteworthy train appeared in this era — the *Indian Imperial Mail* from Bombay to Calcutta, a superbly luxurious express whose thirty-two passengers were well out-numbered by the staff which attended them.

During the Second World War many Indian locomotives and much stock was transferred to the Middle East while the whole system was under great strain with the Japanese virtually hammering at the gates. Then in 1947 independence and partition arrived, and a few years later the mileage which remained in India proper was re-organised into regions. Familiar names like the East Indian and the Bombay, Baroda & Central India vanished, as did the exalted 'Nizam's'. But if the old names went, steam remained and indeed flourished. The last steam locomotive was built in a new works near Calcutta as late as 1971, and India hence remains a happy hunting ground for lovers of 'big steam'.

Of the nine regions into which India's railways are now divided, the Central railway based on Bombay is the largest of the broad-gauge systems and feeds Hyderabad, Nagpur, Delhi and Allahabad. The Eastern railway, based on Calcutta, serves the lower Ganges and is largely of metre gauge. The South Eastern is again based on Calcutta but runs south to Madras. The Southern, with Madras as its centre, covers the whole of the southern portion of the peninsula, two thirds of its routes being on the metre gauge. The Western railway, running out from Bombay, covers the area up to Agra and the Pakistan border: more than three quarters of it is of metre gauge or narrower. The Northern railway is based on Delhi, works up to Amritsar and includes Lucknow and Allahabad: its metre gauge section runs south-west of the capital. The North Eastern, North-East Frontier and South Central systems complete the roll-call.

In addition, of course, there are the railways of Pakistan, which date from 1862 and were divided off from the main Indian system after partition. East Pakistan — now itself the independent nation of Bangladesh — was never rich in major lines, but the western part of the state took over most of the old North Western railway of India. Extensive electrification has recently taken place on these lines, and the *Tezgam Express* now links Rawalpindi and Karachi — a distance of about 960 miles — in the respectable time of 26 hours.

But both scenically and from the standpoint of railway politics the most interesting line in Pakistan is perhaps that which heads westward from Spezand junction through the mountains of the Afghan border, and which has already attained Zahidan over the border in Iran. For across the deserts from here an obvious target is the marvellously-engineered line which links the Persian Gulf with Teheran and the USSR, whilst another possibility is a connection into Iraq to join the standard-gauge line from Basra and Baghdad and so attain Haydarpasa for Istanbul. Whether the initiative comes from oil traffic or from a desire to link the Islam world and lead toward Mecca (for Medina is in the same general orbit), that vision of a through service between Europe and southern Asia which was first adumbrated by a French visionary in an 1836ish flush of enthusiasm has not yet been abandoned.

Meanwhile, on most of the systems of India itself there are still 'great' trains to be encountered and travelled on. The pride of the nation's railways is probably the *Rajdhani Express* which connects New Delhi and Calcutta. It has day and sleeping cars, both luxuriously equipped and fully air-conditioned. And it travels at up to 80 mph on the largely-electrified route between the two cities, a distance of 1,020 miles.

Indeed, the overall speeds of Indian trains are being progressively accelerated over the next few years, and it is promised that the principal expresses over the main broad-gauge routes will be operating at up to 100 mph by the middle of 1975. These routes will connect New Delhi with Howrah for Calcutta, with Bombay (using the *Frontier Mail* path by way of Baroda), and with Madras

The *Poona Express*, familiar to generations of servants of the *raj*, in 1907.

Fruit stall in Pakistan.

The pride of the lines of the sub-continent in their high standards of maintenance is evidenced by the stressing of the fact that this diesel of the West Pakistan railways has completed more than a million miles in service.

This steam locomotive of the West Pakistan system is also well-tended, as well as demonstrating the nation's adherence to the Moslem faith.

by the old Grand Trunk railway, whilst another will link Bombay with Nagpur and Howrah. Meanwhile, in 1973 the fastest *steam-hauled* passenger train in the country was the *Golconda Express* which covered the 200 miles from Secunderabad to Vijayawada in 6 hours. Other important trains then were the *Madras–Howrah Express* linking southern India's leading city with the heart of West Bengal, and the *Grand Trunk Express* which connects Madras with Delhi.

Furthermore, the best of these trains are extremely comfortable and well-attended in their air-conditioned class, and in many ordinary first-class coaches too. In the late 1960s, for instance, the writer travelled from Bombay to Delhi on the *Frontier Mail*, steam-hauled by well-kept Pacifics for most of a journey of some 950 miles accomplished in a creditable 23 hours. The sleeping-berth compartment was fully air-conditioned (plus a large electric fan), and by day one had the full length of the couch — which is a better word than seat — to relax on. The bed, prepared by a servant trained in the traditions of the *raj*, was remarkably comfortable. In a panelled dining car which had the space and opulence of older days I had a good meal, rapidly served, at low cost. That I had to walk along the platform at a suitable stop was no hardship at all, since as well as being a survival of early practice it was quicker and steadier than going along the corridors as in European or American trains. Breakfast was brought to my compartment complete with elaborate salt and pepper dishes and a teapot of mammoth proportions.

By contrast, on the daily *Taj Express* between Delhi and Agra I enjoyed a hearty breakfast at my seat in an air-conditioned modern coach: only when the plant developed troubles did things begin to get a little unpleasant. The highlight of my trip on that occasion, though, was the overnight metre-gauge service from Agra to Jaipur where I had a complete suite to myself — a bed-sitting room and a bathroom with shower. Add to this a servant who seemed to anticipate every wish, and you will appreciate why I think highly of Indian rail travel.

Finally, no description of the trains of the sub-continent would be complete without some reference to such hill and mountain railways as the spectacular Nilgiri line which takes the leisurely, steam-hauled *Blue Mountain Express* up to Ootacamund from near Trichinopoly in the far south, or the Kalka-Simla railway in the Himalayan foothills which serves Simla, the summer capital during the days of the *raj*. The most famous and interesting of all was (and is) the Darjeeling line in the tea-growing area of West Bengal. With its 2 ft gauge and its curves as sharp as 50 ft in radius it puffs its adhesive way up the 51 miles from Siliguri to Darjeeling, hauled by 0–4–0 saddle-tanks which are crewed by no fewer than six people — driver, fireman, two assistant firemen to pass fuel and two 'sandmen' who sit in front sanding the track, a very necessary task since in the 40 miles from Sukna to Ghum the line rises 6,600 ft on an average gradient of 1 in 26. Scenically this is one of the most spectacular routes in all India, a land which specialises in the spectacular.

206

A semi-streamlined 'Pacific' locomotive north of Bombay on the Delhi Pacific railway.

Great Trains of the World

'Alur', a well-kept locomotive of the East African railway waits at Mwanza station on Lake Victoria with the three-weekly express for Dar-es-Salaam.

A life which began in the South Seas has truly been fortunate to me so far as trains are concerned, for it has shown me more than my fair share of railways great and small. The small ones come first, though; for the first locomotive I ever saw was a diamond-stacked 2 ft gauge machine, polished like a mirror and billowing clouds of smoke as it charged across the sugar-cane fields of Fiji.

Then came the war, schooldays, and New Zealand. The steep, 3 ft 6 in lines of the NZR seemed at that time to have everything — expresses with enormous romance (if no dining cars), teeming local trains, lengthy freights running almost nose-to-tail, and virtually every engine built since 1900 still hard at work. Above all there was the unique 1–in–15 Rimutaka incline which represented the last survivor of the Fell system of boosting power through the use of horizontal wheels gripping a central rail. I can still hear the arythmic, shuffling bellow of those engines, and remember the kippering one got in the tunnels.

European trains were remote wonders read about in books; and though I finally discovered them in 1945 there was another new and rare railway encounter to be made first. For we travelled by way of the Panama Canal. Since this takes the voyager from the Pacific to the Atlantic in an east-to-west direction it provides a surprise of its own; and this is augmented when one finds one's ship taken in tow by a number of narrow-gauge electric rack locomotives with winches mounted on top and so hauled through the locks. But even more was to follow.

For, as we rose inch by inch through the lock at Miraflores, a train came stamping up the grade from Panama City and terminated in the station nearby. While the passengers swarmed off the four long wooden cars and another load climbed aboard — all shouting and singing and passing the time of day with itinerant vendors of peanuts, chewing-gum, *frijoles*, Coca-Cola and the like — the engine uncoupled and ran ahead to a water tank, where it stood simmering peacefully while the fireman filled the tender and the driver bustled round with his oilcan; a pleasant sylvan scene, common enough the world over in those happier days. Then all of a sudden the coaches started rolling back down the grade on their own. A catastrophe, I thought, and envisaged the headline: 'Great Runaway Train Disaster'. But it turned out to be an everyday routine on this line. Up at the top of the yard the engine hooted and set off in pursuit. The coaches ran steadily on; the locomotive followed, gaining and then overtaking on a loop and

Railways in Chile — the crossing of the Bia Bia river near Concepción.

pulling ahead. Then it slowed down. As the rake of cars caught up with it the engine started to accelerate again; the automatic couplings banged together; there was a hoot; and, already doing 15 or 20 miles an hour, the driver opened up once more. The Miraflores local was on its customary way back to Panama City. Obviously this was the way the Panama railroad turned it round every day. In most other parts of the world it would have been regarded as the perfect way to turn it over.

The Panama railroad has the distinction of being the shortest transcontinental route in the world (47½ miles), though retaining the 5 ft gauge it was given by its builders from the Confederate states. But in other aspects it is an archetypal small Latin-American line. And although things have changed a little since 1945, the sight later that day of one of its main-line trains overtaking the ship where the railway ran down beside the canal on the other side of the continental divide, belting along behind a bellowing little 2–6–0 with bell clanging and black smoke scudding back along the grimy green coaches or swaying and clattering across an inadequate-looking bridge over an arm of the canal lake, was another one that has recorded itself firmly into my mental file of Great Trains I have Seen. Humble in itself, it had spirit.

One cannot, of course, do more than make generalisations and cite random instances when one compresses tens of thousands of miles of line into a few pages. Sweepingly to generalise, then, the railways of South America illustrate the fragmented nature of the continent's trade and politics. Not only are there few international rail links; in many countries there is not even a coherent *national* railway system, but only a series of isolated and independent lines running inland from various ports to serve particular traffic objectives in the interior, although it is true that in parts of Brazil, in Argentina, and in Chile, there are more comprehensive networks.

A consequence of this is that though there are many interesting and even grand railways in Latin America, there is a shortage of identifiably great *trains*. The nations are, by and large, poor: the lines were built mainly for the transport of freight: and some of the longer and international links are less than thirty years old, so that the prospective first-class customer thinks first in terms of flying. Where long-distance passenger trains run, then, they tend to be slow, infrequent, and packed with peasants and proletarians; if they do boast a dining car (which is by no means certain) there is no nonsense about *cordon bleu* cooking and wine bins. Perhaps the fact that the continent's railways were mainly built by foreign capital has also detracted somewhat from national pride in them. There are exceptions, and some very respectable trains run in the three major nations mentioned above with such luxuries as cinema cars. But there are not many of them.

Railways in the northern half of the continent tend to be as short and exotic as was the Panama line. Here Colombia is the country which comes nearest to having a national system, with even its gauges now standardised at 3 ft. These lines do not fall below the high continental standards in such matters as steep grades

Galera in Peru on the Lima to Muancayo line is one claimant
to the title of the highest railway station in the world.

and altitudes. The former British Guiana has the oldest railway on the continent — a short, standard-gauge, coastal-plain affair which still precariously survives on passenger traffic only; Surinam, next door, has an even more precarious narrow-gauge steam tram. Venezuela got rich on oil, and almost the first thing it did with the money was to build a megalomaniac motorway from port to capital over the ruins of the narrow-gauge La Guaira & Caracas line. Even the various Caribbean railways are in similar categories, for first Barbados and then Trinidad extirpated them entirely and Jamaica now runs second-hand British Railways diesel railcars. One cannot hope for great trains in such conditions.

On the southern mainland Ecuador provides a surprise in the Guayaquil & Quito, on whose 3 ft 6 in main line 2–8–0s zig-zag their way up the 1 in 19 of the Devil's Nose with successive four-car instalments of the daily mixed. Amazonian Brazil has the world's undeniably remotest railway in the 227 mile Madeira-Mamore: although long closed as far as the organs of the distant central government are concerned this still runs, thanks to the army, a twice-weekly train hauled by whichever of the line's original sixteen metric locomotives has been temporarily reclaimed from the jungle undergrowth. Marvellous though these lines may be, though, none of their trains are in the Baedeker class except for enthusiasts.

The railways of Peru have been more written about than any others in South America. There is admittedly something colossal about the Peruvian Central line, which in a mere 107 miles from the coast at Callao climbs, by way of zig-zag after zig-zag and miles of relentless grades of up to 1 in 22, through and over Andean gorges and chasms to what is usually claimed as the highest through-railway summit in the world, 15,690 ft up. With its small but robust 2–8–0s constantly thrashed within an inch of their lives its trains got up the hills very smartly, though the quickest way *down* was by way of the plate-layers' truck which preceded the first train every day and was impelled by gravity alone, but this merely made the altitude shock the worse, and hence oxygen cylinders were — and still are — provided in each coach for the sustenance of gasping passengers. Being a partly British-built line the Peruvian Central used vacuum brakes; but since at those altitudes the ambient air pressure roughly equalled that in the vacuum cylinders at sea level the system was chronically inoperative and the trains effectively had no continuous brakes at all and depended on agile men running along the box car roofs. Alas: though it took them some time, the diesel builders finally devised a turbo-charger which copes with the pressure variation and their product's noxious breath was then drawn even on the Andean heights.

There remain the systems of Brazil, Argentina, Chile, Bolivia, Uruguay and Paraguay. These, however riven by breaks of gauge, are all in some sort connected, though sometimes very recently and sometimes only by train ferries. Brazil is mainly metre-gauge country, though with two substantial 5 ft 3 in lines running inland from Rio de Janeiro and Santos. The latter (originally the Sao Paulo railway), though now mainly electrified, still has perhaps the

Above: Paraguay's only passenger train 'express' covers the route between Asunción and Encarnación on alternate days, taking a through coach to Buenos-Aires once a week. The picture above was taken during one of the not-uncommon minor derailments.

Right: *El Corrientino* — Argentina's ferry-borne train — seen taking on water in 1968, still hauled by a locomotive built in 1913 by the British firm of Kerr-Stuart.

Below: Wooden-bodied American-style coaches round a sharp bend on the Bolivian La Paz–Cochabamba line.

South Africa's *Blue Train* — a '5-star hotel on wheels' — is by common consent the most luxurious train in the modern world. Four styles of accommodation are offered — Super-luxury (private bathroom, sitting-room and bedroom), luxury (private bath with toilet), semi-luxury (shower and private toilet), and standard (with use of shower and toilet). The picture above shows the 46-seat dining-car.

A typical South African platform scene near Pietermaritzburg.

most remarkable thing on the South American railway scene — the rope-worked 1 in 12 incline between Piassaguera and Paranapia-caba, on the main line not far from the coast. This coelacanth of railway evolution, the last of its kind anywhere, is now being replaced by a rack line; but the old system will be kept as a stand by.

For the Brazilians are believers in railways. They have some ultra-modern, high-capacity, narrow-gauge iron-ore lines. And although they committed the eccentricity of deciding to build a capital city in a jungle which twenty years ago was accessible only after hundreds of miles on muleback or by helicopter, they have not since omitted to construct a railway to Brasilia and to run nightly sleeping-car expresses to it.

The Argentine railways, and to some extent the smaller Uruguay system, are alone on the southern continent in having developed on the American Midwest model. On the vast wheat-growing plains there the object was to have a railway siding sufficiently close to every square mile of land for a farmer to work a load to it with horse and cart and return home in one day. Iowa, Illinois, Kansas and Indiana thus each have a significant percentage of the world's railway route-mileage; and so does the province of Buenos Aires, though on three gauges. And in all these places there is now the classic branch-line problem. One still finds a single daily two-coach train creeping slowly across the illimitable pampas between points A and B (neither of them much more than railway junctions), tracing its way along metals almost invisible in the grass yet sometimes taking each of three different routes on each of three successive days. Even on the trunk haul between the two main cities of Buenos Aires and Bahia Blanca, some 300 miles apart, the 5 ft 6 in Ferrocarril General Roca (erstwhile, and more descrip-tively, known as the Buenos Aires Great Southern) still operates three parallel main lines.

Add to this the facts that in these parts stone ballast is rare and expensive, a certain lack of continuity of government policy, and a certain trade-union militancy, and one correctly expects decrepitude and demoralisation despite the appearance of a number of cosmetic diesels. This part of South America may indeed be comparatively full of trains, but one senses that few of them are objects of anybody's pride. A retired British civil engineer, who had given his life to the railways of a land larger than India, once reminisced about sitting on the rear platform of the observation car of an express of the Buenos Aires & Pacific line during the rains, consolatory gin in hand, and glumly watching his permanent way float soggily up to the surface of the sea of mud as the train's weight passed off.

And yet there are many fine things about the Argentine rail-ways, not least that they set out comprehensively to serve a nation's needs, that they boast some seventy-year-old diners which were perhaps the most ornate vehicles which Britain ever exported, that their foreign financiers were not loth to build some grand stations, and that the best of their modern equipment is very good. There is, of course, the gauge problem, always the consequence of letting expatriate engineers loose to design a railway network piecemeal.

Hauled by triple electric locomotives the *Blue Train* climbs the steep
and winding track near Tulbachkloof in Cape province.

The *Mail train de luxe* at Canumbeia on the Benguela railway which connected Lobin Bay to the Congo border in Portuguese West Africa.

A vernacular moment as passengers board a sleeping car on Nigeria's Lagos — Kano line

Most of the central lines are of 5 ft 6 in gauge, and the remoter and more mountainous ones are mainly metric. But there is some overlapping and a single long standard-gauge line, converted from a giant version of the type of rural tramway described in Geoffrey Household's *A Thing of Love*, snakes out of Buenos Aires — westwards at first before turning north, making a long journey up the river Plate, and then developing into a network serving two Argentinian provinces, southern Paraguay, and Uruguay. This line was originally horse-operated — but even in its equine days it boasted sleeping cars for the three-day journey.

Chile is almost the ideal shape for a railway system — long and narrow, with habitation and communication hemmed into valleys running parallel with the coast and fierce mountains discouraging alternative routes. Even the gauge problem was minimised by geography here, so that almost everything south of the capital of Santiago is of 5 ft 6 in gauge and almost everything north of it is metric. Travellers speak well of Chilean expresses — at least in the south, where they are smooth-running, quite fast, often electric but with some of the few modern steam locomotives in the continent. Matters in the north are complicated by the fact that much of the traffic comes through from Bolivia, which itself has a dramatic series of railways sufficiently illustrated by the two competing lines climbing out of the capital (La Paz, already 12,000 ft above sea level) to Viacha on the lip of the *altiplano*. One of these ascends at 1 in 25, following a long and indirect course to allow the gradient to be eased to this moderate figure: the other line, electrified, scorns indirection at the rate of 1 in 16. In recent years, largely thanks to the demand for oil transport, new international lines have been built between Bolivia and both Brazil and Argentina.

Formally, the term *Trans-Andine Express* is reserved for the train which (with assistance from a rack) works the 880 miles from Valparaiso to Buenos Aires in some 36 hours, all being well. But to my mind more distinguished lines are to be found on the borderlands of Bolivia, Chile and Argentina — all of them claimants to be the highest railways in the world, for in several places sections reach nearly to the 16,000 ft contour. Here are three metre-gauge international lines forming a triangle — the Antofagasta (Chili) & Bolivia, the General Belgrano line from Tucuman and Jujuy in Argentina joining the A(C)&B at Uyuni, and the Salta-Socompa branch of the Belgrano — the Northern Trans-Andine, completed only in 1948 — providing the newer of the two links between Chile and Argentina. This last is remote and spectacular in the extreme, and carries very little traffic. Its weekly passenger train, crowded to the rooftops, still consists of four or five ancient wooden coaches and a string of vans, and a relatively modern 2–10–2 drags it ever upwards over dizzy ledges and viaducts to the high and endless desert. Perhaps neither the Chilean nor the Argentine state railways are very proud of it; but whether two or twenty hours late this is to my mind one of the great trains of the world. Long may it labour half-way to the stratosphere under its towering pillar of smoke...

In many ways the African railway situation is similar to the South American one, since over most of the continent there is the same pattern of isolated lines linking port and hinterland. The exceptions, where at least a rudimentary grid of rails *does* exist, are to be found in the old-established nations along the Mediterranean coast and in the newer lands of European settlement in the south: something is said of the former systems elsewhere in this book, though mention should also be made of the service once offered by the *Casablanca–Algiers Express*. Yet things might have been different had two great colonial dreams been realised.

One of these was French, the concept of a Trans-Saharan railway from Morocco to the Niger. This received a fillip during the Second World War when the Germans realised that it would give them a fairly secure overland route to Dakar by taking in the 800 miles of track running inland from that port which had been constructed (and even provided with a *wagons-lits* service) before 1939. But despite the use of forced labour the Chemin de Fer Mediterranée-Niger petered out some 500 miles south of the Mediterranean, just as a rather similar fate had overtaken Cecil Rhodes' better-known vision of a Cape-to-Cairo route. Here construction began in 1897; but though this was itself speedy considering the work involved, the direct route was deviated from more than once in order to serve mining needs. Eventually Kindu in the Congo was attained; but from there on there remains a gap of some 1,000 miles before the lines of the Sudan are reached, and a further 150 miles separate these from the Egyptian system.

Despite the resemblances between the railways of Africa and of Latin America, there are of course differences as well; for instance (except along the Mediterranean again), all African gauges are narrow. Save for some purely local instances break-of-gauge problems do not exist either — *as yet*, for one long foreseen will come about when the railway from Zambia to Tanzania links the 3 ft 6 in Cape system with the metre gauge of East Africa. Another difference is that, in the absence of natural barriers, lines from the ports tend to be longer and to throw out more branches. But, as in South America, most African railways strong.y reflect the practice of the European countries which built them — generally Britain or France, though a little Italian influence survives and there are a few traces of pre-1914 Germany. The French lines are most common in the west; their only railway in the east, the 487-mile Franco-Ethiopian railway from Djibouti to Addis Ababa, got rough treatment from Evelyn Waugh in *Black Mischief* and was fictionally sold off to an Armenian junk merchant in the last chapter — though in actuality it has survived to run its second generation of diesels and some new lines are being built or planned in and around Ethiopia. The French cleaned steam power out of their African possessions rather rapidly, but it survives in some strength where the British influence determined matters.

To make another sweeping generalization, though there are trains which cover great distances and offer all the civilised amenities (especially, perhaps, the elegant steam-hauled expresses of the

Narrow-gauge express in Mozambique.

One of Africa's typical Beyer-Garratt articulated locomotives heading an express at Salisbury, Rhodesia.

The Wagons-Lits company's first agency at Pekin (opened in 1902 after the Trans-Siberian line had brought a direct link from Europe).

A scene on the Canton railway in 1911. The locomotive is an American-built 4—4—0, and the stock also betrays a strong US influence.

Benguela railway and some of the best on the Kenya & Uganda line), central, eastern and western Africa leave one with no very clear impression of character or magnificence in their railways. There is much of interest, including such a fragment of history as that on the Mombasa/Lake Victoria line in 1898 a lion entered the first-class car and selected the superintendent of police for its dinner, and much that is effective and well-designed. But there are no recognisably great trains between the tropics of Capricorn and Cancer — or beyond.

The republic of South Africa, whatever one may think of its politics, is another matter though; for it possesses, with the possible exception of Japan, the narrow-gauge railway system with the heaviest traffic and finest equipment in the world. This is no new development either, for South Africa and Rhodesia have a tradition of luxury travel. Thus, in 1902 Rhodes introduced the *Zambesi Express de Luxe* between Bulawayo and Cape Town whose twelve bogie coaches included a buffet car into which was squeezed a library and reading room, a writing room, a card room, a smoking room and finally an observation balcony: wine coolers, crimson leather and electric light added to the décor. Almost equally luxurious — and indeed offering the extra amenity of hot and cold showers — were the Cape Town boat trains.

Since those days there have been enormous developments in electrification, modernisation and the entire reconstruction of routes, so that there is now a well-grown network covering the whole country. This country has its own character and history, and it is tragic that today that history should have led to the absurdities (to say the least) which are evident even in nagging details of the railway system. Viewed purely with an economist's eye, it is irritating to see allegedly skilful — and certainly scarce — white labour used to fire the engine of a pick-up freight on an obscure branch line when all over the land the signs of things not done through lack of manpower are so striking, or to notice the racially-separate footbridges expensively built side by side across tracks in even the remotest places.

South African long-distance expresses may not be startlingly fast — the very best do not by much better 40 mph overall — but this is inseparable from their 3 ft 6 in gauge, and some of them must rank as great trains however one defines the term. They travel long distances, running through country which is wild and sometimes splendid: they aim high in matters of comfort: and they place emphasis on their prestige value overseas. The very best of them test the limits of the technology, and are driven through the network at speeds which put some force on the flanges and are certainly well beyond the most economic points on the engineers' speed-versus-fuel-and-maintenance-cost curves. To my mind, South Africa's *Blue Train* conveys the excitement of the *Super Chief*, the *Silver Jubilee*, the *Mistral* and other lordly expresses past and present — an excitement which the trans-Siberian trains, jogging along as if fully knowing their proletarian place in the intervals between freights, fail to convey despite their immense runs.

There are, of course, at least two *Blue Trains* in the world. The French one is now just another in a nightly procession of sleeping-car expresses flashing nose-to-tail down the electrified PLM main line and is no longer even blue. But the South African one, covering the close-on-a-thousand miles from Johannesburg to Cape Town twice weekly in some 25 hours, scores by being so unlikely as well as so splendid — for it was only inaugurated some two decades ago, when the world seemed to belong to the aeroplane. It was even, in 1973, still steam-hauled for part of the way. Judged purely on a commercial basis, this train which has a right to be regarded as the most luxurious in today's world (it has, for example, three private, full-sized baths, and many passengers still dress for their magnificent dinners) ought not to exist — but one rejoices that it does. For man starves on a diet of only what is commercially viable; one has to do something for the sake of excellence, and honour is satisfied in its doing. The *Blue Train* was even re-equipped in 1972 with 16 new coaches costing over £2 million though carrying few more than 100 passengers served by a staff of 26, and its earlier stock was then transferred to another fine train, the *Orange Express* from Cape Town to Durban.

In spite of their narrow gauge, the South African railways have side-corridor compartment stock on all long-distance workings; and where there are no separate sleeping cars, first- and second-class passengers are given fold-down bunks. There are third-class cars lacking this day/night convertibility, reserved for non-whites: such lesser breeds do, however, also have their 'separate but equal' firsts and seconds.

In general, though a great deal of new stock has been built for South Africa, pre-1914 vehicles can still be found in express duty indiscriminately mixed in with the newer, and some of the nation's coaches date back to the start of the century and are hence among the world's oldest in main-line use. Dining cars also vary in age and comfort, but either way serve very adequate and absurdly cheap meals. All accommodation is automatically reserved, and at the larger stations the train conductor mounts a pulpit on the platform, directing passengers to their appointed seats and turning away those for whom there is no room. For though most trains are slow (the Cape Town/Port Elizabeth service is an extreme case, taking 39 hours to cover 675 miles on a roundabout route between cities a comfortable half-day's car drive apart), they still fill with passengers. This is perhaps because they are cheap. South Africa may be the richest state in the continent; but it is still the poorest English-speaking country in the world, and car owners are a minority even among whites.

And so, for the most part, one becomes content to climb aboard and relax: one might as well, since one is likely to be there for some time. Even where steam power has been replaced by diesel — or, more often, electric — traction, running is usually faster only because watering and fire-cleaning stops are not needed. (Burning the cheap but ashy local coal, locomotives need a pause for this purpose every few hours.) But if one is in the right frame of mind

British builders supplied many standard-gauge locomotives to China — a country, where, as in the USA, main lines not infrequently run through streets and warning bells are hence a necessity. This 6-coupled locomotive was built for the Yueh Han railway prior to 1939.

it is a pleasant enough way of passing the time, especially if one cares for the last survivors of the steam age.

The general manager of the South African railways recently went on record as saying that main-line steam locomotion had no place in the final third of the twentieth century. No doubt — though *laet uns bid* or not — he will prove himself right well before the year 2000; but for the present there is still a splendid herd of snorting, smoking beasts in his stable demonstrating otherwise. And while the twice-weekly Mossel Bay/Johannesburg train still snakes its way along the high mountain ledge to the summit of the Lootsberg pass behind a pair of light 4–8–2s with half the world spread out below — having done much the same thing the evening before in climbing over the Montagu pass behind a 4–8–2 + 2–8–4 Garratt — and the vast and extraordinary turbo-blown condensing 4–8–4s still whine like mercifully-distant jet aircraft across the Karoo on the Cape Town/Johannesburg main line, he is going to continue to have to keep looking over his shoulder and crossing his fingers.

From South Africa to the Far East is almost half way around the world; and it is hard to present a picture of the largest land there if only because China's trains have been little reported for at least the last thirty years for various unhappy reasons. Before the 'avoidance line' from Chita was opened in 1914 and the *Trans-Manchurian Express*, with its various connections southward became independent of the 'Trans-Siberian' proper, travellers' books described how the latter penetrated the frozen forests to connect with the remarkable and Japanese-built Manchurian system at Harbin — at which point there were also some purely Chinese trains if anybody happened to notice them. But though they had some remarkable locomotives — including the last of the 'singles', 4–2–2s built by Kerr-Stuart in 1910 — the Chinese railways themselves hardly got going before 1914, and they were then promptly knocked about by various major and minor wars and turmoils and confused by British, German and Japanese ownership. The last of these nations did, however, achieve a 40 mph service between Pekin and Mukden by 1939.

In recent years the Communist Government has radically overhauled and extended the system. By all accounts it still depends very heavily on steam power, with many American-built and second-hand Russian engines and still a fair number of British ones — all sporting Chinese builders' plates as well as the ubiquitous red star and maybe a portrait of the Chairman. The best timing appears to be about 45 mph over the 750 miles between Pekin and Hankow; but beyond remarking on the nostalgic power of whistles in the night, travellers report little save the uncontrollable public address system booming martial music in each compartment and the sight of waiters and platelayers looking at their little red books.

Even these impressions may now be somewhat out of date. But during the 'glorious cultural revolution' the writer met another retired railway engineer, a locomotive man lately returned from a visit to China where he had worked for many years. His comment

Surabaya station on the Indonesian railways, showing well-shaded rolling stock with simple but effective air-cooling devices hung outside to be re-dampened.

on a recent announcement by the New China news agency that, through taking heed of the thoughts of Chairman Mao, the crew of an elderly 2–8–2 had succeeded in doubling its haulage capacity, was that this was just the type of experience he had himself had many times. The Chinese did not lack for courtesy (or, perhaps, a sense of humour directed at the ardour of the highly-educated), and were fond of putting down in statistical returns figures that it was known would, for some arcane reason, give pleasure to the recipient.

So whether there are great trains in China we do not know. I doubt it, though, if we adopt the definition that some expenditure of effort and aim at an excellence beyond the economic is called for, since this would seem in conflict with the theory and ethos of the materialist dialectic. Rice and rockets would have to come first — or long sluggish freight trains fulfilling high norms of ton-mileage per worker-hour but getting in the way of anything spectacular.

Japan, however, is another affair again: and however unrepentant a sentimentalist for the old ways of running trains one may be, one must grant to the Japanese that those which cover the 400-odd miles of the New Tokaido line at intervals of about half-an-hour meet almost completely our definition of great trains. They certainly tested the limits of railway technology to their utmost. A whole new line was built from the ground up (or down) with the sole object of running expresses on it at speeds far higher than anybody had ever achieved before; and it was hence necessary to tackle such novel problems as rail and wheel behaviour at regular speeds of 150 mph, or the shock waves set up by trains diving into long tunnels at the same rate or passing each other at a combined speed almost half that of sound. The cost penalties exacted by this pursuit of excellence are considerable; yet my definition's requirement that economic limits should be exceeded does not demand that profits must not be made. The crowning honour to the Japanese has been that their new electrified 'bullet trains', expensive to build and to run though they are, nevertheless make a profit because their earning power is even greater.

With their service of refreshing towels supplied by *geisha*-like stewardesses, such 'Hikari' flyers recall aspects of the European past and have already become the centre of a myth. For the rest, Japan is narrow-gauge country — and, like South Africa, one which combines a spectacular landscape with heavy-duty railroading whilst adding dense traffic to the mixture. For the highways in this densely-populated and industrialised land are so poor that guidebooks express the distances between towns in such terms as 'By road, 4 hours: by train, 100 minutes'. Long-distance trains on the 3 ft 6 in lines set high standards of speed and comfort, whether electrically-hauled or not, though voyagers from European countries may tense slightly at the fact that the Japanese possess a number of those fearsome-sounding beasts, diesel-multiple-unit sleeping cars. Nobody else has as yet dared to build such a thing, though the French and Russians have thought about them. A sleeper is (or should be) a sleeper, unitary and locomotive-hauled.

A narrow-gauge diesel heading an express at Djakarta on the Javanese railways.

Welcome pineapples being taken aboard modern rolling stock at Palembang, on the Pandjang line in Sumatra.

The interior of a modern train on the Japanese National Railways. The flower-girl with her trolley at the end of the corridor introduces a local accent to an international scene.

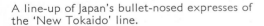

A line-up of Japan's bullet-nosed expresses of the 'New Tokaido' line.

Before the Second World War, the Indonesian (or, to be more particular, the Javanese) railways had the reputation of running some of the best trains in the world on the 3 ft 6 in gauge. A quarter-century of post-colonial upheaval, plus a collision with a water-buffalo which put an end to night running, has altered all that; and as Indonesia emerges again into the comity of nations its railways, though they run some smartly-worked diesel-powered expresses, are reported chiefly for their marvellous variety of active relics. The Dutch, living in a homeland which presented to the railway engineer few challenges except in the design of mobile bridges and adequate drains, seemed to put all their thwarted daring and brilliance into designing for Java and Sumatra not only civil engineering works but some remarkable locomotives, and many of these are still hard at work. Ancient 2–4–0 tender engines simmer cheek-by-jowl with giant 2–8–8–0s and 2–12–2Ts, while perhaps a compound 4–4–0 clanks off down the line under the verdigris-covered, creeper-wound remains of some ancient electric catenary. It all makes for a railway scene of great interest.

Across the Malacca Straits, in Malaya and Thailand, matters are more closely regulated. Both countries have fairly small metre-gauge systems; and in the days when it operated an *International Express* that of Malaya was something of a model of tropical railway operation, with a strong flavouring of England's Great Western railway manifesting itself in such things as the shape of the signals, the colour of the coaches and the copper-capped chimneys of the locomotives. Nowadays there seems a tendency there to demonstrate freedom from imperial oppression by refusing to clean the engines — which is odd, especially as Thailand, which was always staunchly independent and uncolonised, undoubtedly has the smartest steam locomotives of any main-line railway in the world. (It can also boast of running air-conditioned sleeping-car trains before 1939, and if one goes back to 1926 one discovers a special luxury saloon, equipped with fans and shower, built to transport the royal white elephants.) These locomotives gleam, they sparkle, they are polished and groomed; and when they grow old they do not die but are erected in well-tended avenues bordering the roads to stations and other places of public resort and entertainment. The scene on approaching Haad Yai Junction is stated to be of especial antiquarian interest.

Malaya appears notable mainly because third-class passengers make a habit of travelling on hot nights with their feet sticking out of the window. But in Burma — it was formerly reported — a different problem arose in that to occupy an upper berth on the *Mandalay Mail* was considered to inflict intolerable loss of 'face' on the person sleeping below one.

And so at last one returns to the distances of the Antipodes. Australia has one thing in common with South America, a confusion of gauges, and it has them for a similar reason. In spite of the fact that the whole continent was British, it was in the middle of the nineteenth century so politically divided that each of its states reserved to itself the right to consider railway policy as a domestic

A 'Hikari' express sweeps between the rice-paddies and the holy mountain of Fujiyama.

Another Japanese luxury train, the *Kegon* express.

The control compartment of a 'Hikari' express is now operated by computer.

matter, engaging its own consultants and engineers and establishing its own practices regardless of what its neighbours were doing. Once started (as Britain itself had discovered in the 1840s) this process is very hard to stop; and overseas only New Zealand and South Africa, having set out with contradictory railway specifications, saw what they were doing in time to pull back from the brink and to standardise.

Hence three gauges survive on the Australian main-line system — 3 ft 6 in at each end of the network in Queensland and Western Australia, the standard 4 ft 8½ in in New South Wales, and 5 ft 3 in shared, more by luck than judgement, by the central states of Victoria and South Australia whose border was until very recently the only one without a break of gauge. Since total conversion was obviously impractical, joining the five capital cities by standard-gauge railway had been mooted for many years, and in fact a new standard-gauge line reached Brisbane in Queensland in the 1930s. But Sydney, Melbourne and Perth have only recently been linked in this way (again as much by new construction as by gauge conversion), while work still continues on a spur to Adelaide.

For such a large and unpopulated country Australia is remarkably urbanised — and with its great cities all being ports, the long-distance railway has had to compete with the ocean liner too. As a result, much of its considerable mileage of track serves remote and faraway places in the 'outback' with correspondingly little traffic. To take an extreme case, the Western Australian railways in 1956 decided in effect to close all their branch lines on which the scheduled service was less frequent than one train *a week* — and as a result the system's route mileage of some 3,000 miles was reduced by nearly a third. Much Australian railwaying, therefore, has always been done on a one-engine-in-steam basis, though without any reprehensible economising in equipment.

Each state, too, went its own way in matters of style, and particularly in locomotive design. During the nineteenth century British influence everywhere predominated, but subsequently native schools developed out of the British root. For instance, Dugald Drummond for a time practised locomotive design in Sydney and left his mark in New South Wales, though signalling and station architecture there tended to follow the practices of the Great Northern and Great Western railways respectively. But Queensland found a locomotive style of its own — and so ultimately did Victoria, whose engineers originated the type of free-standing smoke deflector which one associates with German practice.

Though such Australian trains as the long chain (*Sunlander, Brisbane Limited, Spirit of Progress, Queenslander...*) which linked Cooktown to Adelaide were never unworthy, they seldom had anything about them meriting the word great. Perhaps of the highest quality were the expresses on the Melbourne–Sydney service: in the latter days of the break of gauge at Albury on this run, the administration of Victoria put on a named and streamlined train, the *Spirit of Progress*, with purpose-built stock and locomotives. There have also been plenty of trains of character, ranging from the

Earlier days in New Zealand are recalled by this picture of the steam-hauled *Napier Express* leaving Palmerston North.

One of the world's finest trains, the Wellington-Auckland *Silver Star* sleeping-car express follows the west bank of the Rangitikei River on New Zealand's North island.

The Australian railways' *Indian Pacific* express en route from Sydney to Perth and here seen near Mambray Creek, South Australia. Such fine trains can only run because at last the Commonwealth has relieved its arterial lines from the plague of a multiplicity of gauges.

weekly narrow-gauge *Ghan* (mixed passenger and freight) which toiled across the arid centre to Alice Springs and took its name from the fact that it replaced a camel-caravan tended by Afghans to the many slow and stolid 'mails' steaming to every corner of New South Wales and the *Tasman Limited* with its famous refreshment stop. Possibly the 2,000-mile run right across the continent offered the most unusual travel, with the journey from Perth to Sydney involving three breaks of gauge. The medium-sized 4–6–0s which once rolled over the famous 300-mile 'straight' across the Nullarbor Plains were dwarfed by the enormous tenders needed to keep them supplied over the immense distances between fuel and water stops, and passengers too solaced themselves with most of the usual amenities plus a piano which could be impressed into any entertainment from a Melba recital to a bar-room rendering of *Waltzing Matilda*. Descendants of that piano have survived into the modern era, being included in the equipment of the *Indian Pacific* expresses (so named, of course, from the oceans which they link) which now cover the recently-completed length of the transcontinental standard-gauge route from Sydney through to Perth in 65 hours.

This service is certainly remarkable enough to deserve special mention, for it is provided by stainless-steel streamliners designed on the most advanced (and, indeed, final) American models, built at the end of the 1960s when its North American progenitors were fast starving into disappearance. Today, as the remaining American long-distance trains struggle for custom, the *Indian Pacific* is booked solidly for months ahead. Perhaps this is so partly because Australians have a feeling of guilt about their vast and empty hinterland and want to see it in more detail than the airlines can offer and in greater comfort than is possible on the dire roads. But a tribute is due to the quality of the trains too.

Looking back over these pages, I realise that I may have concentrated too much on my own view of a great train and too little on the titled aristocrats of the lines. But the luxury express is, by definition, of benefit to the few only; and railways sprang and grew out of their ability to serve the daily needs of ordinary people, carrying their produce, fuel, ore, and bodies — clerks on the daily grind, farmers' wives to market, grandchildren to grandparents. Much of this trade has been eroded away during the last half-century, and for better or worse we appear in the age of the road. In particular it is the dull, drab, humdrum, workaday rural train, once so much a part of everybody's experience, which has steadily declined all over the world and is already extinct in many places and which ought to be honoured and remembered. So, though this book is designed to commemorate the thoroughbreds, let us not forget the mongrels. And may one such be chosen to serve as a memorial for them all.

During my childhood in New Zealand in the Second World War, I for some time stayed in a remote township in the Urewera country, the broken land between the Bay of Plenty and Poverty Bay. The town had been founded around the turn of the century to serve the sawmills then busily stripping timber from erodable,

Early days on the Commonwealth railway, Australia. Above, the parlour-observation car on the Melbourne-Sydney express. Right, the lounge bar with its famous piano which could almost play *Waltzing Matilda* unaided and which has descendants today, and below, a remarkably homely 'Saloon special car'.

New Zealand railways' *Southerner*, which runs between Christchurch and Invercargill on the South island. This is one of the new luxury trains on New Zealand lines, which features four-position reclining seats.

infertile and geologically-recent hills; now, with the timber exhausted save for blackened trunks fallen or standing desolate in parts swept by fire, some determined characters were trying without enormous success to make a living out of sheep. The transport needs of the scattered communities were served by a road, full of hairpin bends and gravel-scree surfaces slipping down to the lips of savage gorges, whose beginning was marked by a sign reading 'Danger; bends for next 35 miles' — and also by a railway, climbing up from Gisborne on the coast.

Like all other railways in New Zealand (including the Auckland-Wellington trunk route, where after more than fifty years during which the country could not show a single operative dining-car the *Silver Star* suddenly appeared as perhaps the world's third finest train), this was of 3 ft 6 in gauge. But it was an isolated section. Plans for its northwards extension to link with the lines of Auckland province had been dropped during the hard times between the wars; the tracks coming up from Napier along the coast had been under construction, on and off, for thirty years and were still a year or two from completion. The once-daily mixed which ran inland the whole 49 mile length of the Gisborne Section was therefore composed of elderly coaches, ferried in during construction and hauled by a little 2–6–2T (one of the first engines built by the New Zealand railways) which had to shed half its load at the edge of the plains before tackling the great climb into the high country — 12 miles of 1 in 35. The quite respectable speeds it attained on the lower reaches, to say nothing of its drunken hurtling on the few down-grades, died away in the hills; the crowded coach, which had started in mid-afternoon by being full of cheerful bustle and song, quietened as night drew on: and the gas light slowly dwindled and died as the carriage creaked and leaned into the curves, first one way and then the other. Finally nothing could be heard but the limping, desperate shouting of the engine as it strained its way to the summit with its wartime overload, a well-matched battle between the force of gravity and the skill of the men on the footplate turning on only a small margin.

The road through the Urewera is now improved out of recognition, but it leads to a different world. My little township's day was once marked and bounded when the locomotive's headlight finally appeared over the crest of the ridge. When a few minutes later, running fast and free again, the daily mixed roared down into the darkened town and panted to a halt at the station it was met by half the inhabitants. Letters, parcels, papers, visitors, prodigal sons had all arrived together. Two years later, and before the war ended, things had already begun to change. Tyres and petrol were coming back: the train was no longer so crowded. Then one day, back at school, I spotted a small paragraph at the foot of the column in the newspaper. Railway passenger services on the Gisborne Section, it said, had been abandoned and a bus had been put on instead. A *bus*? To carry that vast and cheerful crowd? Over that impossible road? I was shattered. It was the first intimation I ever had that trains, too, were mortal.

1913 Contemporary Viewpoint

On Monday, 6 August, 1888 — one of Britain's rare public holidays — a London clerk named J. P. Pearson paid ten shillings to take the first day excursion to Calais. He and the French met and parted on the insular terms to be expected of such an occasion. But it sowed in Pearson's mind the seed of what was to become an interest, a hobby and soon an obsession.

As a boy in Carlisle, Pearson had been fascinated by the Midland railway. Less expectedly, what intrigued him most was a tidiness of appearance which extended even to the telegraph posts: all his life, indeed, Pearson's first approach to a railway was to consider its track maintenance, the standards of its station furniture, its unglamorous neatness. Such qualities were not often to be found in France. But at least the young man began to realise that overseas countries did *have* railways, and between his first serious trip to Europe in 1892 and the outbreak of the First World War he made some seventy journeys in search of them.

As early as 1893 he could be seen in Chicago, where his nominal *but de voyage* was the World's Fair (which, like most such exhibitions, he found to be uncompleted) but where he was more interested in the railroad station. And as the years passed and his resources increased — for in his early days Pearson had been unable to afford even a penny guidebook before sailing off into the unknown — the names of foreign parts piled up in his diary. Talahuano, Lower Umkomaas, Cripple Creek, Mount Carmel, Wakatipu, Skagway and Chang-Chung took their place beside Newhaven, Southampton and Liverpool now.

Some of these journeys lasted up to four months; but when they were not possible Pearson would still make the 80 minute crossing from Dover of a Saturday afternoon simply to look at continental trains. More even than his exemplar, R. L. Stevenson, he loved travel for travel's sake; but he was also the prototype of that particular type of railway enthusiast — most commonly found, perhaps, in Britain — who must be forever refreshing himself with the sight of overseas railways but who has little interest in the life around them. The cities of the world were for him little more than caravanserais where one changed to a new timetable, and he rarely spent more than one night in a station hotel (noting, perhaps, the selection of musical-comedy hits played in its Palm Court) before boarding his next connection.

After the 1918 Armistice, Pearson's compulsion took hold of him again; but his heyday was Britain's Edwardian age, and when in 1932 he published an account of his voyages it was pre-war years which received first attention. He titled this book *Railways and Scenery*, though a great deal of it is devoted to sea voyages. And perhaps, too, the very word 'book' is a misnomer, for this is a vast and shapeless assembly, as rambling as its author's journeys themselves, of over one and a half million words broken into four volumes purely as a bookbinder's convenience. Pearson was no writer (and no artist either, despite his compulsion to draw little sketches of anything remotely suited to a diagram), his topography went unchecked, and even his railway knowledge was unsystematic: he was a magpie of facts and impressions and presented them in a way which has a certain naive appeal but which is too often (and inappropriate as the word may seem) *pedestrian*.

'Pearson' is in fact a mad, bad, almost unreadable book. And yet it is indispensable to anybody who wants to know what it felt like to travel over the railways of fifty countries in what were, in many ways, the years of their greatness nearly a lifetime ago. The following four excerpts, which represent the author in various moods and lands, deal with 'express' journeys made just before the First World War. Topographical nomenclature has, of course, been left unchanged.

For a little way now we were on double track and the hills around us were lower, rising soon, however, to a greater height on our left. At Schwarzach-St. Veit the 12.5 stopping train to Innsbruck got away practically up to time with quite a heavy train (for such gradients) of 12 coaches (averaging 15 to 18 tons each) and an eight-wheeler of 32 tons. As we followed this train out to the south-west, I noticed, to my great satisfaction, that the sun was trying to emerge from the clouds.

The Tauern line takes the same course as the other for quite a long way, but has the Salzach and the Innsbruck line far below it, as our ascent is rapid. St. Veit looked very pretty behind, and, after traversing a tunnel and crossing a viaduct, there is a view back to the portal of a tunnel of the other line now far below us. Beyond the third kilometre post out of Schwarzach the view in front of the narrow valley of the Salzach, with high hills on either side shelving very steeply down with finely-wooded slopes, is glorious, but soon we turned away from this fine spectacle and directed our course southward after passing Loifarn, taking a last glimpse backward to the overlapping wooded heights on the farther side of the Salzach as we altered our course to enter the Gasteiner Klamm. In front the view was equally splendid — the great peak of what I took to be the Bernkogel being visible. We passed through at least three tunnels (two of them are 800 and 814 yards), noticing, between a pair of them, a superb waterfall roaring below and sending its waters down to join the foaming stream, the grey waters of which were far below on our right. As we ran along the narrow, but level, valley floor to Dorfgastein on much easier grades than our previous 1 in 40, etc, the sun lit up everything finely and I began to think that my crossing of the Tauernbahn was going to be a success after all.

Beyond Dorfgastein high and savage-looking mountains — the Höhe Tauern connecting from the Schareck to the Ankogel — seem to (and actually do) bar our way in front, but the great tunnel is not yet. These great mountain forms receded almost altogether into the mist after Hofgastein, and I was able to concentrate my admiring gaze on the beautiful valley to the left in which the pretty village of that name, which is situated well to the south of the station, lies, far below the level of the railway track. Crossing several viaducts (respectively 78, 60, 72, 80, and 40 metres in length) before the 24th kilometre, we came, between the 25th and 26th, to the magnificent Anger-brücke, a metal span of 110 metres which crosses the torrent coming down from the Angerthal (here a turbid rush of wildly-descending brown waters) at a height of no less than 85 metres — a bridge quite worthy to rank those of the Gotthard line over the Reuss. From here, there is a fine retrospect to the grand black snow-streaked peaks closing the valley view in the direction from which we have come (these would be the Bernkogel and the Arlspitz), while, in front and to the left, the Kötschachthal is seen opening its gloomy way into the recesses of the Tauern. The head of our own valley — wooded and wild — is of similarly sombre, yet imposing, character and, but for the occasional villas and hotels of Badgastein, which we were now approaching and which lies on our left, would present an aspect of gloomy grandeur. The Gasteiner-Ache foams and roars, quite white in colour, on the farther side of the valley, a general view of which . . . was obtainable on the left. Near the 29th kilometre post, there was a small waterfall over rocks, close to the line on our right and then in front the spray from the great waterfall (round which villas are congregated in a semi-circle) is visible on the other side. Unfortunately, here rain was again descending, and now heavily, but did not very greatly mar the views. Beyond Badgastein, after crossing the Gasteiner-Ache, there was a grand high waterfall on the right and several smaller ones, and then keeping upward with the valley now on our right, the dim Ankogel glaciers were seen, very vaguely it is true, high up and just above us. At Böckstein Halte the mountain wall through which we were to tunnel our way was right in front of us, as also was the continuation of the narrow valley — as wild and savage a sight in the down-coming rain as could well be imagined. Then, turning into the Anlaufthal, a side valley equally as wild as the other, we crossed the grey Anlaufbach, foaming most furiously and, passing several fine waterfalls on our left, plunged, in a furious wind storm, into the great tunnel.

Emerging from our journey of 8,550 metres underground, the line comes out at an elevation of about 4,000 ft above sea, north of Mallnitz, with a retrospect behind us, on the left, up the Seebachthal, to the Ankogel glaciers towering above. The side valley of the Tauernbach is then seen to the right, dim snowy peaks closing it, and the foaming brown Mallnitzbach dashes along below, on the same side. Beyond Mallnitz a fine spiky peak is seen on the left and then we enter the Dössen tunnel (881 metres) and cross a viaduct of much similar type to those seen on the Arlberg line. A stupendous cone now comes into view in front and dim snow mountains close the view of the glorious valley of the Möll seen at a fearsome depth below us on the right — the turbid brown river here rushing along at top speed, swollen by the recent rains. Away to the west the view up the valley of the Möll was indescribably fine, and was closed by a peak and snowclad mountains. Opposite, as we neared Obervellach, stupendous peaks — the Polinik and others — pushed their summits up into the clouds, some dense masses of which also hung below our elevated rail-track and between us and the valley depths.

At Obervellach we passed the northbound express, running punctually, and then on to Kolbnitz is one of the most interesting parts of the line for engineering works, as, accordingly to my notebook, we here traverse a viaduct, a tunnel, a long tunnel, a short galleried tunnel, about five other tunnels, and a grand viaduct (see below), in this short distance of about twelve miles and perhaps some other viaducts were not noticed owing to our running in cloud-mists here and there. The first viaduct (over a turbid brown waterfall) and the tunnel following it are visible after leaving Obervellach some time before reaching them, and the scenery here, with the line high up above the Möllthal, is magnificent in the extreme, though occasionally all was obscured by our running into cloud-banks which, apart from the tunnels, too frequently blotted out the view. Between tunnels Nos. 15 and 16 is the grand metal Pfaffenberg-Zwenberg viaduct (referred to above) — the finest yet seen, I thought — which spans the white Wildbach far below us. The openings here are of 33, 58 and 33 metres and the height, 68 metres. Still running high above the valley I took a last glimpse of the opening of the upper valley of the Möll, which I had first seen before we reached Obervellach. A peak with a dim snowy range and a grand cone to the right of these closed this opening. The peaks right opposite us before we reached Kolbnitz were very high and extremely wild in appearance.

CHICAGO — ST. LOUIS, 1912

The morning of April 10th opened with gloriously fine, sunny and warm weather in Chicago, and after going down by tram to Dearborn terminus (where I saw a Santa Fe express with seven cars), to pick up my luggage, I had it conveyed to the Union depot by the Parmelee 'bus. [I was to travel to] St. Louis by the 'Alton Limited' — one of the crack trains of that road — [284 miles in 8 hours, with 12 stops]...

Our motive power on this run was engine No. 629 (a 4–6–2 of Class 15A), as far as Bloomington, and No. 632 (of the same type) thence. The load was the substantial one of one eight-wheeled day car, three twelve-wheeled day cars, and four twelve-wheeled parlour cars as far as Chenoa, at which point a twelve-wheeler was put off for Peoria. It is, of course, rather difficult to estimate the loads of these American trains, owing to car weights not being marked, but the minimum at the start would be quite 430 tons, and from Chenoa about 375. The maximum would be considerably greater.

Criticism of a run without the gradient profile must always be haphazard, and in this case, where slacks were so frequent at the beginning and in the later stages of the journey and where a part of the run (despite the statement in the 'Alton' folders for April, 1912, that Chicago to St. Louis is double track all the way) was performed over a single track, it seems hardly likely to serve any useful purpose. It would appear, however, from its name that 'Summit' station probably stands at the apex of two ascents and, apart from this, I noted ascents out of both Joliet and Lincoln. I clocked a few miles towards the end of the run and these I give for the benefit of any of my readers who are fortunate enough to have a gradient profile. Thus, 237 to 243 took 8 minutes 23 seconds and between Edwardsville and the slack over the river I noted a mile in 62 seconds and, after the slack, another in 80, both these latter being clocked from posts on an adjacent parallel line, while, nearing Granite City, I got a mile in 63 seconds.

Some salient facts of the journey may now be set forth briefly. Firstly, in spite of an almost heartbreaking series of slacks, coupled with occasional probable over-stoppages at stations, the two locomotives converted slightly late starts into handsomely too-early arrivals at their respective destinations. Thus, although nearly 14 minutes late at Joliet, we were so much before time at Bloomington — only about 89 miles away — that we nearly got stopped outside the latter station for being too early, and indeed actually pulled up there more than 3 minutes before time. This bit (from Joliet to Bloomington) was the only really unhindered part of the whole run, and part of it, namely the start-to-stop runs from Joliet to Dwight in 43 minutes 36 seconds (36.4 miles) and from Pontiac to Chenoa (14 minutes 13 seconds for 10.4 miles) were really very creditable with such a load. Secondly, the performance furnishes one more illustration of the fact that actual work in the United States far surpasses what seems to be called for in the time-table. Quite moderate-looking schedules, such as this one, in actuality often demand fine work from the locomotive, by reason of heavy train-loads, delays en route of the most serious nature, and over-stoppages at stations. I made this journey in a very fine Chicago and Alton Chair car, which had the seats, arranged two and two on each side of the central corridor, quite distinct from one another, both having armrests on either side. They were also not so uncomfortably close behind one another as is customary in the American day cars. Each seat had a very large window at the side of it, of which the upper part was (like a Grand Trunk car noticed some days earlier) arched, as seen from the outside. This window-sash was fitted with double panes, and above it the ornamental brass luggage rack was fitted. The car roof was unusual in shape ... and had eleven single electric lights each side ... and six quadruple ones in the centre... Two large mirrors brightened up the ends of the car, and the lavatory accommodation was reached by a swinging door from the main part of the car interior.

Since leaving the Great Lakes, fine scenery had been conspicuous by its absence, and to-day's run formed no exception to that rule. The weather, luckily, was again glorious right through from the dawn to the fall of a perfectly quiet and soft night, and so the otherwise quite ordinary scenery was transmuted into something most pleasant to look upon. Going out of Chicago there was — just as on entering it — a wilderness of railway tracks which I, with my very short experience of that great town, did not attempt to unravel, and even as far out as Lambert an electric line was paralleling us to left. Near Joliet we crossed the Rock Island road which had rather a poor-looking signal-box below us. Flat maize-growing country is soon entered on and before Braidwood we crossed the fairly wide Kankakee River. Between Dwight and Pontiac an electric line paralleled us on our left, and then, still with the most beautiful weather, we went on past Lexington, where there were maize fields everywhere, crossing the Illinois Central road at Normal 'at grade' — a practice very rare indeed in England but quite common in the USA — and again at Lawndale (that road having a wooden station here painted in white and brown). Beyond Lincoln we passed the northbound train, due there at 3.15 (about half an hour late), and saw an electric road, with fine cars, close to us on the left. Still the flat country and still the glorious weather continued, the former, beyond Nilwood, with its maize fields, looking very fine in the lovely soft light of a perfectly-quiet evening. This glorious mellow light, in the east, lit up beyond Plainfield many trees which had retained last year's leaves and was preparatory, so to speak, to a splendid sunset, the orb of day going down like a red ball. Farther on, near Wood River, many lines, converging, herald the approach to St. Louis and the very broad Mississippi appears on the right. Near Edwardsville a tributary of the great stream (probably the Wood River) is crossed, and at Mitchell several tracks come alongside of us, seemingly belonging to various roads. We then crossed the very wide Mississippi, with many neighbouring evidences of floods, and thereafter had the great river on our left, the journey soon coming to an end after this. Arrived in St. Louis, I put up at the Terminal Hotel. With the evening already well advanced and having to leave at a fairly early hour in the morning, I was quite unable to see anything of the town at all and so devoted my time to an examination of the great terminal station here.

HAMBURG — BERLIN, 1913

Rising at half past five, I found splendid weather. Joining the Berlin express at Altona, I noted the arrival of the Kiel express, with five 'D' eight-wheelers and a small eight, just before its due time of 6.51. Our times on to Berlin [287 kilometres in 3 hours 26 minutes, with one stop, made] one of my finest runs up till now on the Continent.

Our engine on this splendid run was an 'Altona' 4–6–0 (No. 1102) and, for a very short distance out of Hamburg, a pusher behind gave us a good send-off with our enormous load (for 1913) of 438 tons empty (I can hardly estimate what the weight 'with passengers' would be, as our eleven heavy eight-wheelers were packed, and people were standing in the corridors as well). With so very heavy a train as this, not to clock would have been to miss a rare opportunity, so I took off a good many kilometres...

The wonderful feature ... is that nowhere (except on the twenty-four kilometres done in 893 seconds) was a 60 mph gait reached, and so slightly above that rate were the twenty-four kilometres done, as a block, that probably many of them did not touch the mile-a-minute rate. And yet the book speed of this train throughout its journey was nearly 54 mph and was slightly improved on! In the absence of a gradient profile, minute criticism is hardly feasible, but one would imagine an upward trend, if anything, from a riverside port like Hamburg to a place in the interior like Berlin. The two blocks, unhindered by slacks and probably unhindered by opposing grades, namely from 247 post to 161 and from 90 to 23 — in all, slightly over 95 miles — were covered in 99 minutes 58 seconds, and in view of the fact that the load (empty) was 438 tons and (full) quite 475, I am not sure whether this run does not surpass my more spectacular feats up to this time on the Nord of France, where some surprising work on uphill grades was accomplished with, however, much lighter loads...

Of notes on scenery, weather, and incidents of the run, there were few. The morning was a glorious one, with trees, grass and shrubs (as seen at Wittenberge) simply sparkling in the sun. Our train-crowd was well looked after at this holiday season, as not only were coffee and beef tea brought round, by means of the corridor, but also beer, port and sherry. On arrival in Berlin, I made my way at once round by the Ringbahn to the Potzdamer station, walking thence to the Anhalt Bahnhof. As seen from the railway, the capital presented a very bright aspect...

Though we got away from Tsitsihar before midday by St. Petersburg time, so great was the discrepancy (about 6 ¼ hours) between that and solar time, that evening was already coming on and a glorious evening too, with cooler air after the earlier great heat. Some twenty-five minutes out from Tsitsihar we slackened speed over a swampy piece of ground, and from here nothing but tall grass or reeds were in view all the way to the western horizon. Stopping at Jen-t'ung-t'un, the night was indeed a lovely one, nothing being audible but the sound of the wind and the singing of birds, while the great expanse of swampy land gave one the idea that the line was running into, or near to, a desolate sea. Some ten minutes later we again slowed down at a point where again the ground seemed treacherous, and then, going on past Hsia-ho-tzu we crossed, at 707 versts from Manchuria, the westbound Siberian express (No. 1), running, with six cars, up to time. An interminable expanse of green grassy country, flat to the very horizon, followed, east of this, on either side. A fine light, tingeing a mass of cloud in front, held sway in the western sky, and, later, the crescent moon appeared. Just before Sartu a small lake was noticed on our right, and then, midway between Sartu and Anda, there was another slowing over a swampy bit of land, the moon glinting finely on water hereabouts. With the gradual oncoming of darkness, little else could be seen, but sparks were coming heavily from our wood-burning locomotive before Anda. Then came the tragedy of the run in the shape of a stop for nearly three-quarters of an hour to pass a train at Sung. Being due at Kharbine at 3.50 p.m. (or about a quarter past ten local time), and being already nearly 50 minutes late and having to see about re-booking my luggage there, I had anticipated that it would be necessary to remain up until our probable (real) time of arrival about 11 p.m. and, with an hour devoted to the luggage, had fully expected to retire by midnight. This irritating stop, however, put everything back about three quarters of an hour, and had a still more serious effect, in that, pulling up near a swamp, the train was invaded by hordes of mosquitoes and grasshoppers, attracted by the lights. Realizing that if these creatures invaded the sleeping berths a night of discomfort would result, I closed my windows (which in common with others throughout the train had been kept open owing to the heat) almost at once, and thus escaped much trouble, although my night's rest was a very short one. Many passengers, however, got no sleep at all as the corridors and berth-compartments were humming with mosquitoes. As regards the grasshoppers, dark green in colour and somewhat repulsive to look upon, they seemed to favour the dining-car and, flopping down in great numbers quite at random on tables, food or even on the persons of the passengers, gave us an unusual opportunity to examine these curious insects.

Crossing the very wide Sungari (at 5.9.30) just outside Kharbine, we ran into that station, where more trouble awaited me. I had noticed, in visiting the berth-compartment adjacent to my own, that its sole occupier had filled it up with all his heavy baggage, which, he told me, had, by means of a tip, been put direct into the compartment at Moscow without being weighed and charged for according to tariff. My luggage having to be re-booked at Kharbine, he advised me to adopt a like procedure, but thinking that even State railways have rights, I refused. At Kharbine, however, I was approached by the sleeping-car conductor, who said he could get it through without payment. At first I declined to have anything to do with it, but seeing that he (fearing to lose my tip for the service) was getting surly and being afraid that, in that state of mind, he might wilfully lose my baggage, I somewhat weakly consented. The baggage therefore disappeared — but not to the baggage room and, up to within about five minutes of our re-start, had not come back. Inquiry in the baggage room proved worse than useless, the conductor suddenly seemed to have lost what little English he had, and I was rapidly becoming quite sure that I had seen the last of my trunks (without the possibility of claiming for their loss, as to do so would involve a confession of my complicity in an effort to 'do' the railway) when, to my great joy, they appeared in the hands of two or three porters from behind a brick wall, and all was safe again. The baggage-room people, thanks to my questioning them, made some inquiries just at the moment of our re-start, which, however, were warded off by our conductor.

Less than two hours sleep had to suffice after getting away from Kharbine, and by about half-past two in the morning I was up, noting some little time thereafter that a lovely morning was promised and having a good view of the sunrise — the red ball being seen coming up out of the horizon...

Our engine for this run (No. 661 — a small 4-6-0) brought us right along from Kharbine and thus had a stretch of over six hours' duty. The load of six cars totalled, as before Karymskaya, 270 tons. The running appears to have been very moderate in character, although it is true that some eleven minutes of lost time were recovered. Criticism, however, seems unnecessary as no gradient information is available, and none was gathered *en route*.

Of other notes I made but few, as somewhat tired by want of sleep, I reserved my energies for notes on the new line (the South Manchurian) beyond Changchun — the Siberian and Chinese Eastern roads having already been fairly fully commented on. At Mei-sha-tzu some of the

Russian State first- and second-class eight-wheelers were seen, which, with very wide corridors, seemed really excellent coaches, athough of the interior of the compartments I could see but little. Of these compartments there were not so many as in the Wagon-Lit stock, and opposite each, outside in the corridor, were a small table and an adjustable seat. A string luggage rack was also provided just under the semi-circular roof of the corridor. Then, as regards the scenery, the flat country seemed well cultivated on the whole, while, nearing Changchun there were some low mountains or hills on the left (the Hu-lan-hê-ta). We completed our long journey at that station 78 hours 35 minutes and 30 seconds after our start from Irkutsk, changing over to the South Manchurian train on the other side of an island platform there, where we were welcomed by a cheery-looking and most obliging set of Japanese porters, nattily dressed in blue and white and carrying the word 'Porter' on their uniform. Practically, with a change of gauge, the Russian part of the run may be held to have ended here, so perhaps this is the most appropriate point at which to give briefly, and in most general terms, my broad impressions of the journey. As regards the speed of the run, there was nothing remarkable anywhere and at times the work was poor, but, considering the remote land that was being travelled through and the respectable weight of the train, I have nothing to complain of, and the performance was quite equal to anticipations. But for dropping behind time on the latter portion of the run, the time-keeping was excellent and schedule was more nearly adhered to than on the transcontinental railways of America. Track, although not remarkable, was certainly better than I had been led to expect, and ballast seemed much more neatly disposed than on some of the western roads, say, of Canada. Verst, gradient and curve indicators were generally good, but their chief feature was the way in which they stood out by the side of the line on coloured surrounds of varying patterns, than which, of the sort, I have seen nothing so good anywhere else. Stations, section-houses and, in fact, all buildings, seemed to have a very high standard of upkeep, and in a great number of cases recent repainting had made all look very spick and span. Of the waiting-room accommodation I made few notes and cannot say if it was good, but platforms were excellent and often very extensive. On the whole, therefore, the general aspect of the line was very fine, and I was well pleased with it. I have, of course, on all these points a very great number of notes, which I have not space to reproduce here.

We went on from Changchun (leaving the station at the end by which we entered it) to An-tung in [16 hours for 360 miles]. The gauge is now 4 feet 8 ½ inches instead of the Russian 5 feet.

Our engines on this run were No. 802 (a 4–6–2 of the South Manchurian Railway) from Changchun to Moukden — a long run of about 6 ½ hours. This engine was painted black and kept very clean, and was succeeded by No. 604 (a 4–6–0) which was still at the head of affairs 5 hours afterwards and probably went right through to Antung, where, although my clocking operations ceased, I noted that No. 402 (a 4–4–0 of the Chosen Railways) took charge for the first part of the night journey. This engine had brass bands round its boiler much like some types on the Etat Belge, and had a eight-wheeled tender. Our load out of Chanchun was six eight-wheeled cars (built by the Pullman Company). Three only of these made our train beyond Fengtien (or Moukden), and we went out of Antung with three. Their weights I did not discover.

Apart from the fact that (even allowing for a probable loss of 3 minutes by my watch during the day) we came into Antung handsomely before time after a late start out of Changchun of nearly 50 minutes (over thirty minutes of this improvement on time was due to curtailing our waiting time very drastically at Tiehling and at Moukden), there is little remarkable about the work done, and in the absence of a full gradient profile, I think detailed criticism is unnecessary. Possibly the long ascent from Shih-chiao-tzu to Chi-chia-pu was not bad. A few miles were clocked off and a few grades picked up from the indicators, but only a few, and these tell us practically nothing...

I made this journey in a train of which, before I saw it, good accounts had reached me — one of these, indeed, going so far as to assert that it was the finest train in the world. That it certainly was not; but undoubtedly it was very comfortable, and was simply but artistically fitted-up. The first-class accommodation was in compartments (rather cramped after the Wagon-Lit stock we had been accustomed to from Moscow), while the second was open. Exteriorly the colouring was green and the appearance (like that of other trains seen to-day, which carried third class as well) was generally that of an American train. My first-class compartment may be more fully described thus. It was upholstered in green plush, which, in some of the compartments, had a cover of holland sheeting, and the woodwork was walnut. The appointments included a (let-down) wash-basin, with hot and cold supply, a writing-table, mirror, towels, water-bottle, and a glass for drinking purposes (this was secreted behind the mirror). An electric fan, three electric lights, and a netting (to prevent flies or other insects entering when the window was open) were also provided. The compartment door could be locked from the inside and the glass in the door leading to the corridor was covered by a green curtain. One of the first-class cars was partly open like an American car and had, besides, two or three compartment sections, and another, instead of washing accommodation in the compartment as described above, had a large general lavatory for the use of the whole car.

Imagined Journeys

Any revolution as great and many-sided as that brought about by the coming of railways was bound to be reflected in contemporary literature; and so, from Fanny Kemble's first observant notes on the opening of the Liverpool & Manchester line and the biographies by Samuel Smiles through to the novels of Mrs Gaskell, George Eliot and a host of others, there is no shortage of references by classic writers to the conditions of the early railway age in Britain alone. Sometimes these are mere *en passant* comments such as Trollope's abuse of the railway sandwich: at other times there is more development or even an argument of approval or denigration. But it is generally — if paradoxically — true that railways began by being taken almost for granted by writers, and that only in their more sophisticated yet romantic age after 1870 do they appear as a subject worth attention for its own sake. And so for anything approaching a literary equivalent of Turner's *Rain, Steam and Speed* the arts had to wait more than three decades.

Even then the approach was coloured by differences of national outlook. In poetry, for instance, Britain (and Horatio Brown) produced well before the end of the nineteenth century an ode to the passing of the broad gauge on the Great Western. This contained some memorable lines ('The splendid stroke of driving wheel / The burnished brass, the shining steel', or 'Drive on then, engine, drive amain, / Wrap me, like love, yet once again / A follower in your fiery train'), as well as an itinerary of the old route past 'Sweet Clifton dreaming in a haze' to where 'The wind blows free / From levels of the Cornish sea.' But what is most notable is that even around 1890 a poem is coloured with affection and nostalgia, those feelings — usually directed towards the branch line rather than the express — which were to dominate the later offerings of the 'Georgian' poets (Yes, we all remember Adlestrop), of the light-verse writers of 'Punch', and of Sir John Betjeman. Respect and admiration for railways are, after the first flurry of heavy-handed wonder at the coming of 'King Steam', emotions which rarely appear in the verse of the nation which gave them birth. And when they do appear the poem is usually less than satisfactory: Spender's 'pylon school' salutation which forms part of the epigraph of this book is one of the better examples, but the single adjective 'jazzy' makes it far more of a period piece than the most pedestrian of nineteenth-century odes.

Unless romance is to be sought in such immortal but subterranean lyrics as 'Eskimo Nell', then, it is but poorly represented in English verse. Certainly one poet at least faced the problems which the very word raises — Rudyard Kipling, with his argument that romance always appears the lord who 'was with us — yesterday' but which in reality still 'brings up the 9.15'. To the present-day reader, though, Kipling's case is flawed in that he wrote in the age of steam, an age now regarded as synonymous with railway romance: would he, one wonders, have found this elusive quality in a computer-signalled shuttle-service of diesel multiple units?

For the rest, the English poets have recognised their railways mainly in lineside glimpses, whilst America is perhaps best represented through such vernacular ballads as 'The Runaway Train' and 'The Little Red Caboose'. Certainly (as the epigraph of this book again shows) Walt Whitman made some gestures towards the great systems which began to span his continent from 1870 onward: but his references are surprisingly few, and such spasms as:

... O the engineer's joys! to go with a locomotive!
To hear the hiss of steam, the merry shriek, the steam-
  whistle, the laughing locomotive,
To push with resistless way and speed off in the distance...

do not show that ludicrously logorrhoeic writer at his best.

In France, by contrast, the great expresses appear in the works of a number of poets who, after the Franco-Prussian war, seemed anxious to atone for the opposition to all railways expressed by such earlier *littérateurs* as Flaubert, de Musset and de Vigny. Verlaine, imprisoned at Mons in 1875 for his assault on Rimbaud, heard in his *nuits blanches* the marshalling of wagons which would soon escape to freedom like fledglings fleeing a nest, and shortly afterwards the Flemish Emile Verhaëren (of whom Raymond Prince wrote 'ses "Villes tentaculaires" sont sillonées de rapides, ses nuits sont illuminées par les feux multicolores des signaux'), Blaise Cendrars, Valéry Larbaud and a number of minor figures were disputing the title of *le poète des wagons-lits* and seeing in the *grandes lignes d'Europe*:

... Tout s'oublie — et les tunnels, et les wagons,
Et les gares de suie et de charbon couvertes —
Devant l'appel fiévreux et fou des horizons
Et les portes du monde en plein ciel ouvertes...

If this note on poetic trains must be restricted to verse in only two languages, any treatment of the roles enacted by the world's great expresses in the world's great (and less-great) novels must be still more cursory: the length of this chapter could be filled many times over from the relevant literature of Russia alone, and a long and learned essay has been written on the incidence of the railway in Dickens. When to this problem of compression there is added the language barrier, it is clear that one must resist the temptation to recount the plot of *By the Night Express — A Psychological Romance of 1889* or even of *The Stolen Boat Train*, published in 1936. In this the *Golden Arrow* in its entirety is stolen by agents who ferry it to Germany, pack it with hostile troops, and return it to Britain for a trip over obscure branch-lines to Victoria. Since this is so convenient for Buckingham Palace... But no: only samples *can* be given from the domain of the express in literature: and, as the latter example above suggests, one of the richest hunting-grounds is the English-language crime-thriller.

For this field is itself wide enough. Even when one has reluctantly discarded some classic short stories (one of which may have anonymously starred Sherlock Holmes himself) as not featuring 'great' trains, such pure detective novels as those of Freeman Wills Croft as over-technical, and a whole host of other works because the express plays only a minor part in them, there is still a recognisable group of tales which might well share the generic title of 'Death on the 11.35'. Those set in Britain itself (and one writes 'Britain' rather than 'England' if only because of Dorothy Sayers's devilish tricks with Scottish ticket-punching in *The Five Red Herrings*) are perhaps the strongest in straightforward detection, though H. R. F. Keating recently sent his delightful Inspector Ghote on a fine crook-chase on the *Bombay–Calcutta Mail*; but if there is to be a little glamour, violence and even seduction thrown in, then one must turn to the trans-European saga. In the hands of an Agatha Christie *(The Mystery of the Blue Train)*, of course, this itself can be a classic legend of logical deduction: in the hands of an Eric Ambler it becomes a more direct action story. This latter school was in the writer's opinion degraded by Ian Fleming, that master of technical inaccuracy: for it was Fleming who contrived to perpetrate, in the very year which saw the inception of the TEE system, a remark about the great trains going out all over Europe. The work involved was *From Russia With Love*, an episode in the life of 007 otherwise memorable mainly for James Bond's seduction by a Russian lady-spy whose idea of appropriate nightwear in a *wagon-lits* was black stockings, a black neckband, *et praeterea nihil*.

There are, however, near-masterpieces in the genre of train crime, and it is interesting to cite here two works which intrude into other chapters of this book. One is *The Wheel Spins* by Ethel Lina White — aunt to the author of the essay which follows this — and the other is Graham Greene's evocative *Stamboul Train*. (The express in the former is fictional, but Greene's passengers follow accurately the route of the through cars from Ostend to Istanbul). For these novels proved parents to a whole family of romances based on the *Orient Expresses*. Somebody lies drugged in a *wagon-lits*: a corpse is substituted (but *by which side?*): the prime minister is being eyed across the aisle of the diner by a communist, a reformed prostitute and a drug-pedlar disguised as a bishop (or *vice-versa*): in the *fourgon* a countess is doing something rather complex with gold ingots: and in the moments when the racing wheels quieten one can hear cartridge-clips being fed into well-oiled automatics, ready for the final shoot-up amid the snows of the frontier... This composite image dominated several novels and even more screenplays of the 1930s: and if there was never such a real-life train of events, most of its components have *some* parallel in the factual history of those expresses which have, for a round century, united Cap Gris Nez to the Golden Horn.

In many of these books crime has had love — or at least lust — as a travelling-companion. It is true that nothing very exciting happened to Lady Chatterley (who, snob that she was, condemned the *Simplon Express* for its 'vulgar depravity') on her way to Venice; but ever since a delicately illustrated fragment of Victorian pornography-plus-flagellation appeared under the title of *Flying Scotsman*, train coupling has meant more than a chain holding two carriages together. And this is so despite the fact that the ordinary sleeper-berth is so narrow as to demand sexual athleticism of a high order (or, alternatively, long-welded rail) if involuntary *coitus interruptus* is to be avoided. James Bond certainly passed a rhapsodic journey from Miami to New York in an episode of seduction of which his creator thought so highly that he used it almost word-for-word in two different stories. But then, 007 had the advantage of one of those private drawing-rooms available on American railroads (at one stage the *Broadway Limited* carried a bridal suite with exquisite Adam-style decor), and it is hard to believe that the click of latches being lifted between adjoining compartments and the pantings of passion mingling with the beat of wheels were ever sounds as common in fact as in fiction — at least in Europe, where these things are less commodiously arranged.

Even in the Old World, however, a pornographic gramophone record was recently released from Denmark under the title of *A Day in the Train with Anita and Jack*, and certainly there is a long-established association between high-speed travel and other pleasures. Dr Johnson (who had a limited choice of transport media) may have considered the height of bliss to be a fast drive in a post-chaise with a pretty woman: in the 1920s impropriety was equated with an Alfa-Romeo: and, since there is little distraction from shuffle-board except shuffle-bed, long sea journeys have had a good fictional showing too. Perhaps only air transport has missed out, on this score as on so many, since the halcyon days of champagne taken in the gondolas of balloons; for though there *are* tales of aerial seduction the tendency has been to sympathise with the lady who sang that 'Flying too high with some guy in the sky is my idea of nothing to do'. Certainly for all the advertising agents' talk of 'VC10-derness', and hints that their oriental hostesses are more oriental than those of the other outfit, the very idea of a jumbo jet is profoundly unaphrodisiac — quite apart from its great lack of privacy. But for *l'amour* in transit rail travel has held first place for at least the century since one Colonel Baker was dishonourably (and, as events proved, quite wrongly) dismissed from the British army, after a *cause célèbre* involving the Queen herself, for kissing a girl in a first-class LSWR compartment. And at the expense of a further digression it is worth looking at another such real-life link.

Towards the end of the last century, then, both London and Paris had recognised routes of assignation. The French ladies — the *hétaïres ambulantes*, the *courtisanes à plein tarif* — worked the long-distance lines, thinking nothing of a run down to Lyons if they saw a likely prey embarking in Paris: 'Si le monsieur est excitable,' noted a contemporary journalist, 'il chauffe à Tonnerre, il s'enflamme à Dijon, il est perdu à Mâcon, et Perrache le voit descendre avec sa nouvelle "conquête".' But in England it could all be done on mass-production lines, thanks to the fact that trains then ran non-stop across London for eight minutes from Cannon Street to Charing Cross.

Innocent travellers waiting at the latter West-End station were indeed often puzzled at the number of ladies who descended from blind-shrouded first-class carriages only to take the next train back to the City terminus, leaving some silk-hatted merchant hastily readjusting his dress. But this trade ended when an intermediate stop was introduced, leaving a run of a quite inadequate five minutes. The specialists then had to set up quarters in an area which soon became known as 'Whoreterloo'.

For all such trade was for hard cash, whilst back in the field of fiction the archetypal train-seductress is an enthusiastic amateur. And *her* archetype entered the world in 1925 in a novelette without mention of which even the most superficial coverage of railway literature would be incomplete — Maurice Dekobra's *La Madone des Sleepings*.

Curious as is the French habit of detaching the gerundive from English composite nouns (but *un sleeping* certainly sounds much naughtier than *un wagon-lits*), it is nothing like as odd as the book itself. The heroine of this, for instance, was a Scots lassie named — though not all at the same time — Lady Winifred Grace Christabel Diana Wynham, and she was described as having received an *éducation sportive* (rather than *sentimentale*, presumably) at Salisbury College: whatever this seminary was it never taught Gracie to un-mix her metaphors, for she declared that her lovers must 'ripen in [her] safe deposit some golden apples from the garden of the Hesperides'. In fact, neither the lady nor the *compagnie internationale des wagons-lits* plays any very decisive part in the plot of this farrago; but it captured the imagination of the public, was translated into the languages of twenty-seven countries — or more even than were served by the CIWL at its peak — and sold over a million copies.

One must here reluctantly pass over a hundred other literary references to railways, ranging from a Dutch version of 'Orient Express' by A. den Doolard to *The Happy Death* of Camus or the dream-journey in *Alice through the Looking-Glass*, or from Nancy Mitford's disconsolate young lady at the Gare du Nord who was *not* an *esclave blanche* to Humbert Humbert hearing the midnight wail of trains in his Missouri motel: a concordance to Proust even includes such tantalising entries as 'psychological superiority of railway over motor-car' and 'the railway timetable the most intoxicating romance in the lover's library'. For crime and sex *are* the most piquant elements in all train fiction, and it is especially fascinating to find them united nearly a century ago in the sole masterpiece which gives to the railway the place which the sea holds in Conrad or Melville. This work (as John Foster White notes) also heads the sub-class of those which deal with the *affaires* of train crews themselves. It is, of course, Emile Zola's classic of the realist school, *La Bête humaine*.

Like many lighter novels, this has been translated into screen terms — and with the usual changes, for its director not only up-dated the story but in one version gave it a happy ending. (He also showed some ingenuity in symbolising the sexual act, not by the usual pounding pistons, but by the mighty orgasm of a water-tower.) But the book would also demand mention in any survey of railways as represented in the visual arts; for in the period between 1870 and 1889 which he spent planning, researching — with 700 pages of notes, many of them based on contemporary court cases — and eventually writing his *roman judiciaire*, Zola prowled around the yards of St. Lazare studying the 2–4–0 'd'une élégance fine et géante, avec ses grandes roues légères réunies par des bras d'acier, son poitrail large, ses reins allongés et puissants, toute cette logique et toute cette certitude...' which became one of his leading characters under the name of 'La Lison', or discussed the project with friends. Since one of those was Claude Monet, the scene has achieved its own immortality.

Monet's group of paintings form part of the homage which was paid by the impressionists to the railway in England as well as in France. But they also provided a fitting prelude to the publication of Zola's long, steam-drenched tale of the jealousy between driver and fireman which led to the pair falling together from the footplate. And behind 'La Lison', bound from Le Havre to the front line of the Franco-Prussian war, the drunken soldiers packed in their cattle-trucks cheered and sang as the express rushed on, past terror-struck faces on the platforms of Rouen, through the hastily-cleared marshalling yards of Sotteville, riding-down signals, firing-off unattended detonators, on to its passengers' doom and its own...

Perhaps this troop-train itself was not by the strictest standards an express. Perhaps the closing pages of *La Bête humaine* are melodrama rather than literature. But they presented, for the first time, a new image of excitement and dynamism — an image which, over the next eighty years, was to be realised as often in the racing forms of the cinema screen as in the rustling pages of the novel.

The Marx Brothers *Go West* — and so does almost everything else in sight.

Blue Horizons

The railway and the cinema have at least one feature in common in that their natural element is movement: and so it is not surprising that the passenger train made its screen *début* in the very first days of the new medium. As early as 1895 the Lumière brothers were showing to their astounded French audiences a fragment called *Arrival of a Train at La Ciotat Station* with sound provided by a compressed-air cylinder to represent the brakes, and in the same period there appeared Thomas Edison's *Black Diamond Express*. Soon such snippets as *Railway Ride over the Tay Bridge* (made only eighteen years after the great disaster) were proliferating on the flickering screen and variety was being provided by the 'phantom rides' in which the audience apparently rode the buffers for a panoramic view of the landscape; a Mr. Hale of Kansas City indeed seated his audiences in saloon coaches whilst they watched a projection of the passing scenery to the accompaniment of sound effects and simulated train-movement. But though a few daring fictional kisses took place in tunnels, it was not until the new century and the beginning of Hollywood's dominance over the young industry that there appeared a full-blown railway drama.

This was Edwin Porter's *The Great Train Robbery*, made in 1903 for the Edison company and described by the historian of railways in the cinema, John Huntley, as 'the most important single film in the first fifteen years of the cinema industry'. Its success launched a whole school of melodramas in which expresses played a prominent part. Many were in serial form and featured such early stars as Pearl ('The Perils of Pauline') White and Helen ('The Hazards of Helen') Holmes as the ladies who got lashed to the line. This was a situation familiar to the heroes and heroines of the nineteenth-century theatre, and the whole *genre* was inevitably parodied by Mack Sennett in *Barney Oldfield's Race for Life* of 1914, with Mabel Normand rescued in the nick of time by the arrival of the Keystone Cops on a hand trolley and the hero in a sports car. Two years later the same director introduced Gloria Swanson to his hazardous tracks as a 'Pullman Bride'.

Though the British had their Lieutenant Daring racing the London/Folkestone express by road and air, the Americans were leading the field; and in 1914 they came up with an exciting new development with the use in *The Wreck* of real locomotives and rolling stock for the crash of a west-bound express into a runaway engine. This proved so popular that many more veterans of the line perished to the wonder of audiences — and, retrospectively, the dismay of latter-day railway enthusiasts. Then, a decade later, the cinema of the railway reached epic status with John Ford's *The Iron Horse*, which told the story of the building of the Union Pacific railroad and its linking with the Central Pacific. The film

A frame from what is probably the world's first film made for entertainment, and certainly its first railway documentary — Lumière's *Arrival of a Train at la Ciotat*, made in 1895.

ran for over two hours, and was another major landmark in cinema history. Fifteen years later still, Cecil B. De Mille was to explore the same theme in *Union Pacific*, with the stellar attractions of Barbara Stanwyck and Joel McCrea.

The Russians made their own notable contribution to screen railway building, if in a more documentary context, with *Turksib* (1929) which deal with the construction of the Turkestan-Siberian railway and its effect on the life of the steppes. There is indeed an affinity between the mounted tribesmen of *Turksib* who gallop exuberantly in pursuit of their first locomotive and the Cheyenne Indians who more aggressively charge the advancing Union Pacific line in *The Iron Horse*.

The impassive features of Buster Keaton presided over *The General* (1927), that comic classic of the silent cinema with its incomparable locomotive chase based on a real-life incident in the American Civil War. In more sombre vein the twenties produced Abel Gance's *La Roue*, while Fritz Lang brought the *Nord Express* to destruction amid a flurry of espionage in the German *Spione*. As for Britain, the silent era was nearing its close when two notable railway subjects reached the screen, both adapted from stage successes and involving the same author; and so this seems the logical moment at which to switch the points towards some consideration of live entertainment, at least in the English language and with an accent on London.

Though Arnold Ridley's comedy-thriller *The Ghost Train* is perhaps the most famous of all railway dramas (it achieved a run of 655 performances on its first appearance in 1925, has since had two London revivals and innumerable provincial and amateur productions, has been filmed three times, shown on television, and even turned into a musical), the railway plays a somewhat mystifying part in its plot. But there is a genuinely blood-chilling moment when the lights of the ghost train flash past the waiting-room windows to the accompaniment of shrieking whistle and deafening roar as the curtain falls on Act II; and perhaps as a result of the effectiveness of this Ridley returned to the tracks two years later (and this time in collaboration with Bernard Merivale) with a much more express-conscious plot in *The Wrecker*, also later filmed.

This play opens in the London office of the Grand Trunk railway's chairman, complete with illuminated route-map and a window view of a signal gantry and the curve of a train-shed roof. The eponymous wrecker has already caused several train smashes on other lines, and now threatens to destroy the Grand Trunk's crack 'Rainbow Express' near a lonely signal-box in Yorkshire. The chairman himself is murdered just as he seems about to reveal the wrecker's identity, and in Act II we reach the signal-box where, after some fine skulduggery, it is left to the hero to toss a coin to decide which lever to pull in order to avert disaster. In the words of *Play Pictorial*, 'the whole scene is one of tremendous thrill and the whirling sound of the train travelling swiftly onwards to its doom is so realistically imagined and carried out that one holds one's breath until the fateful moment is passed'.

240

Vintage American railwayana, re-created for a 1972 production of a musical version of *Gone with the Wind* at London's Drury Lane theatre.

A scene from the 1909 production of *The Whip*, a melodrama which had as its highlight a railway crash on the stage.

It is a boat express which acts as catalyst in Noel Coward's *Still Life* (1936), set in the refreshment room of an imaginary Milford Junction station and telling the story of an ill-starred romance between a middle-aged lady and a doctor who are both already married. Alec meets Laura because she gets a smut in her eye as the train rushes through and he volunteers to remove it. At the end of the play, after the lovers have parted for ever, the same boat train is heard approaching again and a distraught Laura rushes out on to the platform — leaving the audience in suspense as to her intentions until it has passed and she returns, white and shaking, with the pathetic line: 'I just wanted to see the express go through.' *Still Life* became one of the most celebrated of British films as *Brief Encounter*, directed by David Lean and with Celia Johnson and Trevor Howard playing the parts created on stage by Gertrude Lawrence and Noel Coward himself. Evocative use was made of LMS locations at Watford Junction and Carnforth, with in the background the steam-hauled locals which have now acquired their own nostalgic *tristesse*. The plot of *Still Life* also returned briefly to London as part of a curious, composite musical, *Mr. and Mrs.*, worth recalling for a set which showed Milford Junction being rebuilt around its refreshment room as the action proceeded.

Noel Coward also introduced a scene at a London terminus during the 1914–18 war in his *Cavalcade* (1931) at the Theatre Royal, Drury Lane, with the arrival and departure of troop and hospital trains effectively simulated from the concourse side of the platform gates. For real Drury Lane spectacle, however, one must return to the days of melodrama — and in particular to 1909, when *The Whip* by Cecil Raleigh and Henry Hamilton presented what was surely the greatest train scene of all. The Whip is a horse, and in an attempt to prevent his running in the classic 2,000 Guineas race at Newmarket the villain uncouples his horse box, leaving it stranded in the path of an immediately-following express. The horse is led to safety just before (and again the words of *Play Pictorial* have an irresistible exuberance) 'a tremendously loud whistle sounds, and the express roaring out of the tunnel dashes into the box and smashes it to atoms'. The stage was strewn with casualties that included the derailed locomotive — but how did the 'goodies' discover the plot? One of them had posed as the image of the murderer Charley Peace in Madame Tussaud's chamber of horrors, and so overheard the wicked Captain de Sartoris plotting the whole operation with a lady whose own callous devilry extended to cynical remarks about 'all third-class passengers'.

Ivor Novello — who had earlier appeared in the film *Sleeping Car* — ran the gamut of true 'Drury Lanery' in his romantic musical plays, and for *Crest of the Wave* (1937) he arranged for the American transcontinental express, the *Chief*, to appear to rush through the night (though actually is was the scenery which moved) and then explode into smoking ruins. And in recent years Harold Fielding has carried on the tradition in his production of *Gone With The Wind* (1972), with a cow-catcher engine drawing into the depot of war-torn Atlanta.

Top left: One of London's brightest stars at the turn of the century was Marie Lloyd, whose *Oh! Mr. Porter* was one of those songs which has survived the years.

Top right: The music-hall performers of Britain's Victorian era found a vein of humour and sentiment in songs dealing with events on trains or with the railway as a background.

Right from the start sleeping cars were associated with naughtiness. This poster advertises a French music-hall performance which regarded the wagons-lits service as just an excuse for pretty girls to take their clothes off.

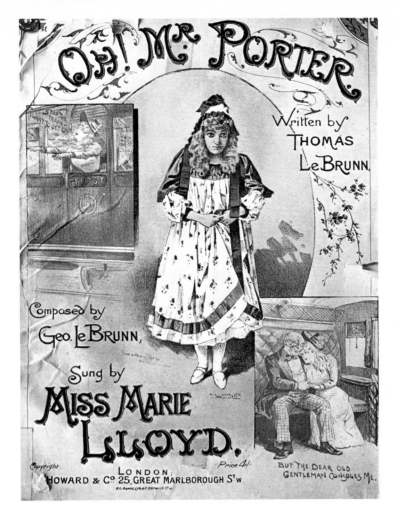

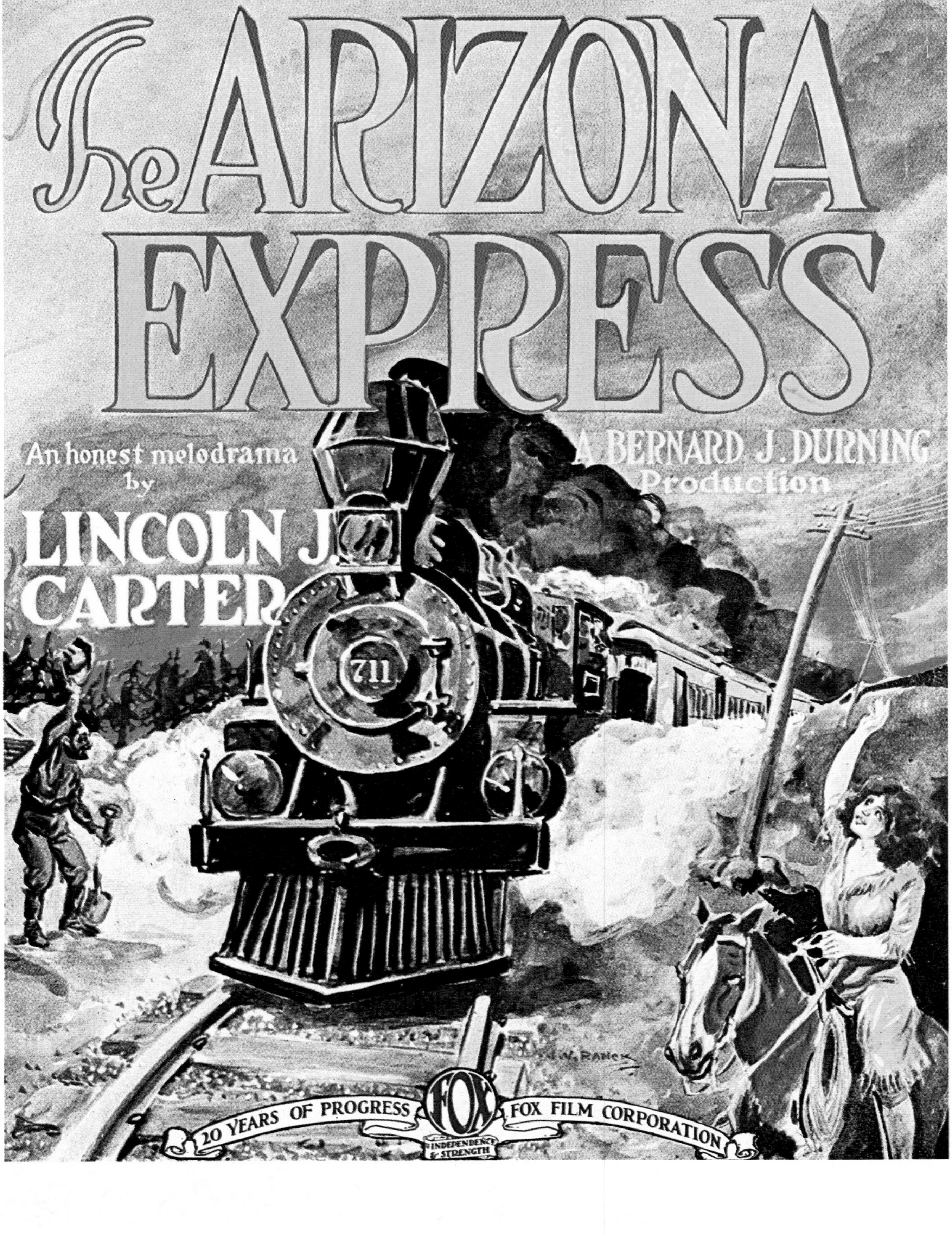

The ARIZONA EXPRESS

An honest melodrama by
LINCOLN J. CARTER

A BERNARD J. DURNING Production

20 YEARS OF PROGRESS — FOX — FOX FILM CORPORATION

INDEPENDENCE & STRENGTH

Drury Lane, however, has no monopoly of trains in this field. In 1910, in the early days of the Gaiety theatre musicals, *The Messenger Boy* had a song celebrating Bradshaw's timetable ('It has trains that dep. and trains that arr., / And trains that take you a lot too far...'), and a couple of years later *The Girl in the Train* saw Phyllis Dare involved in divorce proceedings as the result of an unfortunately locked door on the night sleeper from Nice to Amsterdam. *The Blue Train* (1927) had only one scene aboard that legendary express, but it brought Lily Elsie back to the stage to sing:

> They call it the Blue Train that goes to the South.
> So if you are blue, don't get down in the mouth.

This show did much for the growing reputation of Bobby Howes, who would soon keep company with Binnie Hale in *Mr. Cinders* and so come to Willow Vale station for 'a tremendous whiz-bang when the express train dashes through'. The music for *Mr. Cinders* was in part by Vivian Ellis, the composer of that perennially popular orchestral piece, 'Coronation Scot'.

Ever since, as far back as 1860, a Parisian music hall mounted a piece set in a station, a vast number of miscellaneous productions have paid their own tribute to the varied appeal of railways, these ranging from Folies Bergère revues through such Broadway productions as *Bye, Bye, Birdie* and *The Music Man* to a London theatre club presentation called *Steam*, which featured a duet between 'Puffing Billy and the Brighton Belle': in this the former sang 'I adore your first-class carriage and your neat upholstery / And if you will not have me then a Blue Train I must be.' Then, as a bridge from the theatre to the music hall and so to the world of popular ballad, we find a royal special in *Sing A Rude Song* (1970), a musical based on the life on Marie Lloyd with a scene on the platform at Crewe where Marie and her fellow artistes sing, none too reverently, of 'Waiting for the Royal Train' which is delaying theirs. And in the great days of London's music halls Dan Leno may have had his song 'The Railway Guard' and the comedian Jack Pleasants may have discoursed with gentle sentiment of 'Watching the Trains Come In', but Marie Lloyd's own 'Oh, Mr. Porter' of 1893 surely makes it plain that only an express could have caused the misfortunes of the young lady who wanted to go to Birmingham but was taken on to Crewe. Less well-remembered in the Lloyd canon, but offering full scope for her incomparable gift of innuendo, is 'What did She know about Railways?' Here 'a reg'lar farmer's daughter' arrived 'at Euston by the midnight train' but ran into trouble 'when someone wanted to punch her ticket'. What knowing nods and winks must have added a double meaning to this, and to such subsequent revelations as that when the police arrived they 'seized her rolling stock'.

In America — though not in Europe — there was a genuine railroad folk music, typified by the hobo ballad extolling that mythological express, 'The Wabash Cannon-Ball', which had 700 cars and eventually took off into space. Running into an age of less apocryphal composers and lyricists, the immortal 'Casey

Shanghai Express. Marlene Dietrich, Anna May Wong, and Clive Brook grouped in the corridor.

An early idea of how the West was won, described as 'an honest melodrama' ...

Jones' of 1909 (by T. Lawrence Seibert and Eddie Newton, though based on older themes) tells of the driver of a fast express and his fatal involvement with 'two locomotives that's a' goin' to *bump*!' For the ragtime era there is Irving Berlin's 'When The Midnight Choo Choo leaves for Alabam' (1912) with an over-eager passenger collaring and hollering at 'that rusty-haired conductor man' in his anxiety to be reunited with his honey lamb down south. Many will remember of another deep-rooted number, 'The Runaway Train' (1925), that 'she blew, she blew', but not perhaps that she ran away 'in the year of '89 on that old Chicago line' as a result of air-brakes not holding on the frozen rails. 'The Sleepy Town Express' (1930) was a somewhat saccharine account of 'an all-night trip on a pillow slip' but sophistication heightens as one approaches the world of Glenn Miller and boards the memorable 'Chattanooga Choo Choo' of 1941 on which: 'You leave the Pennsylvania Station 'bout a quarter to four 'Read a magazine and then you're in Baltimore 'Dinner in the diner, nothing could be finer than to have your ham'n eggs in Carolina...,' and the fireman is enjoined to: 'Shovel all the coal in, gotta keep it rollin'...,' so that a more comfortable journey to Tennessee can be enjoyed than by the participants in that great chase of 1862.

In 'Sentimental Journey' (1944) the train leaves at seven and the traveller has a reservation on which he has 'spent each dime I could afford'. In 'On the Atchison, Topeka and the Santa Fe' (included in a film of 1946 called *The Harvey Girls*, the saga of a restaurant chain which brought refreshment to railroad travellers in the West), the great Judy Garland sang the words and music of those almost-equally-great tunesmiths Harry Warren and Johnny Mercer. But, as in the theatre, one could roll on for ever: 'Alabamy Bound' in 1925, counting 'The wail of midnight trains in empty stations' among Eric Maschwitz's 'These Foolish Things' in 1935, or exploring the 'Rock Island Line' in the company of Lonnie Donegan in 1956. So, according to your fancy, 'Take the "A" Train' (1944) or do yourself proud on a fox-trotting 'Orient Express' (1933) — and maybe we will all arrive at 'Tuxedo Junction' (1940), singing lustily: 'I'm a Train, I'm a Train, I'm a Chuffer Choo Train' (1967).

A few 'serious' composers are also to be found working on the railroad, if not to the same extent as their more 'popular' brethren: between these two worlds, perhaps, one finds the Strauss family with Johann (Jr) contributing his 'Excursion Train' polka and Edouard a 'musical train ride' complete with guard's whistle. Thus, Villa-Lobos included 'The Little Train of the Caipira' in his 'Brachianas Brasileiras No. 2', and although this is the most modest of country trains — the word 'caipira' meaning 'yokel' or 'rustic' — it nonetheless inspired a singularly haunting and evocative piece of railway music in which, to quote Sir Eugene Goosens, 'the little train puffs and chugs along, and save for a solitary emergency stop (with great squealing of brakes) towards the middle of the journey, proceeds to its distant destination which it reaches safely in a process of gradual deceleration and much exhaust steam'. And there is something about it which suggests that not only peons but also some more sinister refugees from the corridors of *wagons-lits* lurk, suitably disguised, among its passengers. Almost a century earlier, Hector Berlioz had provided a cantata, 'Chant des Chemins de Fer' for the inauguration of the French Northern railway in 1846 — a spirited piece which was revived in the Brighton train-shed in 1972, with the participation of the massed bands of Britain's Guards regiments, to mark the last run of the *Brighton Belle*.

Looming austerely over all these *jeux d'esprit* is Arthur Honegger's 'Pacific 231' of 1923. Honegger loved locomotives 'as others love women or horses', and as a native of Le Havre knew well the 4–6–2s (or, in continental notation, 2–3–1s) which hauled many of the great expresses of the Ouest. In an interview with the Geneva journal *Dissonance* he said: 'What I have endeavoured to describe in "Pacific 231" is not an imitation of the sounds of the locomotive, but the translation into musical terms of the visual impression and the physical sensation of it.'

Yet in his dialogues with the *Figaro* music critic Bernard Gavoty he seems to have become more elusive and even contrary, suggesting that others had imposed their own interpretations whereas he was really on the trail of a very abstract and quite ideal concept by giving the impression of a mathematical acceleration of rhythm while the movement itself slowed. 'Musically, I composed a sort of big diversified chorale, strewn with counterpoint in the manner of J. S. Bach.'

Even deeper mystery surrounds what is (if one excepts the fictional and unproduced 'Gare du Nord' which forms a running joke in the novels of Caryl Brahms and S. J. Simon) almost certainly a train's only 'appearance' in the ballet. The work in question is 'Le Train Bleu', which Jean Cocteau devised to Darius Milhaud's music for the young Anton Dolin and the Diaghilev company; the costumes were by Chanel, the *rideau* by Picasso, and the first night was at the Champs-Elysées Theatre in 1924.

The train itself, alas, did *not* appear, the athletic action taking place on a *plage*. The ballet historian C. W. Beaumont quotes Diaghilev's own explanation for this fact: 'This being the age of speed, [the train] has already reached its destination and disembarked its passengers.'

To complicate matters, however, Diaghilev also tells us that after the first performance 'everybody was unaccountably seized with the desire to take the Blue Train to Deauville and perform refreshing exercises'. But why Deauville, on the Channel coast, when the *Train Bleu* heads south for the Côte d'Azur? Few balletomanes are likely to have dwelt on the questions posed by this insouciant mis-routing, and no one could deny that in the 'twenties everything about that train was terribly, terribly smart.

Later in this decade the cinema found its voice, and its trains were heard as well as seen. Many appeared in films using the evocative word 'express' in the title; and usually these were thrillers, sometimes adapted from novels. Thus, *Rome Express* (1932)

Many films in the 'thriller' category had a railway background, such as *Rome Express* . . .

had Conrad Veidt in a tale of theft and murder on the Paris–Rome run, combining effective studio sets with actual shots of the PLM. In Josef von Sternberg's *Shanghai Express* (1932), Marlene Dietrich as a lady with a past all but sacrificed herself to the bandit Warner Oland for the sake of a gallant captain played by Clive Brook. (*Sight and Sound* records here that the director established his Chinese atmosphere with 'a sequence in which the train puffed out of [Pekin], through an impossibly narrow street crowded with animals and people, while overhead hung hundreds of oriental banners'.) *The Phantom Express* (1932) dealt with the destructive activities of a supposedly-supernatural train, and *Orient Express* (1934) was a screen adaptation of Graham Greene's *Stamboul Train*. For *Streamline Express* (1936) the makers devised a 150 mph double-decker 'train of the future'. There were yet more spies in *Exile Express* (1939), while *Berlin Express* (1948) found Merle Oberon journeying through occupied Germany.

Alfred Hitchcock made considerable use of trains in his films, as in *The Thirty-Nine Steps* (1935), *The Secret Agent* (1936, with a spectacular crash in Switzerland), *Shadow of a Doubt* (1943, with the villain's villainy symbolised by the engine's black smoke), *Strangers on a Train* (1951), and — perhaps most memorably *The Lady Vanishes* (1938), where virtually the whole action took place on an unnamed train (*not* the *Orient Express*, as has so often been said) from an equally anonymous Balkan state. The passengers included Margaret Lockwood, Michael Redgrave and May Whitty as an endearingly mature British agent whose disappearance was the nub of the plot. In this film Sydney Gilliat and Frank Launder made a brilliant adaptation of a novel by Ethel Lina White, *The Wheel Spins*, and created the characters of two English cricket fanatics played by Naunton Wayne and Basil Radford. So popular did these obsessives prove that they resumed their transcontinental adventures in *Night Train to Munich* — this time in company with Rex Harrison — and other entertainments.

The passions and personal problems of engine-drivers and their firemen have provided a recurrent theme. *The Flying Scotsman* (1930) was only the third British talkie ever made (the first half-hour indeed remained silent), and in it the driver found his last run bedevilled by a vengeful former fireman dismissed for drunkeness and by his suspicions that the new fireman (Ray Milland's first screen role) was doing wrong by his own daughter. The director, Castleton Knight, was granted special running powers over the King's Cross/Edinburgh line together with the loan of the Gresley 'Pacific' No. 4472, and his authentic shooting of much of the run made up for an outrageously melodramatic script. In *The Last Journey*, made in 1936 with special trains provided by the Great Western, the driver became deranged by the belief there was an affair in progress between the fireman and his own young wife, with the result that a brain-specialist had to clamber perilously on to the footplate and reason him out of crashing the Mulchester express into the buffers.

In Jean Renoir's classic *La Bête humaine* of 1938 — titled in its English edited version *Judas was a Woman* — Jean Gabin as the

... and *Orient Express*, adapted from an 'entertainment' by Graham Greene. This frame shows most of the principal characters assembled in the dining-car.

Jean Gabin in Jean Renoir's adaptation of Zola's *La Bête humaine*.

driver suffered from homicidal tendencies. He eventually murdered his mistress, played by Simone Simon as the errant wife of a no-less-lethal sub-stationmaster, and then knocked his fireman unconscious before leaping to his death. Things worked out better for the driver in *Train of Events*, which began with the wreck of a London to Liverpool express and then flashed back into the four separate stories of those involved. Train films have always lent themselves to the composite plot, another example being *Broadway Limited* which rang the Los Angeles/New York changes on a temperamental film director, a missing baby, and a spot of romance for the engineer.

Such films can represent *only* a selection; for virtually every country in the world with a major rail network has seen it featured on the screen, from Canada in *49th Parallel* to India in *North-West Frontier* and *Bhowani Junction*. Conversely, every land with a tradition of film-making has produced its own railway dramas. The world of film *comedy* is smaller, and tends to have favoured branch lines of the more leisurely and bucolic sort. However, *The Titfield Thunderbolt* (1952) brought the veteran 1838 'Lion' out of retirement for a fine burst of speed along the Limpley Stoke/Camerton branch-line which had previously been used in *Kate Plus Ten* and the first sound version of *The Ghost Train*. Will Hay aspired to put on an excursion train from 'Buggleskelly on the Southern Railway of Northern Ireland' (otherwise the already-doomed Basingstoke-Alton branch) in his hilarious *Oh! Mr. Porter*. And certainly the Marx Brothers may be said to have burned up the track, along with most of the rolling stock, in their *Go West*.

This chapter cannot begin to touch on the worlds of radio, of television — though mention should be made that both large and small screens have done notably well by E. Nesbit's *The Railway Children* — or even of such documentaries as *Night Mail* (with music by Benjamin Britten), *Terminus*, or the four separate factual films all named after *The Flying Scotsman*. For even in the realm of film drama the mind flickers on and on. Garbo's *Anna Karenina* stands for ever wreathed in steam. Many a heart has been broken in parting at the principal stations of Vienna. Glenn Ford and Van Heflin must always make the *3.10 to Yuma*, Spencer Tracy arrives in streamline splendour for his *Bad Day at Black Rock*, and Alec Guinness be executed by a signal-arm in *The Lady Killers*. But at the end it is the music that comes surging up again. There goes Ruby Keeler, shuffling off to Buffalo with all those Busby Berkeley chorines in *42nd Street*. And here, at last and incomparably, comes Jeanette Macdonald in Ernst Lubitsch's *Monte Carlo* of 1930 — a runaway countess in the fullest of full voices, singing through a window of the *Train Bleu* to a melody that blends with the sound of the wheels and is then taken up by a choral peasantry in the fields along the line.

So 'Blow, whistle, blow away...' and 'Go engine, anywhere, I don't care how fast'. Rest assured that 'Beyond the blue horizon waits a beautiful day'. And, as surely, there waits yet another play, film or song that has in it the sight or sound of the express train.

Envoi

. . . Voiles de vapeur et de fumée
Se fanent au fond de l'horizon.
Train qui entend ton cri triste ou clair?
Où sont les grands express d'antan?

The very word 'envoi' suggests some 'Ballade des trains morts'; but perhaps the final note in this book should not be too elegiac, too reminiscent of the chime whistle fading beyond the fir-clad crest. For if the sights and sounds and smells of steam have passed from the trunk lines of the world, the two-tone diesel note sounds clear and electrification has brought one evocative sound of its own in the hot dry crackle as the pantograph breaks contact at some lonely frontier station. And in any case this book was not conceived as yet another tribute to the steam locomotive or even to railways as such, but as a tribute to *trains*.

And, writing of the trains they have travelled on or long to have travelled on, many of the contributors here have found themselves between two moods. One such is indeed threnodic: it knows that certain standards can never return, that the trains which were 'great' in the sense of possessing a marked individuality or quality of service passed with (or even before) the age of steam. But the other mood suggests that after fifty years a corner has been turned and a pendulum is swinging back — that we have become sick of the stink of immobile automobiles and the sound of screaming skies, and that with technical advances keeping pace with this environmental concern the passenger train has before it an illustrious future.

Today's world is divided between the developed and the developing. With new railways being built as gaps in a global map of over 750,000 miles of track are still filled in, it may be that the future will see great expresses — trains, that is, which cover long distances at reasonably high speeds and offer worthy standards of accommodation — appearing in China, in central Africa, and in other theatres which have as yet witnessed little more dramatic than the twice-a-week mixed freight working its way over a bumpy single track. But meanwhile the industrialized world seems at the edge of a spectacular and splendid railway renaissance as it witnesses the *début* of a new railway race between various forms of ultra-high-speed passenger express.

Such trains first left the drawing-board in Japan — the country which (with the possible exception of Switzerland) has remained most faithful of all to the railway. But as this book was published there was hardly one industrialised land which was not experimenting — or keenly watching the experiments of others — with such new railway techniques as pneumatic or magnetic cushioning, linear motors and novel suspension systems. Even the USA, so long kept out of this progress by out-dated practices and by a low-quality management which lacked men of the vision of Europe's

Francis den Hollander and Louis Armand, has now undergone — perhaps just in time — a change of heart. And although all aspects of rail technology are nowadays closely linked, the primary beneficiary of such devices will be the passenger express.

So the needle on the meter of putative average speeds moves on from 150 to 175 or more mph; the peak readings sweep up from 200 to 250 or above: and every such increase extends the range below which the train has the advantage in time over that dubious and demotic medium which (whilst itself remaining in so many respects set in the earliest railway age) has apparently destroyed all the romance of speed and distance — the medium of the air. The sceptical may point out that much of this is *only* putative, that technical possibilities are not economic realities, that there are perhaps rather too many new railway techniques currently under development. But bearing in mind the world's present dissatisfaction with the structure of its transport, the chances would seem to favour the introduction of some form of express regularly operating around the 250 mph mark well before the end of the twentieth century, and probably first in Japan or in a Channel-tunnel-linked Europe.

Great trains, then, will still be with us, and moving at speeds which will reduce the achievements of the past to the racing of snails. But what of the glory which those of old trailed in their wake like their vanished clouds of steam? What of the bright liveries and lavish decor, the noble meals and golden names and attentive but unobsequious staff which, perhaps, were never combined on any real train on this imperfect earth?

Despite all the excellencies of such expresses as South Africa's *Blue Train*, Australia's *Indian Pacific* and New Zealand's *Silver Star*, that world whose standards have dominated this book can *not* return. But — if only so that these pages may close on another note of comfort — it should not be forgotten that the splendours of rail travel were never entirely those of luxurious service. Much of its attraction derived from the lineside flashes of other lives — the vineyard worker bent over his crop, the city clerk at supper behind a lit window — and even more came from those landscapes which were (and which, in an increasingly-uniform world, are still) swept out by the tracks of the great expresses. Nothing in the foreseeable future is likely to diminish the excitement of such moments as bring the flash of morning sunlight reflected from Lac Léman a thousand feet below through the wide windows of *wagon-restaurant* or hail the first glimpse of the Rockies after a day of rolling plains: and such moments can never be provided by any means of transport other than the railway nor enjoyed in any other surroundings than those of the passenger express. The great trains, then, are no more dead than are those ringing names immortalised in Villon's ballade. Instead:

> *Princess, in their own regal way,*
> *By field and city they sweep on*
> *And serve the voyager of today*
> *As did* les grands express d'antan.

Contributors

BRYAN MORGAN (Editor) received a scientific education, but since 1947 has devoted himself entirely to working as a writer and editor. Although he has published books and articles covering a very wide range, he has made a speciality of travel and transport matters. The present work, following on his best-selling *The Railway-Lover's Companion*, is his fifth to deal with one or another aspect of the railway scene.

ALAN A JACKSON (Assistant Editor), although by profession a civil servant working in the British Treasury, is well known as an expert in two fields — railways, and the recent history of London and its suburbs. He has written authoritatively on these subjects in *London's Termini*, *Semi-Detached London*, and other books.

JOHN SNELL broke off a career in public transport, which included some years with British Railways, to qualify as a barrister-at-law. He nevertheless retained his interest in resuscitating small but historic railways, and today combines his qualifications as managing director of the Romney, Hythe & Dymchurch line.

ARTHUR D DUBIN is an American architect with an important practice based on Chicago. To the public of two continents he is, however, best known as the leading expert on the great trains of the United States, with his *Some Classic Trains* and *More Classic Trains* being themselves classics.

CHARLES OWEN has written extensively about travel, following his varied work in the Royal Navy, industry and government, and management consultancy. His journeys by rail have covered most of Europe, some of them being made specially for this book.

JOHN FOSTER WHITE, after spending 25 years in London publishing, now devotes himself to writing and freelance editorial work. His interests include the theatre, popular arts, architecture, local history and topography.

K WESTCOTT JONES has, in the course of some three million miles of travel, visited Russia six times. He is the travel correspondent for a number of widely-read British regional newspapers.

PHILIP UNWIN was senior director of a publishing house whose list includes many railway books. He has had a lifetime's interest in travel by sea and rail.

DAVID TENNANT, a Scots-born journalist, is travel editor of the *Illustrated London News*, a correspondent for other periodicals, and a former chairman of Britain's Guild of Travel Writers.

DAVID ELLIOT, though actively engaged in producing children's books, finds time to pursue his interests in railways and their early history.

SIR JOHN ELLIOT moved from journalism in 1925 to become Britain's first public relations officer. This was for the Southern railway, of which he was eventually general manager and so responsible for surface links between England and the continent. His later career in transport led him to the chairmanship of Britain's Railway Executive, of London Transport, and of Thos Cook Ltd, as well as to a seat on the board of the Wagons-Lits company. As vice-president of the UIR after the Second World War he played a major part in the re-establishment of express and luxury trains in Europe, where he was instrumental in setting up the TEE services: in Australia he advised on railway organisation and the problems of gauge differences. He is a past president of the British Institute of Transport.

Index

Note: References to illustrations give the page number of the *caption*, which is not necessarily that on which the picture appears. A separate index of *Train Names* follows the General Index.

GENERAL INDEX

INDEX OF NAMED TRAINS

Acknowledgements

The publishers and editor of this book are deeply indebted to John Price, editor of *Cooks Continental Timetable*, for the great assistance which he has rendered in ensuring the accuracy of its text; George Behrend performed a similar service for the 'Two Pioneers' chapter. The editor would also like to thank Cyril Cobbett for his help with special library research and Elizabeth Kerr for her unfailing secretarial services.

Many dozens of other individuals and bodies in three continents have aided in the compilation of *The Great Trains*, whether by providing facilities for research, by lending documents, by offering expert scrutiny of drafts, by answering specific queries, or in other ways. Prominent among these (and with apologies for any accidental omissions) are the following:

Railway Administrations, etc.

M. Savary and M. de Quatrebarbes, and the staff of the Compagnie internationale de wagons-lits et du tourisme.

M. Wenger of the Union internationale des chemins de fer.

Mr T. Preston of British Railways Board, and the staff of the public relations departments of all regions of British Railways.

Mr J. Scholes and the staff of the British Transport Museum.

M. Desailly and M. C. Roche of the Société nationale des chemins de fer français.

Dr. Glaser of the Deutsche Bundesbahn.

Herr A. Amstein of the Schweizerische Bundesbahnen.

M. Doerr and the Association du Musée Français du chemin de fer, Mulhouse.

M. Alfred Waldis and the staff of the Verkehrshaus, Lucerne.

Mr Omer Lavallée of the Canadian Pacific.

M. G. Tauxe of the Montreux-Oberland Bernois.

New Zealand Railways Publicity and Advertising Branch.

The General Manager, South African Railways.

Publishers, etc.

M. P. Delacroix and the staff of *La Vie du Rail*.

Mr J. Slater of the *Railway Magazine*.

Mr John Murray of John Murray Ltd.

The British Film Institute

The Performing Right Society.

The Mander and Mitchenson Theatrical Collection.

The Librarian and staff of the London Library.

The Japanese Embassy, Berne.

Individuals

M. R. Commault.

Mr C. Hart of the Railway Philatelic Group.

Mr P. Stephens of Patrick Stephens, Ltd.

Mr I. MacBey.

Mr D. Bower.

Dr. Fritz Stöckl

Lt. Col. R. Bucknall.

Sir Arthur Elton.

A number of contributors have also asked that thanks be extended to their wives, secretaries and research assistants.

The authors and publishers are also grateful to the following for their help in supplying illustrations:
(Note: T = Top, C = Centre, B = Bottom, L = Left, R = Right.)

COLOUR ILLUSTRATIONS

This book is published under the direction of
Ami Guichard

Editorial responsibility and supervision by
Tim Chilvers

Produced under the direction of
Charles Riesen and Willy Dubois
and designed by Max Thommen

Printed in Italy
by Grafiche Editoriali Ambrosiane S.p.A. - Milan
Bound in Switzerland
by Maurice Busenhart, Lausanne

Printed in Italy and bound in Switzerland